Other books by Kathleen A. Brehony

Awakening at Midlife
Ordinary Grace
After the Darkest Hour

Cowritten with Robert Gass

Chanting

Living a Connected Life

KATHLEEN A. BREHONY

Living a Connected Life

Creating and
Maintaining
Relationships
That Last

An Owl Book

Henry Holt and Company · New York

The names and specific identifying characteristics of individuals described in this book have been altered to protect their privacy. These are real individuals and not composites. When first and last names are used, it is with permission.

Henry Holt and Company, LLC
Publishers since 1866
115 West 18th Street
New York, New York 10011

Henry Holt® is a registered trademark
of Henry Holt and Company, LLC.

Permission to quote has been granted to reprint "The Pattern Improves," from *The Soul of Rumi*, Coleman Barks (trans.). New York: HarperCollins, 2001, p. 33. "House of Belonging" from *The House of Belonging* by David Whyte. Copyright © 1997 by David Whyte. Used by permission of the author and Many Rivers Press.

Library of Congress Cataloging-in-Publication Data

Brehony, Kathleen A.
    Living a connected life : creating and maintaining relationships
  that last / Kathleen Brehony.
       p. cm.
    Includes index.
    ISBN 0-8050-7023-0
     1. Interpersonal relations.   2. Social interaction.   3. Friendship.
  4. Interpersonal communication.   5. Community.   I. Title:
  Relationships that last.   II. Title.

HM1106.B74 2003
302—dc21   2003051721

Henry Holt books are available for special promotions and premiums. For details contact: Director, Special Markets.

First Edition 2003

Designed by Victoria Hartman

Printed in the United States of America
10 9 8 7 6 5 4 3 2 1

*This book is lovingly dedicated
to the memories of
my sweet friends of the heart,
Buck May, Joanne Harris,
and George Munn.*

Love is the way messengers
From the mystery tell us things.

Love is the mother
We are her children.

She shines inside us,
Visible-invisible, as we trust
Or lose trust, or feel it start to grow again.

—Jalal al-Din Rumi,
"The Pattern Improves"

Contents

Living a Connected Life

Introduction

We are here to awaken from the illusion
of our separateness.

—*Thich Nhat Hanh, Vietnamese Buddhist monk*

A story from India tells about a young apprentice who was always complaining about the difficulties of life. Early one morning, his ancient Hindu master sent the young man to town to buy a bag of salt. When he returned, the master put a handful of the salt in a glass of water and asked the apprentice to drink it.

"How does it taste?" asked the master.

"It's bitter," said the apprentice as he spat the salty water onto the ground.

The master smiled and walked toward a nearby lake. When they arrived at the edge of the water, the master asked the apprentice to take another handful of salt and throw it into the lake. The apprentice did not understand the lesson he was learning, but he did so at his master's request.

"Now drink from this water," the master said.

As the young man drank, the master asked, "How does it taste?"

"Fresh and sweet," the young man replied.

"Do you taste the salt?"

"No."

The master sat beside the young man and offered his teaching. "The pain of life is pure salt; no more, no less. The amount of pain in life remains the same, exactly the same. But the amount of bitterness we taste depends on the container we put the pain in. So when you are in pain, the only thing you can do is enlarge your sense of things. Stop being a glass. Become a lake."[1]

In isolation—whether real or emotional—we lose perspective on life. Our sense of who we are becomes distorted, as though trapped in a house of mirrors, with a thousand reflections, but only of ourselves. It seems strange to realize, especially in our individualistic society ("Have it your way!" "You are your own best friend!"), that we are most able to develop fully into the person we are meant to be, in connection with others. And we are most at peace—biologically, psychologically, and emotionally—supported and buoyed by a body of personal connections. Life's challenges and blessings are sweeter, as the monk suggests, when we are contained by relationships with others.

Eileen's life was more like a glass than a lake, but she didn't know it because everything seemed to be perfect. My friend, for years a single mom, had at last found love. Two years ago, she married Andy on New Year's Day. They moved to a small valley in the Blue Ridge Mountains where they designed and built a beautiful home. Together they were raising her son from her previous marriage and their new baby daughter, now almost a year old.

Good fortune, good health, beautiful family. While I was visiting her, Eileen told me about how perfect her life had become. We hiked through the mountains near her home in rural Virginia and, as the sun was going down, we looked down on the valley from a small ridge. We could see her house, smoke curling from the chimney, yellow light casting a warm glow across the brown winter field. Eileen was right. Her life did seem to be perfect.

Eileen had solved many of the problems of career and motherhood: too many responsibilities, too little time, too many decisions about where to put her attention and energy. She told me that she often felt like one of those circus jugglers who spin and balance plates on sticks. Just when she thought everything was steady, one of the plates would threaten to fall. In spite of lots of demands in her life, Eileen was very happy.

Andy was very busy in his work and traveled a great deal, but still he was a great dad and did his share and more of child care and housework.

Eileen's career as an editor had momentum—a new publishing contract and several projects that she had worked hard to develop had come to fruition. A promotion and raise were expected at the end of the year. Her kids were healthy and her son was an honor student. Eileen's life was abundantly blessed until late one night when she awakened with a searing pain in her gut.

An ambulance rushed Eileen to the hospital, where it was discovered that her appendix had ruptured and infection had spread through her body. She was seriously ill in the hospital for two days and her recovery was touch-and-go at first. Andy raced home from a meeting on the West Coast. Antibiotics and expert medical care saved her life but her doctor insisted that she spend the next two weeks in bed. No lifting. No bathing babies. No driving her son to school. No work.

Eileen and Andy tried to figure out how they were going to cope with the next two weeks. With a baby-sitter who had limited time to work for them, Andy's work schedule, taking care of kids, and paying the bills, they were stunned to realize just how disconnected they were from any sense of community in their lives. They were content, and most definitely busy, and it was only with this unexpected challenge that they looked around and realized that they were "going it alone."

Now, let's be clear that Eileen and Andy do not live like Unabomber Ted Kaczynski—pathologically isolated in their mountain home, emotionally detached from all human life. They are normal people—highly functioning people, in fact. They have casual friends and neighbors who wave as they drive by. They are quite friendly with the parents of their son's classmates who share play dates and school activities together. They both have lots of great colleagues at their jobs. They even have some fairly close friends scattered around the country. Friends who would want to help them out in this crisis but whose lives are equally jam-packed with responsibilities to families and jobs.

What Eileen and Andy don't have is the containment of nearby family or intimate friends—attached-at-the-heart friends—the kinds of friends you can call at three o'clock in the morning. They don't have the kinds of friends they can ask to help care for Eileen in her recovery, or run to the grocery store, or pick up their son from school, or give their baby a bath. They don't have the kinds of friends who will anticipate some of the things they'll need over the next few weeks, who will show up at the door with a pan of lasagna or watch the baby in the morning so Eileen can get some rest. What they don't have is a vibrant community, tribe, or clan. It wasn't until Eileen got sick, when life threw a curve, that they realized they were living more in a glass than in a lake. And the salt was bitter.

Like Eileen's, Larry's life appears to be entirely successful. He is healthy, handsome, and loaded with money. As a high-level executive with a prosperous technology company, he enjoys the good life: regular travel to exotic locations around the world, expensive cars, flat-screen TVs, digital everything, and exquisitely decorated homes on both coasts with astonishing views of the oceans.

But in other parts of his life, Larry is not quite so successful. He's not particularly close to his parents and sister. Divorced twice, he has no ongoing or meaningful relationships with his ex-wives or his teenage daughter who lives a thousand miles away. Though he regularly sends child support checks and birthday gifts, he is not really connected to her life and couldn't really tell you a thing about her interests, friends, or dreams for the future.

Following an intense business meeting, Larry and I went for coffee at a nearby restaurant to sort through the decisions that had been made. It was a teeth-chattering freezing afternoon. Blustery winds swayed the trees and we hurried to close the door behind us as we hunted for seats in the crowded bistro. It was mid-November, just a week away from Thanksgiving. As we sipped our coffee, I asked Larry what he was going to do for the holiday.

"Nothing special," he said. He then explained that he had reservations at a posh restaurant in Santa Barbara. "I'll drive up in the morning, have a gourmet meal, then head home to get ready for my trip on Monday."

"Meeting some friends for dinner?" I asked.

"No. Just dinner. Just me."

· · ·

I was thinking about Eileen and Larry the other night when a solitary great egret soared over the little lake behind my house and landed gracefully on the highest bough of a pine tree. I was entranced by the elegance of its flight and sat quietly watching. Within minutes, six more of these large white birds settled on nearby branches of that same tree.

In the waning light they appeared as luminous ornaments clustered together and, as many birds do just before sundown, they called out to one another. Their sharp, yelping chatter sliced through the air for fifteen minutes until it gradually subsided and then all was still.

Seeing those magnificent birds collected together on that tree, as the sky turned black, was a comforting and powerful symbol for me. It spoke of the need to belong, for connection with others of our flock, in order to feel the comfort of one another and protection from the darkness. These egrets had found their safe harbor for the night.

These birds took the need for connection so naturally and easily that I envied them. While human beings have the same needs for belongingness as they do, we don't seem to soar so easily into our collections. We don't seem to find our flock as effortlessly. Many of us seem to have lost our ability to connect and to maintain the strong tribal attachments that are critical for living as a true human being. And yet, we have the same needs for connection and belongingness as these birds. And the results of this social disconnection are profoundly sad and sometimes even deadly.

As a psychotherapist for the past twenty-two years, I have witnessed the effects of isolation and loneliness. I have seen that most clients who come to me with painful symptoms of depression or anxiety do not suffer so much from biochemical imbalances—as those ubiquitous pharmaceutical television commercials would have you believe—but from the ravages of feeling alone in the world, from the failure to feel connected to others or to give and receive love. And while this disconnection may be most apparent when we experience a crisis, for lots of us, it's there in the sadness of everyday moments—when we yearn for close friends with whom to celebrate our successes, to share a quiet moment, or to have a meaningful conversation about our feelings and our lives.

With the wild, swirling pace of today's world, it can be easy to ignore our deep and innate needs for relationship and community. We sometimes forget that belongingness—the sense of being accepted and embraced by others—is not a luxury in life. It's our lifeblood. It's like air. We need it to live. An abundance of scientific research shows how we are born biologically predisposed to seek connection with others. The physiological systems of our bodies—brain and nervous system, our hearts, and breathing—regulate in close proximity to others. There is also much scientific data to show how we suffer in body, mind, and spirit when we are unable to feel a solid sense of connection to other human beings. The bad news is that by almost every measure we have become increasingly disconnected from one another. The good news is that when we find our tribe, we live longer and happier and our ordinary lives become extraordinary. The best news is that we can make changes in our values and behaviors that create bonds and relationships that can last a lifetime.

I want to be clear that this book is not a clinical discourse about people who are particularly isolated, have a psychological disorder that causes them to fail to connect, or suffer from pathological shyness. I'm interested in understanding more about our normal, everyday, rushing and spinning modern world. I want to explore the reality of the times in which we live: socially, culturally, economically, and, thus, psychologically. I'm curious about modern life and—in spite of the many wonderful things that progress and technology have given us—getting a better grasp on just how far away we have traveled from the necessary skills and consciousness required to meet some of our fundamental human needs. But most important, I want to discover practical ideas—real action steps—that can help us improve the relationships in our lives and keep them growing and blooming throughout our lifetime.

This is a book that, I hope, will become deeply personal to you—not just by reading about the importance of connectedness, but also by reflecting on where your life is at the moment and where it is going. It will help you to live more fully and more consciously when you honestly appraise where you are strong and where the tender strings that bind you to others need repair or shoring up.

Chapter One explores the biological and psychological underpinnings for our human need for connection. The evidence is overwhelming that we are social animals that require deep and abiding connections. Just as we are born with an innate need for food and air, we are born with a need for each other.

Chapter Two, "Are We Bowling Alone?," is a snapshot of where we stand now. How are we doing as a society? What kinds of structures contain us and give us a sense of belongingness? What are the social constructs and values that block our way to creating twenty-first-century tribes? Does life in America in the early twenty-first century support our need for connections?

If we see the terrorist attacks of September 11 as a wake-up call, a tragedy that causes us to take stock of our lives, as individuals and as a country, what have we learned? I want to consider whether the tragedy and horror of those terrorist attacks changed us in any permanent way. The immediate reaction to these unthinkable events seemed to be a greater sense of unity among Americans. Even now, the media are flooded with images of people of all races, ages, and economic classes hugging and giving each other comfort. We wave flags and say we feel different, more connected as Americans. For a moment, it seemed like we *had* become a tribe, caring for one another from the heart, collectively wrenching something good from a shocking and heartbreaking tragedy. It seems that we did change for a while but whether those changes are permanent or were merely a transient reaction to a series of unthinkable events in our collective experience is not yet clear as I write this. Chapter Three, "A Changed and Changing World?," looks at our post–September 11 world and both the bright and dark sides of belongingness.

Chapter Four, "A Thousand Words for Snow," presents a model for understanding the nature of our relationships and, although it's simple in structure, I hope it will help you organize your thinking about your own relationships and containers. This chapter also contains a series of inventories and questions that will help you probe deeper and give you the opportunity to reflect on your own life with a mind to becoming really aware of the true state of your connections. But it's not enough to get a handle on how well you are connected if there are no plans or steps to revitalize them.

The rest of this book is devoted to just that—to practical suggestions and prescriptive ideas about creating and maintaining enduring relationships. I am not so arrogant as to presume that these are the only strategies or that I am the only one who knows them. But these are action steps that I have seen work both in my own life and the lives of many clients I have been honored to work with as a therapist. These are approaches to life that I've learned from people who seem to me to be particularly good at soulful living, people who have become expert at forging deep and meaningful relationships and who have found their safe harbor.

PART I

The Landscape of Connection

ONE

The Psychology and Biology of Belonging

Loneliness breaks the spirit.

—*Jewish proverb*

Imagine yourself as one of our most ancient ancestors looking out across a vast, golden savannah. Fast food chains and grocery stores are still millions of years in the future, so your life is pretty much built around two important activities: finding food and staying out of the way of pythons, saber-toothed cats, and crocodiles. You've recently learned to walk on two legs, which, of course, gives you much greater freedom to use your hands, but it's going to take a long, long time before you realize that a spear, club, or some other kind of tool will dramatically improve your hunting skills. It doesn't take long to figure out that you're not very good at bringing down a large animal by yourself since most of them have sharper teeth and claws or can outrun you by a country mile. And then there are those long, lonely nights. You won't discover fire for another few million years and it's dark out there. The howls of wild animals pierce the night and you wonder: Will I live to see another sunrise?

You're a smart animal and you quickly figure out that the only real solution to solving the problems of hunting for food and protecting yourself is to hang out with others just like you. Of course, you did not reason all this out consciously; your behavior is rooted in biology and evolution and you are being driven to congregate. Everything you do is instinctively directed toward your survival, adaptation, and perpetuation of the species, and by now it's very clear that those will depend upon connections with others just like you. Together you can bring home dinner. Together you can defend yourselves against predators. Alone, your species will go the way of the dinosaurs.

By our very natures, humans are prepared to be social animals. We are biologically and psychologically prewired for attachment and bonding. Our need for connection is—from birth and beyond—a fundamental survival need. We have this need, as this chapter will show, throughout our lives.

Nicolae Ceauşescu, the former president of Romania, created generations of "throw-away children" and proved beyond any doubt that attachment and bonding are necessary for human survival. Now more than a dozen years after his overthrow and execution, this point is clear as the misery continues. Today, there are more than 100,000 orphans in Romania, a country the size of Colorado.

Ceauşescus despotic vision for his country included increasing the population of "pure Romanians" as well as a "robot workforce" from the "impure children"—mainly Hungarians, Bulgarians, and Gypsies. Beginning in the 1960s, he starved his own people in order to export food and then banned contraception for women with fewer than four children, despite the wretched poverty of most Romanians. Parents unable to feed their children handed them over to state-run orphanages—cavernous warehouses where few were fed or clothed and none was given nurturance or love. Ceauşescu reasoned that it was the "impure" children who had ended up as wards of his state, and he decreed that food, medicine, and clothing would not be "wasted" on them.

Even those infants who were fed were provided with only the bare necessities—simply given a bottle, propped up with filthy blankets. There was no one to hold, touch, or comfort them. Many died before their first birthday from preventable illnesses. Those who physically survived slept on rags on the floor, ate scraps of bread, and preyed on smaller kids to secure a bit of food. All of them failed to thrive—they were seriously stunted in their growth and development, and even older children were not toilet trained. It was not uncommon for two-year-olds to weigh less than ten pounds.

Nancy and Brian Geoghegan of Lincoln University, Pennsylvania, didn't know much about the conditions of orphanages in Romania. They were in their early thirties when they learned they could not conceive a birth-child of their own, news that left them heartbroken. They longed for a family and children to love. Down but not out, they considered adopting an American child but were terrified that one of the birth parents might show up in the future and seek custody. Several high-profile cases in the United States convinced them that this was a distinct possibility. So they began to explore an international adoption.

They were told that there were thousands of Romanian children in need of loving families. What they were not told was that these babies and kids were housed in vast warehouses, barely fed, and given no loving attachments with adults. To merely call these children "high risk" for healthy development was a serious understatement.

They understood that a Romanian baby would require extra TLC, but their reluctance to adopt one of these children vanished when they saw a photograph of little Nicolae. They fell in love with him in spite of the fact that they wanted an infant or toddler under age two and this little boy was almost four years old. Nevertheless, they wanted him for their son. They decided to keep the name his birth mother had given him and call him Niki. The decision made, in April 1996 they flew to Bucharest to bring Niki home.

"We went into this place in Bucharest—an apartment, like a ghetto, a third-world country," Nancy told me. "That's where we first saw him and we were shocked." Niki was tiny, underweight, stunted—in the twenty-fifth percentile for height. He made no eye contact and would not come to them. Instead, he sat in the middle of the floor rocking and chanting. "But, as soon as we saw him, I knew he would be our son in spite of how he appeared," Nancy said. Once they got to the safety of their home in southeastern Pennsylvania, he would feel protected and know how much he was loved. Niki would be fine, they thought. But then things got much worse.

At his new home surrounded by toys, pets, safety, and loving parents, Niki still wouldn't stop his repetitive chanting and rocking. Many times a day, he would fly into terrible rages. He was disobedient and angry and needed to be in control of every situation. Nancy said that he knew, from the start, how to "push their buttons" with his anger and defiance. Niki couldn't focus on anything and showed severe signs of ADHD (Attention

Deficit Hyperactivity Disorder). He was hateful, destructive, loud, violent, filled with rage, and a whirlwind of hyperactivity—grabbing everything and knocking it down. Perhaps most difficult of all was that no one seemed to understand. To neighbors and friends, Niki appeared to be a sweet, "normal" child. Nancy and Brian felt isolated.

Nancy would try to put Niki down for a nap and he would run around the bed screaming. She tried to hold him and he stiffened or ran away. He was joyless and never laughed or smiled. He didn't seem to have any kind of conscience. He showed no empathy for anyone or anything. One day, he kicked their old cat Perry down the stairs, then sneered at him. The Geoghegans had to child-proof the house because Niki would pull things out of drawers and scatter them around the room or hide them in secret places. "He was starved for sensory input," Nancy said. "He would turn the TV on/off, on/off, on/off, until we had to unplug it."

Nancy would try to hug her son and he would turn his back to her, though he could be indiscriminately affectionate with total strangers. She had taken care of children since she was nineteen, but nothing she knew about good parenting seemed to make any difference. They tried behavior modification—encouraging and rewarding Niki whenever he did something good. But he didn't respond. They tried time-outs for punishment, but he didn't care. Nancy read parenting book after parenting book but nothing worked with Niki. "I started to think it was my fault, that I wasn't loving him enough, that I needed to give him more time and be more patient," Nancy said.

By the time Niki was in kindergarten and then first grade, he was a constant behavior problem. An astute teacher told Nancy to check the Internet for information on issues that international adoptees raised in institutions might face. That's when she stumbled across a list of the symptoms of Reactive Attachment Disorder (RAD). At first she was excited, because Niki fit every one of the criteria for this disorder. At last she had some answers; she wasn't crazy. But the more she read, the more frightened she became. She learned that RAD is a serious disorder and recovery is very difficult.

Nancy and Brian began to understand that Niki was a deeply wounded child who had never learned to trust anyone. Abandoned by his birth mother, his first four years were spent in a terrifying environment where little children had to fend for themselves. "It was survival of the fittest," Nancy said. "It was like *Lord of the Flies* where older kids were left to their own devices and abused younger ones. Where the kids wore rags and peed and pooped on the floor." The staff would throw bread and water to these children, but there was no one there to comfort them when they cried. There was no one to love or hold them. These children learned that they were on their own. Isolated in an unsafe world with no connection or attachments to anyone, they never learned to trust.

The Geoghegans went for professional help and Niki was diagnosed with RAD. He began what would be years of intensive and specialized therapy. Niki began to make progress but it wasn't fast and it wasn't a smooth course. He would seem to be getting better, then take a turn for the worse. When he was seven years old, he almost killed himself by sticking metal objects into electrical outlets. Nancy and Brian turned off the electricity in his room and pushed on with therapy. "I believe in the power of the human spirit," Nancy said. "I prayed and trusted that Niki would come to know that he was loved and safe with us. I knew that this kid's life depended upon our getting this right."

Today, Niki is ten years old and it's hard to believe this is the same little boy who came rocking and chanting into Nancy and Brian's world. Sure, he still has some difficulty with trust—this may be something he will have to work on for the rest of his life. But he has friends now and is learning to get along with others. He is gentle and loving with his baby brother, Ben (a Guatemalan child adopted at four months of age). Niki laughs, smiles, trusts, and can look you in the eye. He also takes care of the family pets with love and tenderness.

Nancy understands the need for attachment and belonging in ways she never did before. She has established a clearinghouse of information and support so that families of attachment-disordered kids can find help (www.attachmentdisorder.net). Nancy summarizes what she's learned from Niki and conversations with many other parents of attachment-disordered children. "Belongingness and attachment are the most crucial things in the world. You have to feel that you belong. Everything else in your life—every other relationship and your feelings about yourself—will be compromised without it," she told me.

The Geoghegans' experience with little Niki gives a graphic example of a fundamental truth for all of us: we are biologically and psychologically constructed to connect with others. Think of the explosive growth and development that occurs in the first three years of life—mental and physical—as a sort of map-drawing process. The map that is drawn early will serve us as individuals throughout our lives as we make our way in the world. What is increasingly clear is that love and connection are the cartographers—the forces that draw the map. A child like Niki received no such connection in this critical period of his life. He came to the Geoghegans at age four, essentially with a blank map, no guide by which to seek or fulfill this imperative we share as a species: to bond and connect with others.

It should be clear that Niki's level of early abandonment and abuse is extreme, but there are many other reasons for the failure of early attachment that don't require tyrants, orphanages, or extreme neglect. Anything that creates the absence of a close loving relationship between an infant and a mother or father ("a parenting one"), whether because of death, illness, postpartum depression, substance abuse, or a hundred other reasons, will have lifelong effects on one's psychological health and the ability to create and maintain lasting relationships.

When I think about Niki and his struggles I have to ask: What does it mean to belong? What are the results when we fail to attain this sense of belonging—our safe harbor? Are there critical developmental periods when the need for attachment is greatest? What critical psychological and spiritual functions do belongingness and connections serve? Is it true that all we need is love?

Science has so much to show us now about this early period of development; the ways in which our ability to find and maintain loving relationships is determined by (or at least dependent on) the quality of our early connections to others. In order to have a detailed "map" for survival and happiness in life—a sort of mental and emotional blueprint for connection—we need attachment and belongingness from birth. This chapter looks not around but inside us, to our first experiences with connection, and how those affect the rest of our lives. Let's look at what science can show us about this fundamental biological and psychological drive for connection in the first few years of life—the ways in which it determines how we develop, who we become, and how equipped we are to fulfill our potential as human beings.

Connection/love/belongingness is what draws the biological and psychological "development map" that will guide us toward loving connection and psychological and spiritual health for the rest of our lives. Is the need there from birth? Yes. Not only that, but our successes and failures to connect at age thirty or fifty are partially determined by what happened in those early years. We saw with Niki what happens when a baby is not loved; now let's look closely at what that connection *does*, early on, and why it is so essential for the person you are going to be. As science clearly shows us, we start our lives craving connection, and those early experiences pave the way to how we will continue our lifelong drive for closeness and community.

Think about This

1. What was your early life like in terms of connections?
2. Do you have memories or images that tell you what it was like when you were an infant, toddler, or young child?
3. What is your first memory? Write about it in your journal.
4. Find some pictures of yourself when you were very young. Look carefully at them. What do they tell you about the infant/child you once were?
5. How would you describe your abilities to trust other people? Use five adjectives to express how you do or do not trust others.

The Biological Need for Attachment and Belongingness

Attachment is a basic human need deeply rooted in millions of years of species evolution. Quickly connecting to caregivers is essential if we are to develop as full human beings. We're biologically hardwired to ripen through loving, secure experiences with caregivers. Compared to every other species on the planet, human beings are born quite premature and must continue to develop outside the womb. There is good evidence that more than 75 percent of the human brain develops only after birth. Although most of the brain's neurons—about 100 billion—are present at birth and trillions of glial cells (the Greek word for "glue") that protect and nourish them are in place, the human brain at this point is still a work in progress. It is not the sheer number of brain cells but the *interconnections* (through dendrites and the spaces between them called synapses) that produce our rich human abilities. And at birth most of these are yet to be formed.

At birth, a baby's brain begins to develop trillions more connections than it can possibly use. "What the brain has done is lay out circuits that are its best guess about what's required for vision, for language, for whatever," according to neurobiologist Carla Shatz of the University of California at Berkeley.[1]

What happens next is a continuation of the exquisite interplay between nature and nurture that began at conception: hereditary potential unfolding in partnership with the environment. This is nature *and* nurture in equilibrium, a complementary and inseparable dance. Not either/or, it is both/and. Now, the critical *interconnections* between brain cells in a newborn are hooked up through floods of sensory experience. During the first few months of life, an infant's developing brain explodes with new connections. The infant's brain changes 100,000 times more rapidly than an adult's and consumes far more calories and energy (about 65 percent compared to 15 percent). By the age of two, babies' brains have twice as many synapses as adults' brains (remember, nature is laying down *all* the wiring here—anything you might ever need). By age three, the toddler's brain has created more than 1,000 trillion connections between cells. Between the ages of four and nine, children's brains are twice as active as adult brains. By about age ten, in a classic "use it or lose it" arrangement, the brain begins to "pinch off" little used connections so that more heavily traveled circuits—the parts of the brain that are stimulated regularly—become even richer. This process—just like in gardening—is called pruning. The human brain has a great deal of plasticity and we continue to learn and change over the entire life span, but positive and negative experiences in the first three years of life have an extraordinary influence on how children will be wired as adults.

Newborns of other species are born with more fully developed brains and are far better able to survive on their own. Think about what it would be like to be a baby sea turtle. These babies are the champions of self-efficacy. The hatchlings start their lives when an adult female sea turtle laboriously pulls her heavy body across a beach to dig a deep nest where she deposits a clutch of a hundred leathery-skinned eggs. She carefully covers the nest and then, her parenting duties complete, heads back to the sea. About two months later, the newly hatched turtles emerge from their Ping-Pong-ball-sized eggs and collectively scratch their way out of the buried nest. They're born with an instinct to stop about an inch before breaking through where they feel the temperature of the sand and do not emerge during the daytime when heat and predators are abundant. If the sand is cool, indicating it is nighttime, they burst through and immediately scramble down the sandy beach, making a beeline toward the relative safety of the ocean. If they have made it this far and have not been eaten by raccoons while still in the nest, if they can dodge birds and crabs and avoid eating plastic wrappers and other litter on the beach, thinking it's real food, they just might make it. In lieu of being taught by their mothers, heredity and evolution have programmed these hatchlings to "run to the light," assuming that the only source of light on lonely beaches will be the moonlight dancing on the waves. But nature didn't plan for the artificial light of highways, stores, and restaurants: so many of these babies head in the wrong direction and instead of finding the ocean and a long happy life eating seaweed and vacationing in blue lagoons, they end up as a splat in a parking lot. Many of the lucky ones who make it to the water will be dinner for hungry fish. If they can avoid those predators, these tiny babies must swim continuously for two or three days to catch a tidal current. Only a few will survive. Years later, the females will return to this very same natal beach to lay their eggs and repeat this ancient saga with their own offspring.

Baby sea turtles might be nature's best at taking care of themselves early in life, but even baby deer, zebras, horses, and wildebeests can stand up and run within minutes of birth. Chimpanzees, our phylogenetically closest cousins (with whom we share 98.7 percent of our DNA), can crawl, climb, and hang on to their mothers when they're only two days old. Human infants don't even come close to these skills until they are half a year old. Just think about the implications for relationships, connections, and the need for safe harbor based on the helplessness of newborn humans. Human infants cannot survive without caretakers, and the absence of attachment and human bonding can kill us.

Like Niki, failures of early attachment—the absence of the pure sense of belongingness, love, and protection that infants require—devastates the cells as well as the soul. Not only does an attachment-deprived child suffer emotional, social, and cognitive delay; his brain and body don't grow and develop as they should and must. Research has shown that children who are rarely touched—who fail to attach to caregivers— develop brains that are 20 to 30 percent smaller than normal and are diminished in height and weight for their age.

An early and frequently cited study by French psychologist Renee Spitz in 1946 demonstrated unexpected, dramatic, and even fatal outcomes resulting from the failure of attachment. Spitz studied a group of infants who had been taken away from felon mothers in prison and placed in a foundling home where they would be given the best professional care. It was believed that moving these infants out of the prison and into a state-of-the-art institution would help them to grow and develop more normally and avoid incarceration in the future. These "state-of-the-art" orphanages, by the way, were spotless and designed to keep children free from germs. The experts called them "sterile nurseries." Babies were fed regularly but they were not handled, cuddled, or played with because it was theorized that human contact would risk exposing the children to infections.

Spitz observed that these institutionalized infants were withdrawn and sickly. Even with good nutrition, they failed to gain weight. Within a year, 25 percent of these infants had died; none of the infants who remained with their mothers died. Ironically, the institutionalized children were specifically vulnerable to infections—lack of physical human contact devastated their immune systems. Forty percent of the children who contracted measles died as a result of this disease at a time when the mortality rate for measles in the surrounding community was only about 0.5 percent.[2]

By the end of the second year, 37 percent of the infants in the foundling home had died, while there were no deaths among those babies who stayed with their mothers. IQ measurements showed that the one-year-old infants who remained with their mothers scored 105 on the Wechsler Intelligence Scale for Children (WISC), compared with a score of 72 for those in the foundling home (90–109 is considered to be "average" intelligence). By age two, all of the toddlers who remained with their mothers were exhibiting normal childhood skills, but those in the foundling home were having grave difficulties: of the twenty-one children studied, only five walked unassisted, only nine could eat with a spoon, only one could speak more than twelve words, and only three were of normal weight for their height.

Before Spitz's research, it was believed that if infants were simply properly fed, they would develop normally. Any attachment between infants and mothers (or another primary caregiver) was presumed to be of secondary importance, the inconsequential result of the mother providing food (reinforcement) for the baby. This was the prevailing behaviorist position. British psychoanalyst John Bowlby—often referred to as the "Father of Attachment Theory"—didn't believe that. Nor did he believe the early psychoanalytic view that mother-infant bonding occurred because the mother gratified the id by feeding the child. In other words, Bowlby saw that there was a lot more going on in the relationship between mother and child than the basic function of satisfying the child's need for food. He saw that the baby needed more from its mother than just milk. Bowlby looked to the ethological position—the idea that behavior serves a function in the process of natural selection and survival. He hypothesized that mother-child bonding served an important biological function.

Bowlby was quite familiar with the work of the Austrian physician and Nobel laureate Konrad Lorenz, who had studied waterfowl and concluded that mother-offspring bonding was instinctual. For example, Lorenz documented the ways in which baby geese will "imprint" or "lock on to" the first moving thing they see. To goslings, that first moving thing becomes "mother" and they'll follow her anywhere. Or in the case of Lorenz and newly hatched geese, they followed *him* anywhere.

Bowlby theorized that the human mother-child bond is much more like imprinting in geese, and less like the reward and punishment schedules that allowed behaviorists to make rats run mazes or train pigeons to peck levers. Instead, Bowlby said that attachment is a result of a complex human "behavioral system" that is innate, neurologically based, and has a function in and of itself—an instinctive reciprocal relationship with implications for the survival of our species. In other words, Bowlby saw that the bond between the mother and infant—the smell, the touch, the gaze, the close proximity of the heartbeats—was just as biologically imperative to the infant as the milk the mother was providing. He asked, "What is the biological function of attachment?" And, "Is there any survival value in keeping a close proximity between infant and mother?"

Bowlby concluded that there was critically important survival value in maintaining close proximity between mother and child—after all, infants can't fend off predators or even feed themselves—so human infants and their mothers engage in a complex set of relationship-building behaviors. He saw that specific behaviors emerged from both infants and mothers that initiated and activated the attachment between them in a mutual way, the infant and the caregiver influencing each other over time. These behaviors and sensory input are "social releasers" in the very same way that goslings imprint on and follow the first moving thing they see or the way young herring gulls instinctively open their mouths when they spy the red spot on the beak of their parent. In humans, infants will smile at the sight of two dark spots on a white circle (probably because it is perceived as a friendly face).

Crying and smiling, he said, were innate ways in which a human infant brings its mother into proximity and contact. Emotional life is dependent upon the formation and maintenance of attachment relationships throughout life and there are especially sensitive periods of development—infancy, childhood, and adolescence, for example—when the quality of the attachment relationships is particularly important to development.

What Bowlby and others have made clear is that attachment and belongingness are not just the concerns of infants and children. Knowing that you are connected to other people is essential throughout the life cycle. In summarizing decades of research, Bowlby described how scientific studies confirmed what most of us have known by instinct about the critical importance of love and contact. He wrote, "Intimate attachments to other human beings are the hub around which a person's life revolves, not only when he is an infant or a toddler or a schoolchild but throughout his adolescence and his years of maturity as well, and on into old age. From these intimate attachments a person draws his strength and enjoyment of life and, through what he contributes, he gives strength and enjoyment to others. These are matters about which current science and traditional wisdom are at one."[3]

Bowlby is right. Science has confirmed what we already know. Any mother who has held a baby close to her, and every child who grows up sure of being loved, confident in connection with others, know the importance of early bonding.

During the 1950s and 1960s, American psychologist Harry Harlow conducted radical experiments that confirmed Bowlby's ideas about the importance of early attachment to the development of healthy adult behavior. Though I disagree with his treatment of animal subjects, the results of Harlow's studies are important. Inspired by the research that showed that infants who were deprived of touch or loving attention failed to thrive, Harlow studied the maternal-offspring bond by separating infant rhesus monkeys from their mothers shortly after birth. His results showed that tactile stimulation (touch) was critical to primate adjustment and even survival.

In his experiments, the baby monkeys were isolated from all other monkeys and fed with a bottle attached to their cage. The cages were kept clean and the bottom of the cage was covered with gauze in order to keep it sanitary. Harlow noticed that these baby monkeys would throw violent temper tantrums when his assistants tried to remove the gauze and replace it with clean material. Upon further observation, it was clear that these monkeys had formed an attachment to the gauze (in the same way that human babies develop strong emotional ties to a stuffed animal or "blankie"). Monkeys raised in a mesh cage with a bare floor did not even survive the first five days of the experiment. When Harlow covered a chicken wire cone with terry cloth, the infants became very attached to this "surrogate mother." In fact, they embraced it, vocalized to it, clung to it, and hid behind it when alarmed. Harlow's research found that infant monkeys spent more time clinging—sometimes twenty-three hours a day—to the terry-cloth-covered "surrogate mother" than to a wire "mother," even when the wire mother held the bottle that contained their food. The wire mother was virtually ignored except at dinnertime.

Harlow's monkeys, deprived of physical contact with their mothers, were sometimes apathetic, sometimes hyperagitated, abnormally aggressive, and given to outbursts of violence. They were socially inept and highly fearful, failed to interact normally with other monkeys, showed inappropriate sexual responses, and often rocked like autistic children. As adults, the females—even those raised with terry-cloth mothers— were unable to care for their offspring, would not breast-feed, and often behaved violently toward their babies. Psychologist James Prescott notes that "what Harlow could not know at the time of his dramatic experiments in the late 1950s and 1960s was that these behavioral disturbances were accompanied by brain damage."[4] We know now that sensory deprivation—e.g., rocking and holding from a mother—during formative periods of brain growth results in incomplete or damaged development of the neuronal systems that control affection. At the same time, these same systems influence brain centers associated with violence. And a deprived infant may have a hard time controlling violent impulses as an adult.

Touching, hugging, and kissing are the human variations of the licking, tooth-combing, and grooming behavior of nonhuman mammal mothers with their babies. In *Touching*, a classic book about the significance of the skin—our body's largest organ—anthropologist and scholar Ashley Montagu says, "It appears probable that for human beings tactile stimulation is of fundamental consequence for the development of healthy emotional or affectional relationships, that licking, in its actual and its figurative sense, and love are closely connected; in short, that one learns to love not by instruction but by being loved."[5]

When I think about our lifelong quest for connection and community, I feel that Montagu's words are the signal lights of the lighthouse drawing us across a dark, immense sea to those safe harbors. Not only does touch, in and of itself, benefit the infant (and mother); touch ensures proximity, which makes good biological sense for a social animal that is doomed to die of hunger or to be dinner for a hungry beast if left alone or banished from the pack.

Newborn reptiles, like sea turtles, have no such need for licking or any other tenderness from their mothers. In fact, sea turtles never even bump into their mothers unless, at some point in their lives, they happen to drift past her on some warm Gulf Stream current. They have no need for the innate interpersonal skills that human infants use to ensure attachment and bonding. But relationships for mammals are not one-way streets. Infants and caregivers are engaged in a dynamic and powerful dance that creates lifesaving and life-giving bonds and attachments. And the experts make a distinction between these two terms: *bonding* refers to the parent's tie to the infant and it is thought to occur within the first few hours of life; *attachment* is the relationship between infant and parent and develops more gradually. But what is important to remember is that both infant and caregiver have important roles to play in the relationship that is formed.

As Bowlby (and others) pointed out, human infants are not "blank slates"—they enter the world with their own unique personalities and though seemingly helpless in many ways, they are equipped with one significant power: the ability to elicit emotional tenderness from other humans, particularly from their mothers. Human infants may not be able to strike out on their own, as do sea turtles, or swing from trees like our chimp cousins, but they are innately social and far from helpless when it comes to forming personal relationships. In fact, infants come handily equipped with the tools they need to survive.

For example, infants will orient preferentially to the odor of their own mother's breast milk. Mothers, in turn, recognize the characteristic odor of their own infants even when they've had limited postnatal contact with them. Mother-infant proximity, stroking, cuddling, and touching as well as breast-feeding, balance levels of cortisol (a stress hormone) in the infant and literally send messages to the brain to make connections. But the infant is not the only one who benefits from this close relationship. Breast-feeding itself results in a flood of prolactin and oxytocin in the mother. These "mothering hormones" are associated with relaxation and motherly feelings—part of the underlying chemistry of the maternal instinct. Oxytocin appears to induce a state of mild sedation and relaxation, reduces anxiety, and promotes prosocial behavior. Prolactin levels have been measured to increase twentyfold within half an hour of beginning breast-feeding. When mother and infant are in close contact, the infant's core body temperature coordinates with that of his/her mother. This thermoregulation is necessary for the healthy neurological and psychological development of the infant. And while a mother and her infant's heart may beat at different rates, the interval of their heartbeats is the same. All of the available data suggest the same things: mothers and infants are made for each other, and each benefits from physically close and tender connections.

Are the benefits of proximity to others limited to infancy? More recent brain research has demonstrated just how important is the proximity of others. Especially in infancy, but throughout our lives, our physical bodies are influencing and being influenced by others with whom we feel a connection. Scientists call this "limbic regulation."[6] Reptiles and other nonmammals lack the limbic sub-brain, which explains the indifferent mothering behavior of female sea turtles and why it can be so hard for our pet goldfish to really become attached to us. But for mammals, every cell in our bodies calls out for closeness and relationship.

When young puppies are separated from their mothers they begin to howl in a universal mammalian protest against separation. I saw this firsthand with my own beloved pet. On the first night that Dorothy—my yellow Labrador retriever who is now twelve years old—came into my home, she was eight weeks old. After several hours of play and getting to know each other, I set her up in the kitchen with fresh food and water, a soft bed, an old sweater of mine, and a windup alarm clock that, I was told, would sound like her mother's own heartbeat. I didn't want to leave her free to roam because she wasn't yet housebroken and because I had an old dog, Clancy—then almost twenty years old—who didn't seem very welcoming to this new family member. That's putting it mildly. He barked and snarled and the fur on his back rose up until it looked a lot like Don King's hairdo.

Dorothy was happy to play well into the night. She tugged on the sweater and bit on the clock, but the minute I left the room, she began to pace and push at the baby gates that enclosed her. She began to bark and then howl in a high-pitched puppy squeal. When I'd go back into the room to comfort her, she bounded over to me, licking and nuzzling my hands. We repeated this numerous times but I knew that eventually I'd have to go to bed. The minute I left her, she'd once again begin the ancient mammalian separation drama. I went to my room, as if I could sleep with my sweet puppy in such a state of frantic agitation. And there I sat wondering what I should do to help her when suddenly it became very quiet in the kitchen. I listened for a few minutes, then silently slipped down the steps and discovered that—like a canine escape artist—she had somehow managed to squeeze through the baby gate into the dining room where Clancy was sleeping. And there they were. Dorothy was curled up against Clancy and both were sound asleep.

What is this about the proximity of another creature that was so important that it made a tiny puppy snuggle up to a curmudgeonly old dog who, only hours earlier, had threatened to eat her? Dorothy took the risk because she had to—she was biologically driven to do so—and when I left the room, she was thrown into the "protest" phase of the "protest-despair response."

The minute I was out of sight, Dorothy's heart rate, blood pressure, and body temperature increased. Her sympathetic nervous system kicked into gear and thus her levels of cortisol, sometimes called the "stress hormone," shot sky high. Some studies show that cortisol levels rise sixfold in some mammals in just a half hour of isolation. And this is a good thing—young animals who can't fend for themselves are better off staying active and vigilant until they find their mother. Wolf pups in the wild and kangaroo babies removed from their mothers' pouches behave in much the same way as Dorothy did that night. All these young ones become agitated, stressed out, and screaming. Even baby rats have been known to emit nonstop ultrasonic cries when their mother goes off to find some cheese. To fight the unfulfilled need Dorothy had for connection (and the resulting stressful physiological and neuroendocrinological changes), she adopted a quick "love the one you're with" attitude by which crotchety old Clancy looked, and was, definitely good enough for a soothing snuggle.

If the separation lasts too long, then protest gives way to despair. The young animal will fall into a lethargic state, stop eating and drinking, stop trying to escape or find its mother, and stop crying. Physiologically, these animals experience a widespread disruption of bodily rhythms, levels of growth hormone plummet, the immune system loses its edge, body temperature falls, and the heart rate slows down dramatically. There is a huge rise (sometimes ten times normal) in stress hormones. I know that scientists frown on anthropomorphizing—attributing human emotions to nonhuman species—but I've seen photographs of rhesus monkeys who are in this despair phase and there is no other way to describe what they seem to be feeling than to say they're grieving, sad, and miserable.

As mammals, we human beings are just as tuned in to the call of our wild physiology as are dogs, wolfs, kangaroos, and even the humble rat. For example, college women who room together (and especially if they are close friends) find that their menstrual cycles synchronize after only a short time of living in the same dorm. The human body is constantly fine-tuning thousands of physiological events—blood pressure, heart rate, body temperature, sugar levels, hormones, salts. We all know that, but most of us may be surprised to learn that our inner physiology affects others and they, in turn, affect us. In an open-loop kind of arrangement, we transmit and receive regulatory information that changes our cardio-vascular functioning, hormone levels, sleep rhythms, immune functions, and more.

We've all experienced the calm that comes over us—slowing our breath and heart rate—just by being near someone who is calm in the same way that we can get stressed out when we're around someone who is biting their nails and pacing the floor. Research has shown that animals prefer to spend time with animals in whose presence they have experienced high levels of brain oxytocin in the past, which is associated with the relaxation response and reduced stress.[7] Tranquillity, like stress, is "catchy," and there is a preference for spending time with others who make us feel this way.

Some research suggests that it is not just the brain and nervous system that are hardwired for intimacy and closeness. In spite of what poets, dreamers, and millions of lovers on Valentine's Day believe about the human heart, modern medicine has held to a theory that it's pretty much just a pump—a very complex and impressive pump, to be sure—and in this way of looking at it, the heart is a fist-sized chunk of muscle outfitted to pump blood. Like a well-regulated fish tank, contraction after contraction (more than two and a half billion in the average life-time), our hearts drive blood around the body in a never-ending cycle of replenishment. But new research by Doc Childre, Howard Martin, and others at the HeartMath Institute in California[8] questions this pump model and shows that the heart—that ubiquitous seat of sentiment and love—has its own intelligence and its own role to play in emotions and human connections. Perhaps our use of the symbol of the heart to mean wisdom, love, compassion, strength, and courage is more on target than we ever considered. The research shows that the heart is certainly more than just a pump. Perhaps the Little Prince was right when he observed, "It is only with the heart that one can see rightly. What is essential is invisible to the eye."[9]

The heart begins to form in the developing fetus before the brain—in the first eighteen days postconception—and a regular heartbeat can be measured within days of that. No one is sure what starts the first heartbeat, but scientists say that it is "autorhythmic," meaning that the heartbeat is self-initiated from within the heart itself. The heart doesn't need any connection to the brain to continue its rhythmic beating.

What's more, the heart generates the strongest electromagnetic field produced by the body, generating 40 to 60 percent more electrical amplitude than the brain. The electricity generated by the heart can be detected and measured in the brain waves of another person when people are touching or near each other. Like a radio station emitting waves filled with information to a waiting receiver, this effect has been measured as far as twelve feet from the body.[10] Just as side-by-side pendulum clocks begin to swing together in exactly the same rhythm—a phenomenon called "entrainment"—two individual muscle cells from different hearts in separate petri dishes will begin to synchronize their rhythm and beat together when they are moved closer together. Though more research is needed, it is possible that heart rhythms are carrier waves of information that help us "synchronize" with others.

Human infants, physiologically ready to relate, begin immediately to play their part in the exquisite dance of attachment. Within minutes of birth, an infant uses its first oral language to signal hunger, pain, frustration, or sensory overload with a loud cry. And, perhaps, as evidence of our innate empathy and need for community and connection, newborn babies will automatically cry at the sound of another baby's cry, something they do not do to computer-simulated cries or animal calls.

Though parents of newborns may have to struggle to remember this, a baby's cry—even at 3:00 A.M.—is his or her way of influencing the world and survival itself. Research has shown that mothers have strong physiological and hormonal responses to the cries of their infants and that these responses are part of the attachment/bonding plan. Even new mothers can readily discriminate between the types of cries from their infants and instinctively know if the baby is crying for food, for a diaper change, or from pain.

The evidence for a biochemically based "fathering hormone" is not so clear, but this is most likely because very little research attention has been paid to the role that men play in infant attachment. Until recently, science tended to look at the human male role in infant development as being somewhat insignificant, more like the many species in which the father sires offspring, then runs off to spread a bit more seed. This expectation that *only* the mother is programmed by nature to care for offspring has obscured some important truths about a father's role in infant attachment.

Recent research has discovered that the males of many species not only dote on their offspring, but also undergo dramatic endocrinological changes in preparation for and after the birth of their young. Hormonal effects of paternity have been well documented in most species of birds and several species of mammals and rodents—like the dwarf hamster species *Phodopus campbelli*. Interestingly, though, a very closely related species of hamster—*Phodopus sungorus*—is best known for his "love 'em and leave 'em" behavior to their mates and plays no role in the rearing of their young. Biologists Katherine Wynne-Edwards and Catharine Reburn at Queen's University in Kingston, Ontario, found that pup-to-father interaction in the *campbelli* hamsters stimulated the release of hormones (including prolactin) that bring about and intensify paternal behavior. Toni Ziegler, from the Wisconsin Regional Primate Research Center in Madison, measured prolactin levels among cotton-top tamarin monkeys ("the dads of all dads") both during gestation and just after the birth of their young and discovered that levels of this "maternal" hormone had risen to the same high level as their nursing mates. Interestingly, prolactin levels were also found to be elevated in the older brothers of these baby monkeys, probably due to their expected baby-sitting duties.[11] Nature has decreed that males in this species will be the primary caregivers—taking on every parenting role except nursing—since females ovulate within two weeks of giving birth.

But what do studies of hamsters and cotton-top tamarins tell us about human fathers and attachment to infants? The research is suggesting that these studies have paved the way for research on the human animal. For example, one recent study found a significant reduction in salivary testosterone in fathers as they were responding to their infants' cries. Lowered testosterone levels are associated with reduced aggression and more relaxation. Another study showed that fathers of two- to twenty-five-week-old infants provided more social and physical stimulation and mothers tended to be more rhythmic and containing.[12] Fathers were more responsive to gross motor cues of their premature infants and touched their babies with rhythmic pats more often than mothers, who were more responsive to social cues like soft sounds.[13]

Biopsychologist Anne Storey of Memorial University in St. John's, Newfoundland, took blood samples from thirty-four couples attending prenatal classes throughout the course of the women's pregnancies. The results of these blood tests showed that the fathers' levels of cortisol, prolactin, and testosterone changed dramatically during their partners' pregnancy. Testosterone levels dropped—a phenomenon associated with greater paternal behavior—by more than a third just after the baby's birth. After listening to a six-minute tape of a newborn's cries, the cortisol levels of these new dads plummeted, just like those of the infants' mothers.[14] Taken as a whole, the emerging research illuminates the fact that fathers have a unique role to play in infant development and that close attachments are formed between infants and their fathers at the same time and in many of the same ways as they are being forged with mothers. It's clear that both parents have important roles to play in healthy attachment.

And it makes sense that one of the initial infant behaviors designed to create these attachments would be sound, because sound is quite familiar to the newborn. Hearing is fully developed at birth—in fact, from the third trimester of pregnancy the developing fetus has been able to take in roughly 60 percent of all the sounds surrounding his/her mother. Studies have shown that even two-day-old infants show a distinct preference for their mother's voice over all others and that all infants have a decided preference for human sounds and music over other kinds of sound or noise.

So, amid the orchestra (or barrage) of new noises babies are exposed to once they leave the womb, they "tune in" most reliably to human sounds. It is as though our senses are designed to help us, from the beginning, to "stick together," to find, and connect with, the human pack.

In addition to our sense of hearing, infants have a preprogrammed disposition to look at—to look for and see—human faces. Babies are particularly attracted to facial expressions. They can detect and distinguish between minuscule changes in emotional responsiveness. Between three and six months—to the delight of new parents—an infant begins to smile at the sight of a human face. It seems clear that this is an instinctive human behavior—an "innate releasing mechanism" in the same way that sea turtles know how to swim without being taught or birds can make nests specific to their species with no instruction. Several early studies have shown that infants will also smile at the sight of a mask resembling a human face so long as it has two eyes, a smooth forehead, and a nose. The mask has to be seen from the front and it has to show movement.

Curiously, the mask doesn't have to have a mouth; the infant's smile, these researchers concluded, was therefore not an imitation.[15]

Other evidence shows that even congenitally blind infants smile during pleasant interactions with their mothers. In *A General Theory of Love*, psychiatrists Thomas Lewis, Fari Amini, and Richard Lannon emphasize the importance of this observation as evidence that mammals are born to be social. "Such a smile comes from a developing creature unable to speak, walk, or even sit up, but he already knows how to express happiness through a configuration of muscular contractions he has never seen on anyone's face. His knowledge has to be innate. A blind baby's smile must reflect the brain's inherited emotional architecture."[16]

By the sixth month, infants are getting good at distinguishing between familiar and unfamiliar, friendly and unfriendly, faces.

And if infants are checking us out, we're doing the same to them. The mere sight of a baby elicits specific psychological and physiological responses in adult women and men. Think about the infant's large head, tiny chin, wide-open eyes with big pupils, chubby cheeks, pug nose, and small mouth. Scientists find that this configuration of stimuli seems to elicit warm, affectionate, and protective responses from adults (not to mention an immediate high-pitched, sing-songy form of speech universally recognized as "baby talk").

It seems clear, from these data and others, that evolution has provided many physiological, neurological, social, and psychological determinants that allow human beings to attach to newborns. When all goes well, an infant is protected and loved and begins to feel connected to others and the world. Held in the arms of a loving mother or father, the baby learns that the world can be safe, predictable, and delightful. He learns that someone responds to his needs. His cries for food or contact do not go unheeded but rather bring a delicious interaction with someone to whom he is attached. When he is loved, a baby is prepared to love, having been helped by innate tendencies that worked to insure connection. Embrace me, fellow human! A human baby begins immediately the dance of loving and being loved that he will need to continue throughout his life.

Ethologists, biologists, and endocrinologists have given us good evidence for the innate and imperative value of human connections. And psychologists confirm our inborn need to connect, to seek community with others.

Psychoanalyst Erik Erikson, in his model of the stages of development, described the basic task of the infancy stage as resolving the problem of "trust versus distrust." An infant learns to trust others, herself, and the environment when her physical and emotional needs are met and she is free from uncertainty, feels safe and protected, develops secure attachments, and knows that others will help and care for her. With this early experience, the infant will grow into a person with abilities to form and maintain relationships. She will have positive expectations about others, and a basic and long-standing belief in her own worthiness and the expectation that the world can be a safe place.

According to Erikson, if for any reason the infant cannot master this challenge, she will carry remnants of this uncompleted task into the next and subsequent stages of development and move through life with high levels of fear and insecurity. As an adult, she will see the world as an unfriendly, unpredictable, and chaotic place and will be unlikely to develop deep and intimate relationships with other people.

During the mid-1970s, developmental psychologist Mary Ainsworth, working with and building on the theories of John Bowlby, observed that some infants seemed relaxed and secure in their relationships, while others seemed anxious or uncertain. She postulated three kinds of enduring patterns of relationships that result from early attachments or the lack of them and that these early attachment patterns predict how that individual will experience love, loneliness, or grief as an adult.

Using a technique Ainsworth called the "strange situation," infants (generally eighteen to twenty months of age) and their mothers were left alone in a room while the infant was left to explore his/her surroundings. A stranger enters and the mother slips out of the room. A few minutes later the mother returns, and greets and comforts the infant. Through these repetitive patterns of separations from and reunions with mothers, Ainsworth and her colleagues—watching through a one-way mirror—observed and identified three discrete patterns of infant behavior, one indicating secure attachment and the other two indicating insecure attachments.

The "secure" pattern of attachment showed an infant who was developing healthy relationships and a strong sense of safety in the world. These babies used their parents as a "secure base" and felt empowered to explore their environment. These were infants whose mothers responded quickly and affectionately when they cried. These were mothers who met the baby's needs and were sensitive to the baby's signals. The other two patterns ("insecure-avoidant" and "insecure-ambivalent") seemed to be associated with mothers who showed little maternal sensitivity and more often responded to their own needs rather than those of the infant. Here's how Mary Ainsworth described them:

+ Secure—the infant was upset at the mother's departure and easily soothed when she returned. Ainsworth found that about 70 percent of infants fell into this category.
+ Insecure-Avoidant—infants avoided their mother. The infant may or may not be distressed by the mother's departure, but avoided or turned away from her on her return.
+ Insecure-Ambivalent—infants either passively or actively showed hostility toward the mother. The infant became highly distressed at the mother's departure but when she returned, the infant simultaneously sought both comfort and distance—crying and reaching to be held and then attempting to get away once picked up.

As we grow up, "secure" adults find it relatively easy to get close to others. They're happy, socially competent people with high levels of resiliency and persistence. They don't worry about being abandoned or having someone close to them. They're "emotionally intelligent," empathetic with others, solve many problems on their own but aren't reluctant to ask others for help when they need it. They maintain close, intimate connections with others.

On the other hand, "insecure-avoidant" adults have difficulty trusting others and can't depend upon anyone. They may become uncomfortable, even nervous, when someone gets too close.

"Insecure-ambivalent" adults are constantly worried that other people don't really like or love them. They are constantly vigilant for signs of abandonment and they are often timid and hypersensitive, and lack self-confidence. Their hunger for closeness may make others describe them as "needy" as adults.

Consider the story of one of my psychotherapy clients. Allison was born into a middle-class family where her physical needs were met very well. Before she was a month old, though, her father was killed in a traffic accident and her mother retreated into a deep depression. Her mom could barely manage to take care of her four young kids and the house.

Allison was always fed and changed but her mother didn't have the energy to respond to her cries for comfort or attention. She tells me that she often dreams about a sad-faced woman who picks her up, then drops her. But Allison is not angry with her mother. She understands that as a young widow, her mother was overwhelmed with responsibilities and deeply grieving the loss of her husband. Allison has forgiven her mother and says that her mother "did the best she could," which I also believe to be true. If you were to meet Allison casually you would never know that she carries scars from her difficulties with early attachment. Allison is a successful person by many measures. She is a professional, has a good job, and earns a lot of money. She has relatively good social skills and a few acquaintances with whom she plays golf or goes to an occasional movie. But she doesn't really trust anyone and has spent most of her life emotionally and psychologically alone. She says, "I just can't seem to get really close to anyone." She came to me for therapy when she was diagnosed with cancer in her late thirties and realized that she didn't have a single person in her life whom she could call on for help or who would really care. Allison suffers from an attachment disorder of the insecure-avoidant kind. She just can't trust anyone enough to get close.

Unlike Allison, Bob hungers for connection with others but pushes people away with his "neediness." But like Allison, he doesn't trust people or his relationships to them either. He is constantly playing "come here, go away" with people who love him—a classic aspect of an insecure-ambivalent attachment disorder.

Bob was raised in a series of foster homes where he was fed and his physical needs taken care of, but there was no consistent person to love and hold him. Just when he would begin to form a relationship with his foster family, he was sent to another one. His whole early life was a series of comings and goings. If you ask him to tell you about his early childhood, he can barely remember the names of the families that took him in. He's been divorced twice and each time his wife told him that she had to leave because she just couldn't stand his clingy, demanding, and controlling behavior. No matter how much attention either of his wives gave him, it was never enough. Bob described to me how anxious he became when his current wife took off for something as simple and nonthreatening as an evening out to a movie with her girlfriends. When she returned, he'd accuse her of wanting to leave him and demand that she tell him exactly where she had been. He'd tell her to leave if she didn't love him anymore when all she'd done was go to a movie with her women friends. In spite of her innocence of betraying him, Bob saw rejection and abandonment in every detail of her behavior. Once he found a credit card charge to a men's store and screamed that she must be having an affair. He wanted her to leave. In fact, his wife had purchased a sport coat for his birthday—still more than a month away—while it was on sale.

His third wife told him that she did love him but couldn't stand his neediness anymore. She threatened to divorce him unless he stopped being so insecure and demanding. He needed help, she told him. Bob came to my office in tears. "I know I'm being paranoid but I just can't stop feeling that I'll come home from work and she'll be gone. I can't trust that she loves me," he said. Bob clearly suffers from an attachment disorder of the insecure/ambivalent type.

As adults, both Allison and Bob show clear symptoms of the adult expression of attachment disorders; while their behavior might be extreme, many people have some elements of these difficulties in creating and maintaining relationships. Two points are important here. First, early problems with attachment are reflected in how we relate to others as adults. Psychotherapists sometimes refer to "object relations" to describe how people develop adult relationship patterns that are very similar to the ones they learned as infants and children. Years of psychological research have given support to Dostoyevsky's insightful words, "It seems, in fact, as though the second half of a man's life is made up of nothing but the habits he has accumulated during the first half."

Habits of attachment and relationships, like all habits, are formed through repetition. Neuroscientist Gerald Edelman (who won the 1972 Nobel Prize for medicine) theorized that our most familiar ways of thinking, feeling, and reacting are based on simple repetitions between brain cells. Those thoughts and feelings that are repeated over and over form into a kind of neurological groove and this becomes our predominant way of responding to the world. This is the neurological take on how patterns are established, how we "get in a rut." Think about taking a certain path through a field. Day after day, year after year, you take the very same path. Over time, that path will be well worn and becomes the easiest one to take—in fact, we take that path automatically. Through the never-ending echoes of repetition, the more the path is beaten down, the more it is used; the more it is used, the more beaten down it becomes. In the meantime, while we're traveling this same deeply etched path, weeds will overgrow the rest of the field. These favored paths—these habits of mind—become the filters through which we experience the world. That's what's happened to Bob, Allison, and Niki. Their early experiences showed them that no one was there to love or comfort them. In order to survive, their brains etched certain pathways and their behavior responded to their reality: "No one is going to answer my cries. I don't expect anyone to love me." They developed certain *schemas*—patterns that began in childhood that keep repeating themselves whether or not they are needed or functional.[17] In fact, without some intervention to break those habits of mind—like specialized therapy—these expectations will continue to be the lens through which they will view the world and their relationships to others.

The point is: we don't leave our past behind. Instead, we wear the residue of early experience in our cells and our memories like a ghostly shroud. If we have grown up in a family where love and expressions of tenderness have been scarce, we are likely to see our current relationships as unreliable, viewing them with mistrust and suspicion. Those who grew up with loving, secure attachments find it easier to be open and trusting as they grow up. As adults, we don't need caretakers in the same ways we did as infants. Most of us can satisfy many of our basic needs—we can usually find our way to the refrigerator—but without deeply felt connections we suffer psychological, physical, and spiritual problems.

The second, more optimistic, point is that people *can* recover from early attachment problems. It's a long, hard road, but with therapy both Allison and Bob have become more conscious of how their difficulties with early attachment affect their present relationships, and they are making willful changes in their behavior. And don't forget about little Niki—raised under the most appalling circumstances in a Romanian orphanage but with a loving family, connections to peers and community, and special therapy, he is learning to create and maintain relationships. He's finding his way in the world. Perhaps the final act of development and maturity is to rewrite the circuits that no longer serve us.

A number of psychological inventories have been developed to assess the nature of adult attachment and relationships. One of the best, the Adult Attachment Scale (AAS), was developed by social psychologists Nancy Collins and Stephen Read in 1990.[18] I'm not using this scale as a scientific test but rather as an opportunity to reflect. Just take a minute to rate yourself on the following questions. Use a 1- to 5-point scale where 1 means "not at all" and 5 means "very much so." Each question refers to a style of adult attachment where Av = Insecure/Avoidant; S = Secure; and Ax = Insecure/Ambivalent. What can you learn about yourself and your own safe harbor by looking at the ways you relate to others? Where do you feel strong and where do you need shoring up?

Think about This

Adult Attachment Scale (AAS) by Collins and Read (1990)
Reprinted with permission.

- I find it difficult to allow myself to depend on others (Av)
- People are never there when you need them (Av)
- I am comfortable depending on others (S)
- I know that others will be there when I need them (S)
- I find it difficult to trust others completely (Av)
- I am not sure that I can always depend on others to be there when I need them (Ax)
- I do not often worry about being abandoned (S)
- I often worry that my partner does not really love me (Ax)
- I find others are reluctant to get as close as I would like (Ax)
- I often worry my partner will not want to stay with me (Ax)
- I want to merge completely with another person (Ax)
- My desire to merge sometimes scares people away (Ax)
- I find it relatively easy to get close to others (S)
- I do not often worry about someone getting close to me (S)
- I am somewhat uncomfortable being close to others (Av)
- I am nervous when anyone gets too close (Av)
- I am comfortable having others depend on me (S)
- Often, love partners want me to be more intimate than I feel comfortable being (Av)

Appreciating the ancient and potent biological need that human beings have for belongingness and attachment is crucial if we want to understand the importance of human connections. We are born biologically ready and predisposed to attach to others and our early experiences draw the map that will serve us (or not) throughout our lives. We have also seen how that map can be rewritten (we need to be loved to learn to love). But the central point is that connection, love, the proximity of others are not luxuries for humans, they are basic needs. Without them, we're in trouble.

Well, You Got to Have Friends

In the spring of 2001, six-year-old Haley Jennifer Zega wandered away from her grandparents while hiking in the Arkansas wilderness. She was lost for three days as her family and search parties frantically combed the Ozark Mountains looking for her. Thankfully, two men riding mules near the confluence of Dug Hollow Creek and the Buffalo National River found her, exhausted but alive. She had lost five pounds (she only weighed forty-eight pounds to begin with), was dehydrated, and was covered with scratches. When she was asked how she was able to survive she told rescuers that she had befriended a caterpillar in the cave where she had sought safety. She said that she named it White Spot after the two white spots on its head and that it kept her company until she was able to find her way out of the steep valley.[19]

In the movie *Castaway*, Tom Hanks plays Chuck Noland, a character trapped on a deserted island. He's swum ashore after his Federal Express cargo plane has crashed into the ocean. With nothing but his resilience, imagination, and the occasional FedEx package that washes ashore containing some nonessential items—at least if you're marooned on a tropical island—like ice skates, videotapes, or a volleyball, he must learn to survive. Before he has even solved the problems of food, water, and shelter (not to mention escape or rescue), he creates a companion—he names the volleyball Wilson and begins to talk to him. I'm reluctant to admit that I cried during the movie when Wilson floated away.

The stories of the real little girl Haley Zega and the fictional Chuck Noland make an interesting point. Companionship—the need to connect with another—may be as important as food, water, and shelter to the human animal. The need for relationship is a fundamental requirement for our species.

The humanistic psychologist Abraham Maslow fervently believed in the positive potential of every human being and of the human species itself. We are psychologically designed to move to ever increasing levels of health, creativity, and self-fulfillment. But human beings have very fundamental physical and psychological needs that must be satisfied before they can live up to their full potential as individuals. It's impossible to contemplate the meaning of your existence or "self-actualize" ("Be all that you can be") if you're fighting off predators or have no access to food or water. In order to understand these human needs, Maslow developed a scale that he called a "Hierarchy of Needs." His scale is often pictured as a pyramid, with the most fundamental human needs at the base. The establishment of each level of this pyramid is dependent on the stability of the levels below. Here's one depiction of what Maslow's pyramid looks like:[20]

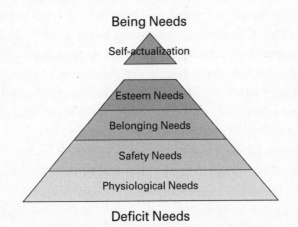

The very base of the pyramid and the most indispensable requirements for human life are physiological needs—air, water, food, sleep—all of those things that are required for existence. Once those needs are satisfied—and in very short order—human beings need safety—protection from wild animals and the elements, the establishment of stability, and consistency in what is often a chaotic world.

Love and belongingness are next in line. Maslow believed that human beings have clear biological needs to love and be loved, to feel a part of a tribe, to need and be needed. In short, people have to belong, and he saw this as an essential aspect of living a human life. "The love need . . . is a deficit need," he wrote. "It is a hole which has to be filled, an emptiness into which love is poured. If this healing necessity is not available, severe pathology results; if it is available at the right time, in the right quantities and with proper style, then pathology is averted."[21] Or in the more poetic words of French author Antoine de Saint-Exupery, "Man is a knot, a web, a mesh into which relationships are tied."[22]

Only when these primary needs are met are we psychologically free to earn respect from others and develop self-confidence, self-esteem, and a sense of mastery for oneself ("esteem needs").

All of these most basic needs Maslow referred to as "deficit needs"—that is, if these needs are not fulfilled, an individual will either die (as with the lack of food, water, or air) or fall into some state of psychological pathology or neurosis (as in the lack of belongingness or esteem). On the other hand, if these needs are satisfied, physical and psychological illness can be averted and the way is cleared for the pursuit of higher-order development as a human being.

The pursuit of self-actualization—being involved in causes outside our own skin and realizing our deepest psychological and spiritual potential—depends upon our basic needs being met and represents a different kind of need. Maslow called this a "Being Need." To Maslow, self-actualizing people are "man [*sic*] at his best," have suitably satisfied their basic needs, and are on a journey of higher developmental possibilities—to "the farther reaches of human nature." Once basic needs are fulfilled, people are free to explore their creativity, their imaginations, and their place in the larger order of the universe. "Musicians must make music, artists must paint, poets must write if they are to be ultimately at peace with themselves. What humans *can* be, they *must* be. They must be true to their own nature," Maslow wrote.[23]

Self-actualizing people are less judgmental and more tolerant, mature, creative, and vibrant. Their sense of existence is both more fully human and more transpersonal, with deep feelings of connection to other people, the world, and to some larger creative intelligence in the universe.

Maslow came to his theory of self-actualization as a result of observing and studying people he believed to be highly functional, psychologically healthy people. He found that these were people who accomplished much, found meaning in their lives, and were moving on a path of self-growth and development. Highly conscious, creative, and—perhaps most important—happy, self-actualized people had a realistic understanding of what it means to live a human life and were doing so with élan.

In addition to the individuals he studied, Maslow looked at historical figures who—in his mind—represented the realization of their full potential. Among those he described were Abraham Lincoln, Thomas Jefferson, Mahatma Gandhi, Albert Einstein, Eleanor Roosevelt, and William James. While Maslow himself avoided the word *spiritual,* values that he often used in describing self-actualization include: beauty, unity, aliveness, uniqueness, perfection, justice, order, simplicity, and transcendence. Here are some of the characteristics Maslow found among self-actualizing people. As you read through them, think about which ones apply to you:

1. Superior perception of reality.
2. Increased acceptance of self, of others, and of nature.
3. Increased spontaneity.
4. Increased problem-solving—a task orientation, rather than self-preoccupation.
5. Increased desire for privacy and solitude.
6. Increased autonomy, and resistance to enculturation. Independence.
7. Greater freshness of appreciation, and richness of emotional reaction.
8. Higher frequency of peak experiences (a term Maslow used to describe the realization that what "ought to be" is, in a way that requires no longing, no straining. It's the blissful feeling of "oneness" or unity with God and life itself that spiritual mystics describe.)[24]
9. Spirituality that is not necessarily religious in a formal sense.
10. Increased identification with mankind.
11. Feelings of intimacy with a few loved ones.
12. Democratic values.
13. Greatly increased creativity.
14. Humor that is philosophical rather than hostile.
15. Nonconformity.[25]

One of Maslow's most important points is that we must satisfy our most basic needs before we can move on to higher levels of psychological development.

With their basic human needs satisfied—the "deficiency needs"—self-actualizing people are able to contemplate the larger questions about life and being. They are prepared to ask the question that British writer Lewis Carroll once put forth: "Who in the world am I? Ah, that's the great puzzle."

It is not too difficult to argue with Maslow's methodology. After all, he based his ideas on observations of people who he selected and decided were "self-actualized." Most people would agree that this process isn't very scientific. In his defense, though, Maslow always said he was just "pointing the way," and that future psychologists could confirm or refute his theory of self-actualization and human development through more empirical means. Although Maslow put his theory into a form that resonates with many people, he's not the only or even the first one to talk about the drives enabling human beings to live up to their greatest psychological and spiritual potentials. For example, psychologist Carl Jung refers to the process of "individuation" (from the Latin *individuus*, for "undivided," "not fragmented," or "whole"). Psychologist Carl Rogers called the same phenomenon "self-realization." Though there are some subtle differences between these concepts, basically they're different words to describe the same thing. Long before twentieth-century psychologists began describing how human beings live up to their fullest potential, spiritual and wisdom traditions in every culture understood this process of human self-growth, of the unfolding of our true natures, and the feelings of unity and goodwill it creates.

This process of coming home to the Self, fulfilling one's destiny by following one's unique path of development, is an idea that has resonated in all cultures throughout the history of the human race. It is a philosophy of growth and development of the personality that can be found throughout Western philosophy since the time of Aristotle, and it appears in the work of Schopenhauer, Aquinas, Leibniz, Spinoza, and Locke, among others. The ancient world is filled with images, myths, fairy tales, poetry, and prayers that outline this spiraling pathway. The Lakota Sioux called this journey the Good Red Road, to the Navajo, it is the Pollen Path, and the Chinese simply say "Tao." Religious and spiritual traditions speak of "being in a state of grace," "enlightenment," "opening the third eye," or finding "nirvana."

But how does Maslow's idea that basic needs (like food and water) must be met in order to realize the higher ones (like love and belongingness) jive with stories of people sharing food with others even when they themselves are starving? How does this idea account for those people in greatly deprived circumstances, such as prisons or concentration camps, who express compassion, generosity, or creativity when their own lives are hanging by a thread? There are many examples of this: the sixth-century Roman philosopher Boethius wrote his brilliant book, *The Consolation of Philosophy*, while unjustly imprisoned (and later executed). Jakow Trachtenberg developed a new system of speed mathematics amid the horror of a German concentration camp.

While imprisoned at Auschwitz and Dachau and subjected to unspeakable atrocities, psychiatrist Viktor Frankl developed his approach to psychotherapy ("We had nothing left to lose but our ridiculously naked lives"). His mother, father, brother, and wife were gassed in German concentration camps, he was starved until his own body "began to devour itself," and yet he somehow found the strength to rise above his conditions and maintain his dignity, grace, and compassion in the process. In his remarkable book *Man's Search for Meaning*, Frankl writes that the only way to survive suffering is to find meaning in it.[26] When he looked around him, he found that the people who physically and psychologically survived the terror and deprivation of the camps were those who found some meaning in their suffering and felt a deep connection to others. These people survived in order to take care of someone else they loved or held a hopeful heart that they would see loved ones again. Some carried on so that they could bear witness to the world about what happened. Frankl observed, "Every man was controlled by one thought only: to keep himself alive for the family waiting for him at home, and to save his friends."[27]

Frankl concluded his horrific experience with the observation that "love is the ultimate and the highest goal to which man can aspire. Then I grasped the meaning of the greatest secret that human poetry and human thought and belief have to impart: The salvation of man is through love and in love."[28]

Frankl's conclusions are stunning, especially in light of the suffering that inspired him. From the depths of pain and sorrow, he realized that compassion and love were central to living a human life—regardless of the circumstances. He understood how important love and connection were if we are ever to master the art of living. What he wrote holds important implications for thinking about the importance of belongingness and connection to the human species. And it seems that our human species is not alone in this need to connect to and look out for one another. As ethologist and zoologist Frans de Waal points out in his book *Good Natured: The Origins of Right and Wrong in Humans and Other Animals*, behaviors that aid the group and foster connections even at peril to the individual are ubiquitous throughout the animal kingdom. "Aiding others at a cost or risk to oneself is widespread in the animal world. The warning calls of birds allow other birds to escape a predator's talons, but attract attention to the caller. Sterile castes in social instincts do little else than serve food to the larvae of their queen or sacrifice themselves in defense of their colony. Assistance by relatives enables a breeding pair of jays to fill more hungry mouths and thus raise more offspring than otherwise possible. Dolphins support injured companions close to the surface in order to keep them from drowning. And so on."[29]

Self-actualization and transcendence are certainly goals to which we should aspire. After all, our lives would be infinitely richer if we were going about the task of becoming our own unique, authentic, and remarkable selves. But what happens when we fail to satisfy our basic needs? Without air, water, food, or protection from wild animals, we'll die.

What is not so obvious is what happens when we fail to satisfy our needs for belongingness, when we are unable to find our safe harbor. A mounting body of evidence has shown that without human contact and connection at critical developmental periods, infants die. And so do adults.

The Power of Connection

If you could do just *one thing* that would lengthen your life, help you stay psychologically and physically healthy, and support your healing when you did become ill, you would maintain strong connections to other people. The effects of belongingness are so potent that if they could be bottled, they would need FDA approval.

And the reverse is also true: If you don't feel loved or have close relationships with other people, statistically you live with a three to five times higher risk of premature death and disease. You have an increased risk of heart attack, stroke, cancer, arthritis, and allergies. You are more susceptible to infectious diseases—everything from tuberculosis to the common cold. Without love and connection you are more likely to suffer from depression, drug abuse, alcoholism, and even suicide.

The evidence for the power of connection is overwhelming and compelling and entire books have been written documenting scientific studies that show the power of love and relationships to heal and extend life.

As early as 1897, French sociologist Emile Durkheim was interested in demonstrating how even what appears to be the most individualistic act can only be understood by examining the social context in which that behavior occurs. During his observations, he noticed that suicide rates varied dramatically between geographic areas and that one could predict rates of suicide (and crime as well) by looking at the quality of social ties in an area. In areas where there was strong "social solidarity" (we might call it "social capital" today), suicide rates were low. Areas where social ties were weak had much higher rates of suicide.

Among his findings was the identification of higher-than-average rates of suicide among unmarried men and women. Durkheim concluded that at least one major factor among people who commit suicide is that they suffer from a lack of social integration, have become "detached from society," and have failed to create bonds that link them to others.[30]

Ironically, more modern-day evidence for the importance of belongingness in extending life and health began with a conversation over a beer in the 1950s. The head of medicine at the University of Oklahoma was visiting a local physician when that country doctor casually mentioned a happy but puzzling observation: heart disease was much less prevalent in Roseto, Pennsylvania, than it was in nearby towns. The local doc also pointed out that Roseto was populated by Italian-American families whose ancestors had left Roseto Val Fortore, a rural village in the foothills of the Apennines in southern Italy, in hopes of finding the American Dream in the slate quarries of eastern Pennsylvania.

Enter the epidemiologists, statisticians, and physicians. Like moths to a flame, researchers rushed to Roseto to try to discover what magic potion accounted for the fact that Rosetans lived longer lives than their neighbors and were virtually free of heart disease. Researchers discovered that there was a near-zero cardiac mortality rate for men aged fifty-five to sixty-four, and for men over the age of sixty-five, the death rate was less than half the national average. Had the residents of Roseto found the alchemical *Elixir Vitae*?

At first, researchers looked to genetic factors. After all, most of the residents of Roseto were descended from the same small group of Italian families that had immigrated to the United States. But this hypothesis didn't stand up when they observed that when members of these families moved away—even to the nearby town of Bangor or Nazareth—their rates of heart disease went up and began to mirror the rest of the nation's.

Researchers knew that Roseto shared its water supply, hospital facilities, and physicians with neighboring towns where heart disease reflected national averages. So those variables didn't explain anything. They next began investigating other health behaviors of Roseto residents, but if you think they found a community of carrot-munching joggers with less than 10 percent body fat, zero cigarette smoking, and little alcohol consumption, you'd be wrong. Instead, the men in Roseto smoked and drank wine freely after a long day at the slate quarries where they scrounged out a living working two hundred feet down at their hazardous, back-breaking jobs. Their dinner tables were a cardiologist's nightmare, groaning with spaghetti and meatballs, potatoes, roast chicken, antipasto, and spaghetti again. Unable to afford their traditional olive oil, the residents of Roseto fried up their meatballs and sausages in lard. They were just as overweight and sedentary as folks in neighboring towns, yet here they were with healthy hearts and long lives.

During their studies, researchers also noticed two other interesting differences between Roseto and nearby communities: both the crime rate and the applications for public assistance were nonexistent.

After ruling out just about every risk factor for heart disease, researchers began to suspect that perhaps it was Roseto's high level of social capital (though they didn't use that term) that was responsible for their superior heart health. They discovered that Roseto was a close-knit community with lots of trust, social cohesion, and mutual respect. The local value system was entirely egalitarian—you couldn't tell the rich from the poor in their manner of dress, the cars they drove, or the houses they lived in. There was a kind of social taboo against conspicuous consumption and ostentatious displays of wealth.

What's more, all of the families in Roseto lived in multigenerational families where elderly people were held in high esteem, their lives centered on family, and they built their houses so close that their front porches almost touched one another. In this town, people knew one another well and got together often, congregating on those front porches, at social clubs, and on evening walks. They had brought the community together by establishing a mutual aid society, sports clubs, labor union, Scout troops, park and athletic field, labor union, and newspaper. Everyone attended big church festivals where they participated in or enjoyed the performance of the town's coronet band that had been started by their ancestors in 1890.

But by the 1960s and 1970s something began to happen in Roseto, and those changes changed everything. The tightly knit family structure and close community began to erode. Young people began to chafe under the rigid, traditional lifestyle of their parents and grandparents and began to move away. Residents—no longer constrained by social taboos that frowned on displays of ostentation and wealth—built large single-family houses with swimming pools and fenced yards on the outskirts of town. Materialism became a stronger value than community. While being interviewed, one person who had moved to the suburbs said, "I'm sorry we moved; everything is modern here and we have everything I need here, except people."[31]

The descendants of those early Italian immigrants had indeed achieved the American dream—and they paid for it. By the early 1970s, there was no longer the strong sense of belonging to a group, no longer the same clear sense of connection and love, and the mortality rate from heart disease in Roseto rose to the same level as that of the rest of the nation. In 1971, the town experienced the first heart attack death of someone under the age of forty-five. In 1985 and for the first time, the town's coronet band demanded to be paid for their performance at the big church festival.

Stewart Wolf (a physician) and J. G. Bruhn (a sociologist) documented the golden age of the Roseto community and its decline from 1935 to 1984 in their book *The Power of Clan*. They concluded, "People are nourished by other people." It seems that the power of connection mitigates against heart disease by reducing stress and isolation. In looking at almost fifty years of data about the Roseto Effect, Stewart Wolf wrote, "Those with the conventional risk factors are more likely to develop myocardial infarction (heart attacks) than are those without the risk factors, but an even larger proportion of the population may have the risk factors and not succumb to myocardial infarction if they are protected by a strong sense of connection and community."[32]

As researchers continued to study the Roseto Effect, they amassed a collection of evidence that confirms that close ties to other people have a protective effect against illness and death, and that social isolation is a killer. Between 1979 and 1994, eight large-scale community-based studies confirmed what those early researchers had found in Roseto.

In a study with cancer patients, Dr. David Spiegel of the Stanford University School of Medicine investigated the effects of psychosocial variables on survival of patients with metastatic breast cancer. Ironically, he had set out to disprove the relationship between social support and cancer survival. But his results caused him to rethink his position. The data showed that women who became involved in a supportive-expressive group not only experienced an improved quality of life and were more hopeful, but they actually lived longer. Using a rigorous scientific methodology, women with breast cancer were randomly assigned to one of two groups. Both groups received state-of-the art surgery, chemotherapy, radiation, and medications. But one group of women met together for ninety minutes once a week. This support group encouraged the women to talk about their feelings and how they were coping with cancer. It provided a safe place in which a woman could cry and laugh in the presence of others who knew exactly what she was going through. In his description of what happened in these groups, Dr. Spiegel observed that the women in the support group clearly felt an intense bonding with one another and a sense of acceptance through sharing a common challenge. The women in the support group on average lived twice as long as the women who were not in a support group.[33] Hundreds of other studies demonstrate the positive effect of connection on health and longevity.

I Get By with a Little Help from My Friends

In spite of dramatic and significant improvements in medical diagnosis and treatment over the past twenty-five years and the fact that Americans actually live longer, there has been a significant decline in *self-reported* health. It seems that we're living longer, but we're feeling worse.[34] During the same period of enhanced health care, levels of social connection have declined and rates of depression and suicide have increased. In any given year, for example, 10 percent of Americans will suffer from major depression. The prevalence of depression is so predictable that public health experts have given it an infectious disease–type name. They call it Agent Blue.

On the other hand, strong social connections create many positive effects. For example, students who are more motivated and achieve high grades experience higher self-esteem and use the least amount of drugs and alcohol; they also feel most connected to their school and classmates.[35] These results have been shown in a wide variety of studies using students from kindergarten all the way through medical and graduate school. For example, the two most significant predictors of health and happiness in old age are the frequency of visits with friends and frequency of attendance at meetings of organizations. Many studies from the business and organizational development literature attest to the profoundly positive effects of belongingness (feeling a part of a "team") on everything from job satisfaction to retention and productivity. Businesses recognize these effects and pay millions each year to consultants and trainers who help their employees boost feelings of community and work together toward shared goals.

A landmark new study has suggested an interesting difference between men and women, stress and connection that holds implications for everyone's health and well-being and may even explain the ubiquitous finding that women outlive men. The creative idea for this study arose—as inspirations so often do in science and medicine—from a serendipitous and everyday observation. Laura Klein and Shelley Taylor—researchers at UCLA—joked about the fact that the women and men who worked in the Stress Research Lab behaved very differently when they were stressed out (yes, people who work in stress research labs can get stressed out). When women were stressed, they came in, cleaned up the lab, had coffee together, and bonded. When the men were stressed out, "they holed up in their offices on their own." These researchers designed a study to look at the differences between men and women responding to stress, and their results showed very clearly that making connections with other people is part of the human behavioral repertoire—at least for women. The findings of this study suggest that there are more behavioral reactions to stress than simply "fighting or fleeing." When women are stressed they respond with a surge of brain chemicals—such as oxytocin—that buffer the "fight or flight" reaction, produce a calming effect, and push them to seek one another's company. (Remember? Oxytocin is the same biochemical that promotes maternal behavior.) Once a woman engages in connecting or befriending behaviors, even more oxytocin is released. And so it goes, in women at least, that stress leads to the release of oxytocin, which leads to social contact, which leads to the release of more oxytocin, which leads to greater relaxation and stress reduction. It seems that estrogen (predominately a female hormone) has an enhancing effect on oxytocin and this "tend and befriend" response, whereas testosterone (predominately a male hormone) reduces it. What's more, Klein's other research suggests that from infancy on, social contact releases a cascade of hormones that reduce stress. Taken in conjunction with the numerous studies that show that social ties lower blood pressure, heart rate, and cholesterol, Dr. Klein (now an assistant professor of biobehavioral health at Penn State) concluded, "There's no doubt. Friends are helping us live longer."[36]

It is abundantly clear that feelings of belonging, connections, and identifying with a community have positive outcomes for every human being on a wide variety of measures and throughout the life cycle.

So what does it mean to be lonely? Surely the pure presence of other people does not make us automatically feel a sense of belonging. We all know that it's quite possible to be lonely in a crowd. And while it certainly helps to have regular, face-to-face interactions with friends and family, we can still enjoy feelings of connection and belongingness—still know that we are loved—while living alone on a mountaintop or tucked away in an ashram or monastery.

Being comfortable with and sometimes being alone are signs of good mental health, and solitude has a profound role in the lives of creative, mature, and self-actualized individuals. Solitude can be spiritually and psychologically enriching, giving opportunities to meditate, pray, and contemplate the larger issues of living a human life. In fact, monks, hermits, and spiritual pilgrims throughout time and across cultures have emphasized the way that God speaks to them in silence and solitude. Lord Byron alluded to this power of aloneness as a path to self-growth and spiritual enlightenment when he wrote, "In solitude, where we are least alone."

Theologian Paul Tillich makes what I consider to be the clearest distinction between loneliness and solitude: "Language has created the word 'loneliness' to express the pain of being alone, and the world 'solitude' to express the glory of being alone."

Feelings of loneliness are not just understood through the statistics of social capital or studies of longevity. Perhaps loneliness is not even best understood by way of its demographics, for the despair of loneliness sears the soul. An isolated heart is of the inner world of the psyche and spirit. And, not surprisingly, there are big differences between *social loneliness* and *emotional loneliness*.

Social loneliness is the feeling you might have when you move to a new town and haven't yet developed a social network or while on an extended business trip and you miss your family or you're so busy that you don't have time to spend with friends. This kind of loneliness might be thought of as *state loneliness*. In this case, a person has attachments and friends but for some external—usually environmental—reason can't hang out with them. This kind of loneliness subsides when you make friends in your new neighborhood, return from that extended trip, or make time in your life for friends and those you love.

Emotional loneliness, on the other hand, is a feeling that follows a person everywhere, like a shadowy specter that surrounds every moment of every day. This is more a *trait loneliness*, and describes a person who is not close to anyone, doesn't trust others, and feels constantly isolated, cut off, rejected, "left out," or "different" from other people. There is no one to share life's struggles and joys. People who experience this kind of loneliness can party for weeks with superficial friends and might never be physically alone but, nevertheless, are not emotionally nourished and so feel isolated and alone. Most often, emotional loneliness leads to depression, low self-esteem, social alienation, and, in some cases, violent, antisocial behavior.

Countless newscasts have followed up on some horrific acts of violence against innocent people, with interviews of neighbors who always seem to say the same thing: "He was so quiet. He kept to himself. No one really knew him very well." Sometime before April 20, 1999, eighteen-year-old Eric Harris could no longer bear his feelings of anger, rejection, and isolation. He scribbled in his journal: "I hate you people for leaving me out of so many fun things. You people had my phone number and I asked and all, but no no no no no don't let the weird-looking Eric kid come along."

At 11:35 A.M. on Tuesday, April 20, 1999—the 110th anniversary of Adolf Hitler's birth—Eric and Dylan Klebold, hiding semiautomatic handguns, shotguns, and explosives under their long black trench coats, calmly walked into the cafeteria of their affluent Columbine High School in Littleton, Colorado, and laughed and hooted as they unloaded their guns into a crowd of students and teachers. Then they headed to the library, screaming, and shooting more students, before killing themselves. In the end, 15 people were dead, 24 injured, many seriously, 160 were treated at the scene, and a nation was shaken to its very core. A suicide note, anonymously e-mailed to the police after the massacre at Columbine High School, made Eric's vitriolic hatred of everyone even more clear: "By now it's over," it began. "If you are reading this, my mission is complete. . . . Your children who have ridiculed me, who have chosen not to accept me, who have treated me like I am not worth their time are dead. They are fucking dead."

In the aftermath of Columbine and other terrible and senseless murders of children by children in American schools, experts have looked for answers. Rage, depression, emotional immaturity, exposure to and obsession with violent film images and video games, an easy access to guns and other weapons lead the list of suspects. It's not my intention to conduct a psychological postmortem on teenagers who are so filled with despair and rage that they cannot imagine anything else to do with their feelings except to explode outward in a final act of self-destruction, desperate violence, and expression of power. But it is clear that in our increasingly alienated world so low in social capital, horrifying events of this kind will be on the increase. Perhaps this is just one of the reasons why the Family and Youth Services Bureau (U.S. Department of Health and Human Services) lists increasing "a sense of belonging" among America's young people as one of the four most critical goals of that agency. A special report, "Toward a Blueprint for Youth: Making Positive Youth Development a National Priority," focuses on the importance of instilling in adolescents a sense of competence (being able to do something well), a sense of usefulness (having something to contribute), a sense of belonging (being part of a community and having relationships with caring adults), and a sense of power (having control over one's future). This report concludes, "If these factors are being addressed, and basic needs are being met (food, clothes, health care, safety, and security), young people can become fully prepared to engage constructively in their communities."[37]

The rather antiseptic definitions the dictionary gives to the word *loneliness* don't convey the shredding pain, the hollowness, of some people's isolation, nor do they reveal the subtleties of different kinds of loneliness. Instead, I think the way this middle-aged woman describes her feelings of emotional loneliness gets more to the point: "Loneliness is a feeling of having no common bond with the people around you. The feeling is akin to being an alien and all those around you are speaking of a language and life that you can see only in magazines. Loneliness is feeling disconnected and lost, even in the midst of family."[38] This woman's words vibrate with the real emotional pain of loneliness in much the same way as those of short-story writer John Cheever: "A lonely man is a lonesome thing, a stone, a bone, a stick, a receptacle for Gilbey's gin, a stooped figure sitting at the edge of a hotel bed, heaving copious sighs like the autumn wind."

Loneliness and a failure of belongingness are most chilling when they are complete—when there is no one to care or comfort, no one to embrace or include us. In spite of what other advantages we may have in life—a warm house, food to eat, money to spend—when we are disconnected, without attachments of the heart, we are psychologically and spiritually destitute. Mother Teresa, who spent her life among the sick, dying, and desperately poor people of Calcutta, India, understood that it is the isolated heart, not a lack of money, that is life's greatest burden. She once said, "Loneliness and the feeling of being unwanted is the most terrible poverty."

Both our instincts and science show us the truth in seventeenth-century British writer John Donne's oft-quoted words: "No man is an island, entire of itself; every man is a piece of the continent, a part of the main." Living well—perhaps even staying alive—not to mention individuating or self-actualizing, requires a surrounding container of loving relationships. In the next chapter, we'll look at where we are now in America with a mind to answering one specific question: Does our society offer opportunities for safe harbors as we embark on the twenty-first century?

TWO

Are We Bowling Alone?

> What makes loneliness an anguish is not that
> I have no one to share my burden, but this:
> I have only my own burden to bear.
>
> *—Dag Hammarskjöld, Secretary-General*
>   *of the United Nations, 1953–1961;*
>   *Nobel Peace Prize recipient, 1961*

We've seen just how fiercely humans are biologically and psychologically designed to connect with one another. We yearn for the feeling that we belong and are loved. But as we'll see, there are many signs that our society is sorely lacking in this deep and essential experience of community. Many of us cannot find our tribe; most of us can't even find the time to try. We're socially isolated and wax nostalgic for the golden days of yore when families spent time together, when friends knew each other intimately, when neighbors cared about one another and—like the theme song from *Cheers*—when we had a place where everybody knows our name. But, for the most part, we're not hanging out together basking in the warm feelings of relatedness to one another, our community, nature, and the world itself. Instead, loneliness is rampant and the majority of us are bowling alone.

Bowling alone?

Did you know that bowling is the most popular sport in America? In 1996, more than 91 million Americans bowled, 25 percent more than voted in the 1998 congressional elections. Bowlers outnumber joggers, skiers, golfers, and soccer players by more than two to one. I had no idea bowling was so popular, even though my Aunt Jeannie ("Gutterball Jeannie") has bowled with the same group of women for more than thirty years. Her nickname hints at her skill level, but the results of her matches are inconsequential to her. She goes every Tuesday night for the friendship and connection. At the Toms River Lanes in New Jersey, Jeannie belongs.

More Americans are bowling than ever before (an increase in 10 percent from 1980 to 1993). Surprisingly, though, league bowling has plummeted by more than 40 percent during this same time period. If this trend continues, league bowling will vanish in the first decade of this new century.

In his whimsically titled though profound book *Bowling Alone*,[1] Harvard professor and political scientist Robert D. Putnam gives encyclopedic references to the changes in community and social connectedness that have occurred in American society since World War II. Putnam draws upon massive data from the Roper Social and Political Trends and the DDB Needham Life Style—surveys that report on details of Americans' changing behavior over the past twenty-five years. What he says isn't pretty. Among other startling findings, Putnam reports that the number of Americans who spent any time at all in informal socializing with friends fell steadily, from about 65 percent in 1965 to less than 39 percent in 1995. From 1974 to 1998, the frequency with which Americans spent a social evening with a neighbor fell by more than one third.

Our connections to friends and neighbors are measurably weaker than even a generation ago, and the evidence is everywhere, from informal socializing, to church attendance, to membership in civic and community organizations. For example, the Charity League of Dallas met every Friday for fifty-seven years to knit, sew, visit, and raise money for good causes. In April 1999 they disbanded. The average member age was eighty, and they just couldn't attract new ones. Similarly, the Roanoke, Virginia, chapter of the NAACP has been an active force for civil rights since 1918. At their peak, they had over twenty-five hundred members, but they're down to fifty-seven now, and most people don't attend the meetings anyway. They're shutting down. Diminishing group participation has eaten away at such bastions of community involvement as the Red Cross, Girl Scouts, Knights of Columbus, and the PTA all across America.

You might be thinking, I don't bowl (league or otherwise) and I don't knit, so why should I care? But something else is lost when we no longer gather together for a shared purpose—whether to help others or to roll gutter balls. Something is missing from our lives when we realize that our web of belonging—our contacts, support, friendship, and activity—is very small; that, in fact, our human connections don't much extend beyond work and family. The women of the Charity League of Dallas, in addition to their good works, got to know their neighbors. They kept up with the news of their community and so felt more connected to it. They knew when one of their group was ill or had suffered a personal loss. And friendships were forged that grew and extended beyond the regular meetings.

All evidence points to the fact that we've come a long way from the kind of tribal relationships that served our ancestors. Indigenous cultures understood how their social fabric was held together by feelings of connection and tribalism. The Iroquois tradition refers to the "long-body"—a felt system of deep relationships between all the members of the tribe. Whether you personally like every other member of the tribe is of no consequence. What does matter is the feeling of belongingness, shared purpose, common values, mutual reciprocity, goodwill, and trust.

Native American cultures hold dear the ideas of relationship and interconnection with others, the land, animals, and spirit itself so that every decision is made with the overriding concern for this great web of being that is the circle of life. These deeply felt connections to the "Seven Generations"—great-grandparents, grandparents, parents, children, grandchildren, great-grandchildren, and our own generation—emphasize respect for previous generations and nurturance of future ones. This philosophy makes clear the power of the tribe, the feeling of belonging and community, that defines one's place in the larger order of things.

So powerful is the idea of human connections to indigenous cultures that sorcerers (shamans) of central Mexico claim to be able to enter into states of nonordinary reality and actually *see* the energy fields that make up the web of interweaving human connections as luminous, shimmering "strings of light." With an uncanny resemblance to the String theory of modern theoretical physics but thousands of years before mathematics, Albert Einstein, or particle accelerators, Mayan and Toltec sorcerers described human beings and the universe itself as being composed of strings or fibers of radiant energy—light—unbounded by the constraints of spacetime and that the relationships between us could be observed as an exquisite dance of that energy. We find this identical idea abounding in indigenous cultures from around the world as well as in many Eastern philosophies, like Taoism, and each has evolved techniques to "tune in to" this energetic dimension. Yaqui shaman don Juan described this phenomenon to anthropologist Carlos Castaneda: "The seer sees that every man is in touch with everything else, not through his hands, but through a bunch of long fibers that shoot out in all directions from the center of his abdomen. Those fibers join a man to his surroundings; they keep his balance; they give him stability."[2]

This is a fascinating worldview, but it is not necessary to accept this complex (and sometimes incomprehensible) metaphysics in order to understand just how essential is our human need for connection to one another.

With far less mystical imagery, and drawing upon the linguistic constructions of empirical social sciences like economics, Western sociologists call the glue that holds societies together "social capital." This term refers to the quality and depth of relationships between people in a family or in a community. The concept of social capital was first given a clear theoretical framework by sociologist James Coleman of the University of Chicago in 1961, and his use of the term focuses on a sense of community, the actual social relationships in that community, common values, shared trust, and a willingness to help one another. Robert Putnam defines social capital simply as "connections among individuals— social networks and the norms of reciprocity and trustworthiness that arise from them."[3]

Despite some academic attempts to arrive at a clear definition, social capital is not a unidimensional concept. Instead, it meanders around our human social realities like trust, civic leadership, giving and volunteering, membership in groups, community involvement, diversity of social networks, social bonds, goodwill, fellowship, and informal socializing. Social capital is reflected in the grand events and everyday particulars of human life—everything from running for public office to organizing a community fund-raiser to playing bridge with a group of friends on Wednesday nights.

I imagine social capital to be like a safe harbor for our little individual boats on the sea of life. When social capital is high enough, we feel protected from the raging winds, the churning waves, and the great expanse of open sea. Here we are intimately connected and live with feelings of belongingness, community, and connection. Here we are better protected from the difficulties and losses of life by a rich network of relationships. Here we live and work together better. Here we are protected from the storm.

For those reasons, it's important to understand the surrounding container in which our own personal psychological and spiritual feelings of belongingness may thrive or may be crippled by the breakdown of our neighborhoods, communities, and even our American society.

What is clear from the research is that a high level of social capital allows communities to solve problems and establishes a rich environment in which individuals, families, and neighborhoods thrive. Numerous studies have shown that communities high in social capital have better educational achievement, more effective governmental institutions, faster economic growth, and less crime and violence. Professor Putnam reflects on the data and highlights the huge benefits of social capital when he speaks about how to make our neighborhoods safer: "Ten percent more cops or ten percent more neighbors who know each other's names? The latter is the better strategy."

What's more, members of these communities high in social capital are happier and healthier, and actually live longer.[4] Communities without much social capital are disconnected and distrustful, walk more dangerous streets, and lack the vibrant sense of aliveness that comes with the recognition that one belongs.

The New Hampshire Charitable Foundation is a nonprofit organization devoted to improving community life in New Hampshire and nearby states. They have assembled a terrific website with many excellent links to information about social capital and helping people make their communities stronger (http://www.bettertogethernh.org/). They've provided some amazing facts about the sheer power of social capital to make our collective and individual lives better.[5]

+ Joining one group cuts your odds of dying over the next year in half. Joining two groups cuts it in quarter.
+ Communities with higher levels of social capital produce children with higher SAT scores and higher performance on a broad range of testing.

+ Communities with higher social capital have lower dropout rates, higher retention, and less youth violence.
+ The more connected we are in our community, the less colds, heart attacks, strokes, cancer, depression, and premature death we experience.
+ The higher the social capital, the less murders and violent crimes in our neighborhood.
+ Representative government is more responsive in communities with higher social capital.
+ Blood donations are higher in communities with high social capital.
+ Road rage is reduced in communities with high social capital.
+ Social capital is the best predictor of tax compliance on a state-by-state basis.
+ Measured happiness goes up when we are socially connected in mutually respectful, trusting relationships based on exchange and reciprocity.

All the evidence points clearly to the fact that social capital and the social trust upon which much of it is based are critical factors in personal happiness as well as the quality of life in our communities. This bears repeating: your personal level of happiness is in large part determined by your surrounding environment and the kinds of connections and feelings of belongingness that you find (or, increasingly, do not find).

A massive survey of more than thirty thousand Americans conducted by the Saguaro Seminar of the John F. Kennedy School of Government at Harvard University concluded that "comparing two persons of identical income, education, race, age, and so on, the one living in a high social capital community typically reports greater personal happiness than his/her twin living in a low social capital community. The same thing is not true of the overall level of community income or education. In other words, your personal happiness is not directly affected by the affluence of your community, but it is quite directly affected by the social connectedness of your community."[6]

What's most important is to understand that neighborhoods and communities are the surrounding containers in which we live. Whether our immediate world is rich in connections and caring or not dramatically impacts our personal happiness and our own feelings of belongingness. So before we move on to looking at the state of health of our immediate world, take a moment to reflect on your own web of connections. This will give you a context for the information that follows and help you to apply these findings in your own life.

Respond honestly to the following questions used by the Saguaro Seminar to assess social capital. Take a pen and paper and actually write down your responses to these questions. There's something about bringing inner thoughts into the outer world through words that helps us see ourselves more clearly. So, take a deep breath and honestly look at the macrocosm of your life.

How Connected Are You?

- How many of your neighbors' first names do you know?
- How often do you attend parades or festivals?
- Do you volunteer at your kids' school? Or help out senior citizens?
- Do you trust your local police?
- Do you know who your U.S. senators are?
- Do you attend religious services? Or go to the theater?
- Do you sign petitions? Or attend neighborhood meetings?
- Do you think the people running your community care about you?
- Can you make a difference?
- How often do you visit with friends or family?

Go to: www.ksg.harvard.edu/saguaro/communitysurvey/ to see how your responses compare to other respondents in American communities.

Reprinted by permission of The Social Capital Community Benchmark Study, The Saguaro Seminar, John F. Kennedy School of Government, Harvard University.

Our Dwindling Social Capital

I don't remember my parents ever talking to me about social capital but I do remember growing up in a neighborhood where everyone knew and cared about me.

I've been thinking a lot about this idea of social capital and how things have changed over time. Then I saw an interview with a representative of a new high-technology product that brought the changes

I've seen in our communities over my lifetime into sharp, if somewhat frightening, relief. It's just one little marker, a small symbol that speaks to our present level of social capital or, rather, the lack of it.

Wherify Wireless, Inc. (www.wherify.com), has developed and is marketing a Personal GPS Locator for Kids. This $400 gadget looks like an oversized Swatch wristwatch and allows parents to keep track of where their kids are at any moment via the U.S. Department of Defense billion-dollar U.S. Global Positioning System. I'm not making this up. In fact, this device won the coveted 2002 Best of Innovations Award from the Consumer Electronics Association. Here's how it works. Your child wears this device on his or her wrist (yes, it also includes an actual watch that changes time when the time zone changes). You snap the lock and send Timmy or Susie off to school. Once you've activated your locator service—about the average monthly cost for a pager or cell phone—you can locate your child within a few feet by calling the Wherify company or logging on to their website. There, on a colorful map of your city streets, you will see the pulsating indicator that shows the exact location of your child.

If you prefer more regular updates, you may choose to go "breadcrumbing," presetting times when "locates" will ensure that your child has arrived at where you think he should be. Beep—made it to soccer practice. Beep—in the middle of my piano lesson. Beep—I'm in the living room, Mom. The GPS Personal Locator for Children is waterproof and currently available in several colors—cosmic purple and galactic blue.

The mere fact that this product exists seems to me an abysmal demonstration of our low level of social capital. When I was growing up, my mother always knew my location without any benefit of consumer electronics. If she couldn't get a visual on me, then she called Jean Sawtelle to see if I was playing in the woods behind her house. Not there? My mom made the quick trip through the garden gate to the next-door Pizalottas to see if their kids could get a bead on me.

Other baby boomers and I grew up in a period when, for most of us, neighbors were friends and watched out for one another. I don't want to wax nostalgic about growing up in the 1950s and 1960s. Our black-and-white television images of *Father Knows Best* and *Leave It to Beaver* don't reflect the entire truth of the times that were not all that idyllic for minorities or women seeking social justice and human rights. But still, when I speak with my similar-aged friends and acquaintances about their experiences growing up, I hear the same things. Regardless of race or ethnicity, growing up middle class or poor, living in a little rural town or bustling inner-city neighborhood, they all speak of "belonging" to a community. They tell me stories of neighbors getting together to solve problems, to comfort one another in crisis, and to make their best potato salad to share at a Fourth of July picnic. We didn't even know what social capital was in those days. But apparently, we had a bunch of it.

Consider today's world and the reasons for Wherify to develop their product. Every year 359,000 children are kidnapped. Sixty percent of the 4 million people who suffer from Alzheimer's disease will wander. Seven billion dollars' worth of vehicles are stolen each year. In our disconnected world, we may need dozens of these devices to keep track of the people and things that are important to us.

Our present state of disconnection is a bit unexpected. Historically, one of the strongest predictors (perhaps, *the* most important predictor) of connected communities and a vibrant civic life has been education. With the exception of informal socializing, the data suggest that the higher the level of education, the higher the level of community involvement, civic participation, voting, associational membership and, thus, social capital. In the years between 1900 and 1940, less than a quarter of Americans went beyond high school, as compared with more than half of those born after 1940. During this same time period, the baby boomers finished high school at twice the rate of their parents and they also went to college in massive numbers (more than 50 percent of this generation holds a college degree). Given the striking changes in education levels throughout our society, our social capital should be higher now than before. Right? Wrong.

The baby boomer generation is among the most educated in the world and yet they are less involved in community and civic life than their less-educated parents. So the question remains: What happened to us? Robert Putnam frames it like this: "Why, beginning in the 1960s and accelerating in the 1970s and 1980s, did the fabric of American community life begin to fray? Why are more Americans bowling alone?"[7]

We can all list various social, cultural, and economic factors (what Putnam calls the "usual suspects") that have contributed to today's sense of isolation: mobility, not enough time, the changing world brought about by technology, increasing disruption of marriage and family ties, increasing numbers of women in the workforce reducing the social bonds of communities, and generational effects. The results of those changes (especially considering how recent many have been) are sometimes less apparent. For example, some people might readily acknowledge that their social circles have narrowed. It is harder to see how that can also constrict their perspective, sense of empathy, self-esteem, psychological happiness, and even humanity.

Social scientists have put the potential causes of decreasing social capital under a bright white light and interrogated these suspects. Some of the results of their studies have drawn unusual conclusions and shown some rather unexpected results.

Putnam's "Usual Suspects"

Mobility and Where You Live

I was in the fifth grade when my parents made a surprising (and totally unacceptable) announcement at our family dinner table. My father had been offered a job in Pittsburgh. My brother, Jimmy, and I sat wide-eyed and I distinctly remember the stinging tears that rolled down my face. How could they do this to us?

We lived in a very nice neighborhood in Westfield, New Jersey, where everyone knew us. How could my parents even consider moving when all of our friends in the whole world lived within walking distance and carpooled with us to Holy Trinity Elementary? Our grandparents, aunts, and uncles, and our gang of first cousins lived in Newark, Union, and East Orange, only a few minutes' drive. Pittsburgh? They had to be kidding.

My parents tempted us by saying that Pittsburgh was a beautiful city with mountains, rivers, and the Pirates—a great baseball team. We'd get season tickets, they promised. My brother and I cried anyway. We'd make lots of close friends in our new neighborhood, my parents argued. We didn't believe them.

Though our tears were those of children, we seemed to have had an innate understanding of the complex variables that affect social capital. According to the theories, social capital declines as expected mobility increases. This uprooting was exactly what Jimmy and I feared. Before the boxes were even packed we were brokenhearted. We grieved for the social connections that we knew would plummet as we watched the heaving smokestacks of north Jersey fade into the distance and headed west. How long would it take our friends and cousins to forget about us once we were living in Pittsburgh? Sure, we'd be eating popcorn and slurping sodas at Forbes Field as we watched the Pirates beat the pants off the Yankees during the 1960 World Series, but it wouldn't matter. We'd be cut off from our extended family, banished to the mountains of Pennsylvania, never again to feel the pure contentment of knowing that we were part of a big family, part of the tribe.

We did make friends in Pittsburgh and we discovered that we remained close and connected to our cousins and extended family, but maybe that was because we burned up the interstate between Pittsburgh and the Garden State to visit for holidays and family events or because my mother talked with her sisters and brothers every few days or because Jimmy and I regularly exchanged goofy letters with our cousins and old friends.

In spite of the sociological research and common sense that argue that mobility may be one of the major reasons for our present state of disconnection in this country, data from the U.S. Census Bureau demonstrate that residential mobility has been exceedingly constant over the past fifty years, and if there have been any measurable changes at all, we relocate slightly *less* now than did generations past. For example, during the 1950s—when social capital was very high by almost every measure— 20 percent of Americans changed their residence each year. In the 1990s, only 16 percent moved. And adding to the stability of present-day communities, home ownership in 1999 was at a record-setting high of 67 percent.

Where we move may have a bigger impact on social capital and feelings of belongingness than does how often we move. The research seems to confirm some of the stereotypes of living in big cities versus small towns. Studies show that residents of large metropolitan areas compared to their small-town counterparts are less likely to join groups, attend club or public meetings, serve as officers or committee members of local organizations, go to church, or even visit with friends.

I live in Dare County, surrounding the historic and tiny town of

Manteo, North Carolina, and even as a recent addition to the community—I moved here just two years ago—I've already had more contact and spent more time with neighbors than I ever did while living in larger cities.

Manteo is one of two towns (the other being Wanchese) that were originally fishing villages on Roanoke Island, which is about twelve miles long by three miles wide. Interestingly, our island is about twenty-three square miles, the same size as the island of Manhattan, the bustling core of New York City. But if the political scientists and sociologists are right, we should expect to find higher levels of civic engagement, more trust and altruism, and a bigger spirit of community here than our more crowded island-dwelling friends find to the north. In the measurement of social capital, the experts say that the rule of thumb for community size is "Smaller is better."

Perhaps there is more to it than the sheer size of one's community. Perhaps feeling of connection in my area arises from the fact that we live on this tiny island just off the North Carolina mainland, surrounded by the Roanoke and Croatan Sounds, and sheltered from the wild Atlantic Ocean only by the strip of sand and shore called the Outer Banks. Perhaps it is waiting for hurricanes and tidal surges—or even the threat of them—that makes for very good neighbors. After all, when the wind is tearing past your house at ninety miles an hour and the sounds are flooding their banks, it's nice to know that friends are nearby and that there has been help in shuttering windows and delivering groceries and bottled water to older folks who don't drive.

The rumor is that Manteo was one of the models for the television town of Mayberry on *The Andy Griffith Show*. Life isn't necessarily as slow here as the stereotypes of small towns might suggest, but there is a feeling of knowing one's neighbors and having an interest in the affairs and decisions of local government. It does matter whether a big chain foodstore is going to locate here and wipe out part of our fragile wetlands and throw the local grocer out of business. My life is brightened considerably by watching the birds that live in the wetlands. Even if I didn't have strong opinions about the importance of environmental responsibility and the unity and sacredness of all life on the planet, the migration of those homeless birds to friendlier surroundings would affect my personal life in very unpleasant ways. I know the people who work at that grocery store and I want them to keep their jobs. I've got a vested—even selfish—interest in caring about what happens in my community.

Here's something else I've learned about living in a small town: communications are inclusive and incredibly fast—one of the signs of good social capital. People keep up with what others are doing and my hairdresser knew that I had been invited to appear on NBC's *Today* show before I even had a chance to call my father to tell him. This *is* like living in Mayberry, I thought. I haven't had any of Aunt Bea's cookies or a blow dry from Floyd the Barber yet and Opie is living his life as Ron Howard and directing award-winning movies like *A Beautiful Mind.* But actor Andy Griffith really does live here and so it's easy to see how the comparisons have been made.

While living in a small town seems to encourage feelings of belongingness and high social capital, it's clear that mobility is not the reason that our society has become so disconnected. And research also shows that the effect of community size is not the culprit for our increasing lack of social connections. Residents of the twelve largest metropolitan areas are only about 10 percent less trusting and report only 10 to 20 percent fewer group memberships than residents of other cities and towns. Big-city dwellers have more nationality-based and political clubs while smaller cities have more veterans', fraternal, service, and church groups. Rural areas have more agricultural organizations. But overall rates of group memberships are not that much different for city dwellers and their rural cousins. The effect of community size has only a moderate effect on social capital.

Maybe one of the advantages in living in a small town is that nothing is very far away. Literally, I can ride my bicycle from one end of Manteo to the other and not break a sweat. On most days, I write at my home office (less than 4 percent of the workforce works at home even one day a week) so I don't spend much time commuting or dealing with the errands of daily life. Most everything I need is close by or a mouse click away on an Internet store. When I lived in a suburb of Washington, D.C., it took me hours to get to jam-packed grocery stores and drive miles more to get my car tuned up or pick up dry cleaning. I regularly drove for more than an hour and fifteen minutes to travel the twelve miles to work in downtown Washington, negotiate the parking-garage traffic, and find a place to plant my car for the day. Commuting Monday through Friday robbed me of two and half hours each day, which was already filled with ten hours at my job. And I wasn't alone. Suburban sprawl has created a spatial environment in which Americans no longer live where they work. The average American commuter spends seventy-two minutes every day behind the wheel. Robert Putnam points out that this represents more time "than we spend cooking and eating and more than twice as much time as the average parent spends with kids."

Unless you're carpooling with friends—and most of us are not, two thirds of all car trips being made alone—it's easy to see how this will cut into available time for socializing with people you care about. And here's an interesting statistic from the scientists who study social capital: every ten minutes of additional commuting time cuts all forms of social capital by 10 percent, which means 10 percent fewer club meetings, 10 percent less churchgoing, and 10 percent fewer evenings with friends.

The data about commuting interfering with social capital lead us to another potential culprit for our eroding social capital. Commuting clearly reduces the amount of time that people can spend with friends or engaged in community affairs. So, maybe the lack of time is the suspect we should look at next.

Not Enough Time

Many people might argue that their social capital is low because the demands on their time are high. We feel as if we're running as fast as we can and still we can hardly keep up. Some say that with the frenetic pace of their lives, it's impossible to socialize with friends or make a commitment to a community organization because they simply don't have enough time.

Think about your own life. Most of us race to work, spend long hours there, speed home at the end of the day to pick up children from baby-sitters or relieve the latchkey kids, make dinner, throw in a load of laundry, help with homework, look over notes for tomorrow's meeting, make lunches for the next day, and fall into bed exhausted. Even people without young children say that there are simply not enough hours in the day to keep up with their responsibilities. So we whirl through one frenetic day after another. The sun goes down, the sun comes up with the alarm clock ringing and heralding yet another day of too much to do and too little time.

Even after we've collapsed onto our beds, we're sleeping less, it seems, than past generations. The 2001 Sleep Survey conducted by the National Sleep Foundation (http://www.sleepfoundation.org) found that less than one third of Americans get the recommended eight hours of sleep a night. More than 30 percent say they sleep less than seven hours a night. So the news at night is not good. But the daytime data are even more distressing. More than 40 percent of people surveyed said that they are constantly tired and that their lack of adequate sleep interferes with their daily activities. A significant proportion of these drowsy folks punch up their alertness level with caffeine (43 percent) or medication (5 percent).[8]

Let's hope that most of our sleep-deprived cohorts are writers or Olympic figure-skating judges and not involved in dangerous occupations or life-threatening situations. Let's hope they are not airline pilots, brain surgeons, or managers at nuclear power plants since sleep deprivation dramatically interferes with mental and physical reaction times, accuracy, coordination, and attention span. In fact, another recent study released by the Center for the Advancement of Health suggests that staying awake for seventeen to nineteen hours—a normal day for most Americans—accounted for more than two thirds of automobile accidents, resulted in reaction times 50 percent slower than for those who are not sleep deprived, and decreased performance on a variety of tasks more profoundly than after consuming 50 mg of alcohol.[9] A 2002 study conducted by the National Sleep Foundation reported that 85 percent of those surveyed said that lack of sleep increased feelings of stress, anger, and pessimism, making it "difficult to get along with others." How do you think that interpersonal attitude affects social capital?

So we're not sleeping well and may be too sleep deprived and cranky to care much about social capital. And we say we don't have enough time to invite a neighbor for dinner at our home, coach our daughter's soccer team, or volunteer for Neighborhood Watch. Social capital and feelings of connection require time and an awakened spirit not racing from pillar to post boosted by endless cups of java. Soulful relationships are created and bonds grow deeper when we can slow down and be fully present to one another, savoring the moments we have with those we love and care about. But what we believe about how little time we have for these purposes and what is true are not always the same.

Although more than half of Americans think their free time has decreased in the past five years, time-use studies don't bear that out. In fact, research comparing leisure time from 1965 to 1985 actually showed a *gain* of about five hours a week of free time. More recent studies suggest that the average American schedule has more than forty free hours a week that could be used to make significant deposits in our social capital account. Apparently, we really do have time for picnics with our kids, running for local office, baking brownies for a church bake sale, and inviting our neighbors to a cookout. But many of us don't use this precious time for those activities. What we do, instead, it seems, is watch television.

Television

The vast majority of people spend far more hours *alone* in front of their TV sets (about three to four hours a day) than in any kind of social activity or conversation with others. These hours of television viewing amount to almost half of all leisure time and account for more than any other activities except work and sleep. People who live to be seventy-five years of age and maintain this schedule of television viewing will have spent more than nine years on the couch watching the tube. How many bags of microwave popcorn do you think went along with that?

As I was growing up, television didn't seem like something that kept my family apart. Instead, it seemed like something that brought our family together for an evening. I fondly remember that on Sunday nights after dinner, we would assemble to watch Walt Disney and then the *Ed Sullivan Show*. It was an event that was often accompanied by cookies and milk or other snacks. I vividly recall having conversations about what we were watching. My parents must have been liberated even then as both my mother and father agreed that the Beatles were fab and never once criticized their mop-top haircuts. But that was then, and now watching television has become an increasingly solitary activity. The proliferation of multiple television sets in a single household (by the late 1980s, 75 percent of all American homes had more than one television set) allows for more private viewing rather than having television as a shared activity among a family or housemates.

Now, don't get me wrong. I'm not advocating ditching your televisions. Perhaps, as a result of my fond memories of the role of television during my growing-up years, my home is dotted with four televisions, four VCRs, digital cable, and a DVD player with six surround-sound speakers. In a way, my house is a virtual theater. I enjoy renting movies—especially small, character-driven imports. My good friends and I have almost weekly "Dinner and a Movie Nights" where one of us will select a movie and we'll enjoy dinner together, conversation (now, there's an idea!), and the shared experience of watching the same film. It's kind of like a book club without the homework.

I believe that television informs, teaches, and entertains. It brings us visual and auditory experiences we are unlikely to ever have—like the birth of a baby whale I saw once on a science show or an astronaut's walk on the moon. Personally, I like television when it is used consciously and with discrimination. That is to say, you love a particular program or sport and you plan your time to include it in your schedule. There's nothing wrong with a little bit of television. But the idea of spending four or more hours a day in front of one makes my head spin.

To consciously use one's time for viewing and make particular decisions about what you will watch (selective viewing) is a far cry from sitting in front of the television every night with the remote at the ready, prepared to watch anything—anything at all—that vaguely strikes your interest (habitual viewing).

And the impact of television on social capital is profound. Research shows that heavy television viewers are less likely to participate in sports, community activities, or spending time with their friends. These viewers are more pessimistic about human nature (that's got to cut into the trust factor so important to fostering a sense of belongingness and community), overestimate crime rates, and are more passive and obese. Among kids between the ages of nine and fourteen, television takes as much of their time as all other leisure activities *combined*, including hobbies, clubs, sports, and just hanging around with their friends. Other studies strongly suggest that heavy television viewing by children results in reduced school achievement, increased aggression, and sexual activity at younger ages (just think about *what* they're watching for a second instead of how much).

Robert Kubey, director of the Center for Media Studies and Rutgers University, and Mihaly Csikszentmihalyi, a psychology professor at

Claremont Graduate University in California, wanted to understand the grand appeal of television viewing, so they conducted a study in which they gave subjects beepers and randomly paged them six to eight times a day. When they were paged, the subjects wrote down what they were doing and how they felt. The results of their study were reported in *Scientific American*[10] and confirmed not only that television is the developed world's favorite leisure activity but also that there were features of regular and chronic viewing that seemed very much like an addiction. By monitoring physiological reactions to watching television (e.g., measuring brain waves by using an electroencephalograph [EEG], heart rate, or galvanic skin response) other scientists have found that subjects show less mental stimulation during viewing compared to reading. The Kubey and Csikszentmihalyi study corroborated those findings through their self-report sampling methods.

Kubey and Csikszentmihalyi believe that heavy television viewing has many of the same characteristics of other addictions. When people turn on a television there is an immediate sense of relaxation and passivity. Thus, people are easily conditioned to associate viewing with rest and a lack of tension. When the TV is turned off, the feelings of relaxation disappear immediately, but feelings of passivity and lowered alertness continue. Many of the subjects in this study reported that television had somehow "absorbed or sucked out their energy." When the screen fades to black, there is a sudden drop in that good feeling of relaxation and, for many people, a twinge of guilt that they aren't doing something more productive with their time. Those are unpleasant feelings, to be sure. But these uncomfortable and negative feelings are easily fixed by turning the TV on again.

A large number of people experience qualms about how much time they spend plopped down in front of the tube. A Gallup poll conducted in 1999 reported that two out of five adults and seven out of ten teenagers admit they spent too much time watching television. About 10 percent of adults described themselves as TV addicts. Interestingly, heavy viewers (more than four hours a day) said they enjoyed watching television less than did moderate or light viewers, became bored more quickly, and were less likely to spend time interacting with others. You may not be surprised to learn that watching television is the *only* leisure activity where doing *more* of it is associated with *lower* social capital.

Heavy television viewing cuts into the time available for creating and maintaining relationships that matter and comes at the expense of social gatherings and informal conversations.

In responding to these troubling observations about the impact of watching television on American communities, Professor Putnam quipped, "Many Americans would rather watch *Friends* than have friends."

Here's an interesting statistic that you wouldn't expect: employed people belong to *more* civic groups than those outside the paid workforce. And, surprisingly, longer work hours are linked to *more*, not less, civic involvement. It's understandable that long work hours will inevitably cut into time available for other things. I mean something's got to give. It's true that people who work longer hours do spend less time reading, eating, sleeping, enjoying hobbies, and just hanging out. But they also have given up watching much television. Compared to their couch potato cohorts, folks who work long hours at their jobs spend 30 percent less time watching television.

As we continue to explore the factors that have impacted on our deteriorating social capital, television is not exonerated.

Technology

Does technology hold the power to reel us back from our disconnected society or does it further threaten our already shaky levels of social capital by creating yet another diversion from human contact? Can the web of interconnected fiber optics and satellite beams transform us into a culture where we feel deeply in touch and able to share information and feelings easily? Or will they foster emotional distance from one another? The answers are not so clear.

It's true that our increasingly wired and digital world offers new and incredible ways to maintain social connections. After all, our most geographically distant friends are only an e-mail click away. Civic organizations and clubs can easily distribute information about meetings and issues by sending e-mail to members. Clubs can solicit new members and let the community know what their group is up to by hosting a website or sending an e-newsletter—all this without the cost, time, or trouble of direct mail.

Today it is possible to keep in contact with our family members and friends by wireless technologies—the ubiquitous cell phone being the most prominent of these—regardless of our location. A few years ago, when I was in Maui, I stood at the summit of the magnificent dormant volcano Mount Haleakala (House of the Sun). Here I was, 10,000 feet above sea level, shivering in the thin, cold air, gazing at clouds beneath me and across the expansive, color-splashed moonscape crater. According to my guidebook, I was standing at the most geographically desolate place on earth.

You can see on a map that the Hawaiian Islands are an isolated dot in the middle of the Pacific Ocean, more than twenty-four hundred miles west of the U.S. mainland, about the same distance from the island groups of the Marquesas, Samoa, and Fiji, and more than four thousand miles from Japan. It's believed that humans first set foot on these islands somewhere between A.D. 300 and 750—brave Polynesians, most likely from Tahiti, who said farewell to friends and family forever (good-bye social capital) as they pushed their fragile outriggers into the lonely sea and sailed thousands of miles on the prevailing trade winds.

In stark contrast to these original settlers who left behind everything and everyone they knew—every drop of their social capital—in order to stand on this very spot, I called my father in Virginia from my cell phone to find out the results of a medical test that were due on that day. (I remembered that he would know the results on this particular day because I had put a reminder on my PDA—personal digital assistant. When the alarm beeped, I made the call to him in spite of the fact that I was standing at the top of a volcano.) I was happy and relieved that the results of his test were excellent and then I described in detail what I was seeing. Our wireless telephone connection was flawless even at this remote spot on earth, and through technology I could relax and not worry about Dad's medical test. As if that weren't enough, my father got a virtual tour of a Hawaiian volcano.

Internet technology allows us to keep in touch in ways that could not have been imagined by generations past. What we easily take for granted now was for them the stuff of science fiction. And it sometimes surprises me to think that the Internet as we know it, with lots of ordinary people connected, is really less than ten years old. And through it, we have enormous opportunities to build social capital through regular connections. Not only can we keep in touch with those we love; we can even extend our reach to people we might otherwise never know and create new relationships and new social capital.

I first met my good friend David after he read my book *Awakening at Midlife* and e-mailed me with a question from his laptop while he was sipping a pint of Guinness in a Dublin pub and I was at home writing on my computer. We IM'd (Instant Messaged) and quickly became friends. After months of electronic communication we finally met in person. It didn't feel like a first meeting. It felt like a homecoming. We've been even closer friends ever since.

According to a study conducted by *The Industry Standard*[11]—until the recent dot-com bust, a leading magazine for e-business—more than 29 percent of Americans have used the Internet for genealogical searches and discussion sites in order to resume contact with far-flung cousins or contact relatives they had not known before. I've communicated with an older "cousin" in Ireland—my new friend Tony Brehony—while searching on-line for my family history. We've kept up with each other, exchanged our books through the mail, and sent e-mail birthday cards to each other; through Tony, I was introduced to other distant relatives in Australia. The Irish diaspora apparently knows no bounds.

My friend Deb is a writer in Tucson, Arizona. She is bright, funny, and enormously talented. She also had polio and uses a wheelchair to get around. In spite of the physical challenges, she frequently goes to lunch with her friends, takes writing classes, participates in the Sufi spiritual community, and enjoys way too much café latte at her local Starbucks. But it is through the technology of the Internet that she has made contact with many people who also are challenged by disability, polio, and postpolio syndrome (PPS).

"The Web has been an expansive experience for me," she told me. "I didn't really know anybody else with polio and hadn't connected with people who were having the same kinds of experiences."

Deb posts some of her writing and provides spiritual and disability resources at her meditative website called Windows to Wisdom (www.wtow.com). She regularly sends and receives e-mails from friends around the country as well as Israel, Australia, and New Zealand. Next week a woman from Delaware, one of her friends she met on-line, is flying to Tucson to visit family. She and Deb will take their virtual friendship into the outer world where, no doubt, they'll talk nonstop while lapping up lattes.

It's clear that technology has added a considerable deposit to Deb's social capital account. She's made friends—good friends—who she was unlikely to ever meet in person. She gives and gets support from others who understand the challenges of physical disability in ways that those of us who do not have those experiences simply cannot, no matter how we try or how much we love her. Deb's story, and many others like hers, emphasizes the way that technology increases our access to community.*

But what about those who don't own or have access to these technologies? In our increasingly wired and digital world, will some people be less able to build social capital? Will some become more and more disconnected from the flow of information and the human connections that allow social capital to thrive? As a society, will we become increasingly splintered into groups of information haves and have-nots where some folks find it easy to know what's going on in their communities and connect with family and friends while others will simply be left behind?

This "digital divide" raises serious questions about the ways in which technology-driven social capital may grow and who will be included in its reverberations. The idealistic belief that the Internet will be a great equalizer among all members of all societies is not holding true. There is great concern and ongoing debate among scholars, governments, technology companies, and social scientists about the social divisions that this technology may exacerbate and even create. Presently, there are an estimated 429 million people on-line around the world. This number seems enormous and has certainly made Internet service providers and technology companies a bunch of rich folks. But it is really just a drop in the bucket globally and represents only about 6 percent of the world's 6 billion people. Forty-one percent of the global on-line population is in the United States and Canada.[12] In fact, with only 15 percent of the world's population, industrialized countries account for more than 88 percent of all Internet users. While the rate of on-line connectedness continues to rise in Milwaukee and Madrid, life remains virtually untouched by information technology in Malawi and Mozambique. It's clear that a great many human beings throughout the world are falling through the Net.

In the early days of Internet technology, the United States on-line

---

*Deb died in 2002.

community was disproportionately young white males with higher incomes and educational levels than average, but that is changing, and changing fast. By September 2001, more than half of the United States was on-line and growing at about 2 million new Internet users a month. Between December 1998 and September 2001, even the lowest-income households (under $15,000 per year) came on-line at a 25 percent annual growth rate. Use among black and Hispanic Americans increased at annual rates of 33 and 30 percent, respectively.[13] The declining cost of personal computers and on-line service along with community-supported Internet access through schools and libraries are reducing the digital divide—at least in the United States.

In his Millennium Report, UN Secretary-General Kofi Annan emphasized the importance of creating global connections by helping developing countries benefit from the economic and social opportunities presented by the digital revolution. To this end, the secretary-general proposed the formation of the United Nations Information Technology Services (UNITeS), a global volunteer program focused on bridging the digital divide between industrialized and developing countries.

In his report, "We the Peoples: The Role of the United Nations in the 21st Century," Annan beautifully embraced the power of information technologies to promote human development, reduce poverty, enhance our human community, and build world social capital. Then he identified the digital divide as a barrier to creating broader social connections and shared values among the world community—the genuine goal of inclusive globalization.

In spite of all the promise for expanded community and enhancing human connections, is it possible that technology has a downside for our human relationships? Will technology make us even more lonely and further reduce our social capital? At face value, this seems like a strange question given the tremendous connectivity offered by the lightning-speed communications of phones and the Internet.

But a 1998 study conducted by psychologists at Carnegie Mellon University suggested that there is indeed a darker side to the digital revolution. Researchers there investigated the impact of Internet usage and painted a frightening picture of the impact of this technology on social capital. The results showed that the use of the Internet, with the capacity for people to keep in contact with friends and family and develop new relationships with people all over the world, was *replacing* vital, everyday human contacts. Their findings showed that spending time on the Internet was associated with declines in talking among family members, reductions in the number of friends and acquaintances, and increases in depression and loneliness. Of all the types of people studied, these negative social effects were stronger for teenagers, who used the Internet more hours per week than did adults.

Professor Robert Kraut, the lead author of this study and a professor of social psychology and human computer interaction at Carnegie Mellon University, said, "We were surprised to find that what is a social technology has such anti-social consequences."[14] Dr. Kraut was quick to point out that the subjects of this study were not Internet addicts or isolated techno-junkies but regular people. Because the research studied the same subjects over several years, the result ruled out the conclusion that it was only people who are particularly socially isolated or depressed who suffered the loss of personal human connections. Instead, the researchers concluded, using the Internet seemed to *cause* this isolation, loneliness, and depression.

In 2000 the Stanford Institute for the Quantitative Study of Society (SIQSS)[15] also investigated the impact of Internet technology on human social interactions. Their preliminary findings received massive media attention and corroborated the Carnegie Mellon study. Their results suggested that regular Internet users—more than five hours a week—report higher levels of depression and say it has significantly reduced the time they spend with friends and families, shopping in stores, or watching television (perhaps not such a bad idea given what we know about the impact of television on social capital). What's more, almost a quarter of regular Internet users who are employed say the Internet has increased the time they spend working at home without cutting back on time spent at the office, thus further reducing time spent with their family and friends.

Stanford professor Norman Nie, director of SIQSS and the principal investigator on this research, summed up the findings: "The more hours people use the Internet, the less time they spend in contact with real human beings. . . . This is an early trend that, as a society, we need to monitor carefully."

Yikes! The results of this research suggest that as our use of Internet technology increases—and it is growing daily—we will become even more isolated, not to mention depressed, and disconnected from warm human moments of face-to-face relationships. Will this remarkable technology be the final demise of tribes? Are we destined for bankruptcy in our social capital accounts?

Some people disagree with the conclusions drawn by these and related studies about the impact of technology on human relationships. Within the academic community and among Internet supporters there has been a great deal of criticism about the scientific methodology used in these studies in order to draw the conclusions that technology is destroying social relationships. First, the studies have been criticized for their reliance on self-report data. Many of the results are based on surveys of subjects' self-reports rather than observations of their actual behavior and, as we all know, people sometimes misrepresent themselves or are inaccurate in reporting their own behavior. Often people rationalize their behavior and, sometimes, they just flat-out lie.

The Stanford study asked respondents whether they spent more, less, or the same amount of time talking on the phone since they went online. The assumption seems to be that "phone time" represents more genuine and closer social interactions than e-mail exchanges, a conjecture that I'm not inclined to agree with. A 2002 study by the Pew Internet and American Life Project discounted the deductions drawn by the Stanford study and, instead, concluded that Internet usage *intensified* social contact rather than reducing it, and those results were especially strong for women, who have been coming on-line in droves. The Pew survey indicated that the more people were involved with the Internet, the more likely they were to enjoy other forms of social interaction as well.[16]

Methodological problems aside, the actual results of the Stanford study are rather weak to draw such strong, and highly reported, conclusions. For example, here are some of the major results: 27 percent of "heavy" Internet users report spending less time talking to friends and family on the phone, 15 percent report spending less time physically with friends and family, and 13 percent report spending less time attending events outside the house. But if you do the math, you'll see that 85 percent of heavy Internet users did not report spending less time with family and friends. And who is to say that telephone communication is inherently more connecting that communicating via e-mail or Instant Messenger (IM)?

There are many reasons to believe that Internet technology holds promise for increasing our social relationships, especially for people who have a desire to connect with others along some important dimension, as my friend Deb has been able to do with others who face the challenges of polio.

Other results from the Pew Internet and American Life study (March 3, 2002) suggest that over the course of a year, Internet users became more comfortable with communicating on-line and that, over time, their use gets more serious and functional. While the number of casual e-mails to friends and families decreases as the "newness" wears off, there is a significant increase in e-mails sharing worries or seeking advice from close friends and family. More than 84 percent of e-mail users say they use it to keep in contact with family members and 80 percent use it to keep in touch with friends. Women, in particular, said they valued the Internet because it strengthened their bonds with family, neighbors, friends, and community. Sixty percent of women claimed that the Internet had improved their connection to parents, siblings, and children with whom they had regular e-mail contact. The study's authors conclude, "The initial excitement and fun of emailing a distant friend or family member is bound to make people at first herald the way the Internet enhances the feeling of closeness. Email has gone from the remarkable to the reliable, but the lower buzz associated with the Internet has not supplanted the clear finding that Americans see the Internet as a good tool for keeping in touch with others."[17]

In summarizing the available data and anecdotal evidence, it seems that telecommunications and the Internet hold both positive and negative possibilities. As always, the impact of technology will come down to human consciousness, how we choose to use any technological advance. Is a sharp knife a weapon, or is it an instrument of healing in the hands of a skilled surgeon? Automobiles pollute the environment, create traffic jams, and give rise to impersonal suburbs that replace smaller neighborhoods where people live and work together. True. But automobiles give us freedom to explore places we've never been and meet new people we may never have met. Automobiles allow us to head home, around the state, or across the country for Thanksgiving dinner with parents and faraway siblings.

Breakdown of Traditional Families

There is abundant evidence that strong families increase social capital. In fact, it's always been assumed that families are at the core of our sense of belongingness, our safe harbors. Developmentally, families are the first place where we learn about social relationships. And marriage is good for social capital. Research from the General Social Survey, reported by Putnam and others, shows higher levels of trust and greater group participation among married people compared to singles. But modern life has seen a change in the basic structure of families: during a twenty-year period, the number of married Americans has declined from 74 percent (in 1974) to 56 percent (in 1998). Almost half of all first marriages in the United States end in divorce. What's also clear is that the *Leave It to Beaver* family of the fifties and sixties is no longer the norm. In fact, this traditional family form—a married heterosexual couple living together with several children—now represents only about one quarter of all U.S. families.

There is an undeniable correlation between the demise of social capital and the century-long increase in divorce rates: as the divorce rate has increased, social capital has decreased. But many other social changes have taken place during this same period of time. So the question becomes: Is there a *causal* relationship between these two? In other words, is it the breakdown in traditional families that has *caused* the decrease in social capital?

It makes a great deal of common sense that as our family structures weaken, so would our social capital. But the evidence doesn't necessarily bear that out. Putnam points out that the sharpest jump in the divorce rate occurred in the 1970s, "long after the cohorts who show the sharpest declines in civic engagement and social trust had left home."[18]

Furthermore, marriage and traditional family structures have been associated with higher levels of organizational affiliation in only two areas of social capital: church and youth-related activities. But marriage appears to have no effect on membership in other kinds of civic groups, service clubs, or business and professional groups. In fact, married people actually attend fewer club meetings than singles and, while they are (slightly) more likely to give or attend dinner parties, they are less likely than singles to spend time informally with friends and neighbors.

Divorced people get together with friends as often as their married cohorts and they don't volunteer, attend club meetings, or work on community projects any less than married folks. In fact, they are more likely to sign petitions, attend public meetings, and write to Congress.

The evidence suggests that divorce and changes in the structure of American families have had only a modest impact on our declining social connections.

Women in the Labor Force

Don't ever suggest, as I once did as a child, that my mother didn't work. But how was I to know? She didn't go off to work each morning snappily dressed and toting a nice leather briefcase as my dad did. Instead, she got up before any of us, made a hot breakfast for everyone, drove my father to the station where he would catch the train into New York City, carpooled a pile of rowdy kids crammed into our station wagon to Holy Trinity Elementary, shopped for groceries, then picked up dry cleaning, stopped by the bank, and ran errands on the way home. Once there, she cleaned the house, paid bills, washed the laundry, prepared snacks, did the prep work for dinner, and headed to a meeting for the Rosary Guild or another volunteer group. She'd race through her schedule in order to pick us up from school at three o'clock. At home, we'd snack on cold milk and freshly baked Toll House cookies and tell her about our day. My brother and I would go outside to play with our friends while Mom was working on dinner. Later, after my father came home, we'd eat dinner together sitting at the dining-room table with cloth napkins and a full complement of flatware.

After dinner, Mom would clean up the dishes, then help us with our math and spelling, making sure that we had completed our work correctly before carefully placing it into our school bags. Some nights our family would watch television before bedtime. Even then, my mother would only watch after hauling the ironing board into the den where she would press our school uniforms, my father's handkerchiefs, sheets, and napkins (all of these items had been previously dampened, rolled up tightly, and chilled in our basement refrigerator so they'd iron up better). At bedtime, my mom would read us a story and tuck us in. I'd fall asleep as I listened to the sweet and comforting sounds of my mother moving around the kitchen making the peanut butter and jelly or tuna fish sandwich that I'd find in my lunch box the next day, always accompanied by a small handwritten note telling me to have a great day and that she loved me. After nine o'clock, when the telephone rates went down, I'd hear her softly talking on the phone to one of her sisters, who I expect was also getting those sandwiches squared away for my cousins' lunches.

Now, just so you don't think that the rest of our family were total slugs, I should mention that my father wasn't just plopped down in front of the TV or reading the newspaper cover to cover (like Ward Cleaver, *Leave It to Beaver*'s father, did) while my mother did all this stuff. When Dad came home from his job, he worked on various projects around our new house and seemed to do a lot of paperwork. My brother, Jimmy, and I had a few chores, too. How do you think the garbage went from the kitchen to the big bin outside or all that carefully arranged flatware graced our dining-room table?

Still, with all that she did, it's no wonder my mother looked at me as if she were considering a foster care placement when I suggested that she had plenty of time to do something or other for me because, after all, she didn't work.

Like most of my mother's contemporaries, raising children and keeping a home in the 1960s was a full-time job. At that time in the United States, only 37 percent of women held jobs outside the home.[19] In addition to the ironing and cooking—not to mention raising children—these women were also doing something incredibly important for our collective sense of belongingness: they made huge investments in social capital. Contrary to a popular contemporary misconception that homemakers must live isolated lives, through volunteer and community groups, creating and maintaining ties with neighbors, and building friendships, my mother and her contemporaries developed communities with strong emotional and social connections.

My mother, like many women of her day, participated in numerous civic and community groups, attended PTA meetings and coffee klatches, and organized our neighborhood's own version of the Welcome Wagon. "Welcome Wagon?" younger readers are probably asking. Ours was a group of neighborhood women who collected coupons from local merchants and put them in a basket with homemade goodies and freshly cut flowers for new neighbors. My mother would write a list of all the neighbors' names, addresses, and phone numbers, roll it up, tie it with a curly ribbon, and carefully place it in the basket. And then a few women delivered this gift in person. Almost always, the recipient of this heartfelt gift—most likely a homemaker like my mother and her friends—would invite them in for a cup of coffee; during the course of this short visit, new friendships were birthed. In those days, that's how incoming families were welcomed to the neighborhood.

I've thought often about my mother and her friends and the way they created our neighborhood by their kindness, desire to reach out, and commitment to inclusion. My mother described her view about welcoming in the stranger when, in a faux Irish brogue, she'd say, "We can always put another potato in the pot, darlin'." We moved into an ordinary middle-class community of lookalike houses on a treeless suburban street, but the women who lived there forged a vibrant tribe with friendships that lasted a lifetime. When my mother died in 1992, many of those same women were there to bid her farewell.

Flash forward to 2003, when more than 60 percent of American women work outside the home, twice as many as when I grew up. Studies show that virtually all of women's rush to outside employment during the past twenty years is a function of financial pressures, not personal fulfillment. In fact, in the United States ninety-nine out of every hundred women will work for pay at some time in their lives. The majority of women, regardless of marital status and including those with young children, work outside their homes. Forty-seven percent of all multiple job holders in 1995 were women (up from 20 percent in 1973).[20]

During the day, most neighborhoods are barren. Kids are at school or day care, both parents are at work, and, by the time everyone arrives home there seems to be little time to welcome a new neighbor into the tribe. Changing social roles in which women have moved out of the home, where they were the social glue of communities, and into the paid workforce is one of the most significant social changes of the last fifty years. Is this the suspect that can explain the demise of our social capital?

Surprisingly, the research says, "No, not really." The data suggest that women do belong to somewhat fewer civic and community associations than do men. Memberships among men have fallen at about 10 to 15 percent a decade, compared to 20 to 25 percent for women. While men join more community groups than women, women spend more time with the ones to which they do belong. Surprisingly, work status among women seems to have very little impact on group membership. It makes sense that working women belong to more professional associations while homemakers tend to join PTAs and other community groups. And the data bear that out. But time-budget studies conducted between 1965 and 1985 showed that women working outside the home were actually spending more time on organizations as time went by than homemakers, who were spending less. Informal socializing with neighbors and friends fell most precipitously among homemakers although, regardless of job or marital status, women still engage in far more informal socializing than men.

The Greatest Generation

On a lazy Sunday afternoon in early December 1941, my father and his friends were hanging out when the news came over the radio that Japanese planes had attacked the U.S. Pacific Fleet at Pearl Harbor. The debate about whether or not America would enter the war to help Britain—the only nation left fighting after France had been defeated—against Nazi Germany was over. For my father and his friends, life as they had known it was over.

On Monday, as President Roosevelt addressed the nation, my father and his best friends Jas Mancini and Joe Cleary headed straight for the Army Air Force recruiting station.

Like my father and his friends, 16 million American men and women rose to the occasion. Millions of men poured out of their factories and offices to line up at recruiting offices and were sent into combat in the Pacific and Europe. Women joined the armed forces as nurses, doctors, WACs, and members of the newly created Women's Auxiliary Army Corps (WAAC). Housewives abandoned their kitchens for the now-deserted factories and arsenals, where they took up the role of "Rosie the Riveter" and manufactured airplanes and bombs, cannons and rifles, trucks and jeeps. Within a year, the number of women in the workforce swelled to more than 20 million.

Those Americans who didn't serve in the military supported the war effort at home through rationing, civil defense, scrap drives, donating blood, buying War Bonds, and waving the American flag. Precious food was reallocated to soldiers and sailors when almost every American family, whether living in the heartland or an apartment in a large city, showed their self-reliance and commitment to the cause by planting a victory garden to feed themselves, their friends, and their neighbors. The mood of the country was one of sacrifice and loss—more than a quarter million Americans were killed during the war, and people had just endured the hard times of the Great Depression. But in spite of everything—or perhaps because of everything that was happening— American society was permeated with a grand sense of unity, patriotism, optimism, connection, caring for neighbors, and commitment to civic duty. Social capital was never higher.

That this "Greatest Generation" made significant deposits into our social capital account is abundantly clear from the data. The contemporary problem seems to be that they were the last generation to do so and they are quickly passing from the scene. Civic involvement, community connections, trust between people, feelings of belongingness, and relationships to neighborhoods and groups were highest in this country in the 1940s and 1950s. Even today, members of this older generation— now in their seventies, eighties, and nineties—have more public spirit, belong to more organizations (twice as many as people born in the 1960s), vote more often (double the rate for other generations), trust people more (60 percent compared to 25 percent for their grandchildren), and are more engaged in civic and neighborhood life.

Guilty as Charged

By inspecting the lineup of usual suspects for our declining social capital, Putnam and others rank generational change—the replacement of the long civic generation by their less involved children (baby boomers) and grandchildren (Gen-Xers)—as the most critical factor and, by their reckoning, this alone accounts for half of the overall decline in our feelings of belongingness and social connections. Interestingly, the baby boomer generation was the first in which social capital began its long, slow decline and also the first to be raised with television as a constant companion.

In his inaugural address in 1963, President John F. Kennedy admonished Americans to participate in our civic and community life. His eloquent words, "Ask not what your country can do for you, ask what you can do for your country," defined his short presidency. In 1979, President Jimmy Carter—in what will forevermore be referred to his "national malaise" speech—pointed out the crisis in confidence that threatened the very institutions of American society and the health and well-being of its citizens. We had changed, he said, from a society that valued hard work, strong families, and close-knit communities, to one that chose instead self-indulgence, consumption, and outrageous materialism. We had changed from a society in which the "Greatest Generation" rushed off to war in a flood of patriotism and responsibility for protecting our country and one another, to one in which less than one third of its citizens exercised their freedom by voting in a national election.[21]

What was he saying? No one particularly liked President Carter's warnings and we certainly didn't heed them. Hey, he was supposed to be giving a speech about the energy crisis, and instead he told us that the emperor had no clothes and insinuated that, as a nation, we had become pessimistic, materialistic, disconnected, and self-indulgent. He was right but, after all, how could we possibly have remained the same?

By 1979, American society had lost faith in its institutions and one another. We had witnessed the murders of John Kennedy, Robert Kennedy, and Martin Luther King. We had seen conflict, too often bloody, as our country began the noble and just integration of its schools and institutions to Americans of *all* races. We had believed that our armies were invincible and our causes just—and then there was Vietnam. We held respect, even awe, for our leaders—and then there was Watergate. Through the magic of television we were now comparing our material wealth, not to those of our neighbors down the block, but to Hollywood celebrities and the rich and famous. Advertisements bombarded us with messages to consume more and more, and so we did.

Jimmy Carter's discourse on that hot summer night in July 1979 was a great speech, an accurate and prophetic assessment of where we were heading—now backed up by reams of data that confirm his early observations.

Although Carter concluded his speech with hopeful expectations for the renewal of the American spirit and his strong confidence in his country and fellow citizens to change the path we were on, no one was listening. Pointing out the emerging truth about the decline of social capital and the state of our connections may have shown Carter's strong sense of history and his powers of social observation, but it was not a good political move. Jimmy Carter decisively lost the presidency in an electoral landslide the following year to the more cheerful Ronald Reagan.

It's true that the Carter administration was plagued with runaway inflation, high unemployment, a massive energy crisis, and a dramatic failed attempt to rescue fifty-five American hostages in Iran. But many political pundits believe that it was this speech, these observations of a declining American society, that chimed the final death toll for a Carter second term.

The Greatest Generation had something that subsequent generations—including the one President Carter was talking about—have not had in the same measure: the sense of comradeship and solidarity that is created through shared adversity. It's well understood by social scientists that external conflict increases internal cohesion. When those Japanese planes launched from their carriers 247 miles off the coast of Oahu on that Sunday morning in December 1941, dropped their bombs, and exploded our ships at Pearl Harbor, something else exploded as well: a new consciousness about our collective responsibilities and need to stick together. Perhaps the first to fully recognize the reverberations of this act of aggression was Japanese admiral Isoroku Yamamoto, who fretted, "I fear we have awakened a sleeping giant and filled him with a terrible resolve."

The admiral was right. The Japanese attack was perceived by Americans as a strike against "us"—not just our navy, not just our government—but against all of "us." Suddenly whatever differences or disconnections there may have been among us seemed trivial and inconsequential in the larger scheme of things. There was now a common cause. Our survival and freedom were at stake and we looked into one another's eyes and saw new connections. In 1943, sociologist Lloyd Warner described the sense of community and connection in one small American town in Indiana as a state of "unconscious well-being" because "everyone is doing something to help in the common desperate enterprise in a cooperative rather than a private spirit."[22]

Unlike the generation who came of age in the 1940s, we have had no such common enemy, no such shared adversity. At the conclusion of *Bowling Alone*, Robert Putnam wrote about the power of crisis to reinvigorate social capital. He prophetically said, "Creating (or re-creating) social capital is no simple task. It would be eased by a palpable national crisis, like war or depression or natural disaster, but for better *and* for worse, America at the dawn of the new century faces no such galvanizing crisis."[23]

We faced no such galvanizing crisis until now.

September 11, 2001: A Reawakening?

The political scientists and sociologists who study social capital and the present state of our disconnection have done a remarkable job of documenting our decline. But they did not, could not, have anticipated the sudden shift of values and feelings of unity that came screeching and flaming from the skies over New York City, northern Virginia, and rural Pennsylvania on September 11, 2001.

The unspeakable tragedy of the terrorist attacks on the United States on that bright fall Tuesday morning was a watershed in our collective life. Suddenly, and without warning, we were awakened from a great sleep of self-interest, an overemphasis on materialism and money, and the social disconnections that derive from a value system that discounts the human need for belonging to a tribe. We woke up all right and the evidence for a new paradigm of human connection is everywhere. Whether those changes will endure is another question altogether and one that we'll pursue in the next chapter. But at this moment, it does seem clear that we no longer want to bowl alone.

THREE

A Changed and Changing World?

We have all known the long loneliness and
we have learned that the only solution is love
and that love comes with community.

—*Dorothy Day, humanitarian and founder
of the Catholic Worker Movement, 1933*

Dan Doyle was setting steel at the new AOL Time Warner Center at Columbus Circle near Central Park on the morning of September 11, 2001. It was a morning like any other for this forty-three-year-old ironworker until he heard that a plane had crashed into the World Trade Center. At first Dan thought it must be a little plane—a small private plane horribly off course for one of the New York airports. Eighteen minutes later, another crane operator screamed, "A jet hit the second tower!" Now Dan felt goosebumps—this was no accident. The job stopped. Dan and the other ironworkers from New York's Local 40 climbed down from their cranes and the skeletal building and gathered to find out what was happening. As they were trying to make sense of the horrifying news, about an hour later the word went out: the South Tower had collapsed, debris plunged to the ground, and a billowing black cloud rose out of lower Manhattan and blocked out the sun.

Dan called home. His wife, Clifta, was hysterical and wanted him home. The city was in chaos. But he couldn't get another phone call through so he walked home to Brooklyn.

Early the next morning, Dan and his fellow ironworkers headed to the site of the disaster. "It was dead. There was nobody there. All I could take in was the smell, the smoke," Dan told me. As they rounded the corner they ran into chaos. There were thousands of eager volunteers and city leaders were scrambling to devise a plan to rescue survivors in this dangerous environment. Dan and his colleagues found someone who appeared to be in some position of authority amid the confusion. "We're ironworkers," Dan said. "We're here to help. We're here to go to work."

"It was my duty to help," Dan said. "We were looking for survivors. That's what kept everyone going. There was nothing else to think about. That's the least I could do. We had the skills. There were lots of pockets, lots of holes, and all surrounded by steel. There might be people alive in there."

Dan kept thinking about people who survived earthquakes, buried in rubble but surviving beyond all hope and finally being pulled out alive from tangles of steel and cement just like this one. That could happen here, he thought. He didn't give up the hope of finding anyone alive until almost six weeks into the rescue effort.

One morning, Dan was asked to go up in the basket with some firemen to look at the steel that had to be removed to get a body out. "I knew he was a Fire Department captain or lieutenant because he was wearing a white shirt. He had his car keys and his wallet. That one really hit home. Now I knew who he was. His name was O'Keefe. William O'Keefe." Later that night, Dan and his friend Mikey walked past the storefronts cluttered with flyers of missing loved ones. They looked for a picture of Captain William O'Keefe, forty-nine, New York Fire Department, Division 15. "I wanted to see what he looked like. What he might have been like," Dan said quietly.

What was most amazing after September 11 was the outpouring of help and love that reverberated across the nation and the world. Like my father, his friends, and millions of other Americans rushing to the recruitment offices after the bombing of Pearl Harbor, people converged on New York City and Washington with only one question: "How can I help?"

Like Dan, more than a thousand ironworkers and members of other trade unions rushed to lower Manhattan. Volunteers from all sixteen New York City Laborers local unions worked frantically with cranes, bulldozers, end loaders, and by hand to sort through the smoking rubble looking for any signs of life. Police, fire, and emergency rescue units from around the country worked twelve-hour shifts, often dropping from exhaustion at the end of the day.

Politicians rose to the occasion to offer both leadership and comfort.

New York City mayor Rudy Giuliani risked his life, saw his friends die, and walked through the trenches urging New Yorkers and Americans everywhere to defiantly rise to the challenge that faced us as he wept publicly for the heart-wrenching loss of life and the devastation of his city. This was, Giuliani said, our darkest day and our finest hour. He spoke of hearts broken and the opportunity to emerge stronger than we have ever been before. He spoke of a newfound commitment to openness, diversity, inclusiveness, and freedom, and that together we would triumph over tyranny and destruction. He spoke with pride about the firefighters and police officers who, impelled by their sense of duty and love of humanity, laid down their lives for strangers.

Within hours of the tragedy, volunteers of the American Red Cross from across the nation set up makeshift command centers—the local chapter had been on site before the second tower went down—to dispense information and loving support for families and friends of the missing. Ordinary citizens brought water and food to the workers. Nearby restaurants opened their doors, swept soot and debris from their tables, and offered hot meals and cold drinks for those who needed them. A swarm of volunteer doctors, nurses, and other medical specialists raced to the designated trauma center at St. Vincent's Hospital on Seventh Avenue to treat early patients—most suffering severe burns—then stood waiting in their green surgical scrubs amid a mass of stretchers, wheelchairs, and ambulances for the legion of wounded survivors that, sadly, never appeared.

And what was happening was something we hadn't seen in a long time. Images surrounded us depicting unity, brotherhood, heroism, and working together. The victims of September 11 came from more than eighty nations and every race and there was an outpouring of support and compassion throughout the world. Amid the rubble, despair, bedlam, and sheer horror of that place, light emerged from the darkness as people grew into a community, helping one another and working toward a common goal. Our collective grief had forged bonds that were stronger than the mighty steel beams that now lay in twisted ruins on the scorched ground. Suddenly the city, the nation, the world itself, seemed very small.

One unnamed rescuer summed up for a magazine reporter what he saw at Ground Zero: "Everybody was so puzzled. Nobody could think.

But there was a beautiful solidarity, digging, digging, digging, passing the buckets. People were appreciating each other, these big men in uniforms, giving a pat on the arm. But there were no words."[1]

Like all Americans and people all over the world, I was horrified and grief-stricken by the terrorist attack on September 11, 2001, and the suffering it created for so many victims and their families and friends. In addition to the tragic loss of life and all the unspeakable individual suffering, there was a collective loss of innocence as well, and an end to the illusion of invulnerability and isolation that had so defined our national character. I felt much the same way I did on the day when President John Kennedy was assassinated more than forty years earlier. It was a sinking and desperate feeling. Life, as we had known it, was now over.

September 11 was a devastating crisis for all of us. The word *crisis* comes from the Greek and means "decision," "choice," or "turning point." And then there is the old adage that the Chinese word for *crisis* is made up of two separate characters that when presented separately stand for two very different concepts, but when combined, they offer a striking new idea. The first character stands for "danger" and the other for "opportunity." In this way of looking at things, a crisis offers an unprecedented opportunity for growth and change.

We all know people—perhaps you are one of them—who, when confronted with a crisis in life, have used it to move forward and transform in ways they never would have expected. Whether initiated by the diagnosis of a serious illness, the loss of an important relationship, or some other unsought and frightening change in our lives, it is possible to use crises as catapults, opportunities, and defining moments that bring us to a whole new way of being, an entirely new worldview. When I interviewed people for my book *After the Darkest Hour: How Suffering Begins the Journey to Wisdom,* I was inspired by countless men and women who had experienced great suffering only to transcend their pain and come through it better than they had ever been before. Through the refiner's fire of their anguish, they emerged as more conscious, more compassionate, wiser, and better prepared to deal with the raggedy edges of living a human life. They discovered a strength and resiliency they had never known. They recognized their most genuine priorities in life and lived those values in ways large and small. They acknowledged each day as a gift, lived more fully in each moment, and opened their hearts to their loved ones. The people I interviewed felt new and fierce connections to others. One after another, they described a grand sense of unity with life itself and liberation from the illusion of separateness. They not only had a clearer understanding of the necessity of a safe harbor, but they put this philosophy into action through their everyday behaviors.

The terrifying events of September 11 have hurled us into exactly this kind of collective crisis. And if crisis truly holds the capacity for both danger and opportunity, we are often far more aware of the danger we are in, whereas opportunity mostly hides in the shadows. But, though it may be well hidden, opportunity is as inexorably woven into the fabric of a crisis as is danger.

Prior to September 11, 2001, our collective feelings of belongingness, our social capital, our sense of connection to and trust in one another, our values, and our commitment to civic responsibility were in deplorable shape. Consider the evidence of the previous chapter in documenting the decline of our communities and our social isolation—the failure at creating belongingness and safe harbors for most of us. What happened immediately after September 11 was a dramatic reversal of the trends toward social isolation and widespread loneliness that had been in motion for more than forty years. It was as if we had been in a collective sleep about the importance of connections among us, about the need we have for one another. Not only did we not have vibrant human connections; most of us didn't even appear to know they'd gone missing.

But by mid-morning on September 11, a new consciousness had arisen. Suddenly we were seeing each other in a new light, rediscovering our family and friends, neighbors and colleagues. We felt new trust in our public institutions and new respect for community servants like firefighters, police officers, and the military. As one pundit aptly put it, the events of September 11 were like a "wake-up call from Hell."

When the World Trade Center came crashing down, so did our illusion of security and our sense of disconnection. If money, status, and rugged individualism were the prevailing values on September 10, they were quickly replaced in the course of that infamous next day by a deeper desire for safety and being alive in the company of loved ones. Awakened with a jolt from that slumber of narcissism and self-interest, we were embarking on a new world. Suddenly, and in everyday conversation, our pronouns shifted from "I" to "we." For the first time since

World War II, there was a palpable feeling of connection, an emerging sense of unity, coming together, community, and seriousness of purpose.

Our changes in priorities and reflection on what really matters suggested that many Americans turned to religion and spirituality—another marker of high social capital and feelings of community and belongingness. They say there are no atheists in foxholes and anecdotal reports suggest that our attitudes and behaviors shifted—as if we were now operating from a terrifying and collective foxhole. Popular wisdom and a slew of news stories showing worshipers flooding into religious services seemed to indicate that churches, synagogues, and mosques were swamped following September 11. According to some surveys, immediately after September 11, 60 percent of Americans attended some kind of memorial service and Bible sales rose by more than 27 percent. But a Gallup poll conducted on September 21–22, 2001—just a week and a half after the tragedy—showed that church and synagogue attendance rose by a mere 6 percent.[2] In fact, there is no evidence that the tragedy of September 11 had any impact on increasing attendance at religious services or on the importance of religion in Americans' daily lives.[3]

A CNN/USA Today/Gallup poll conducted in January 2002 showed that for one third of Americans, September 11 was a "life-altering" event and as a result they have changed their priorities in life. Spending more time with loved ones seemed to be the major effect of these changing priorities.[4]

On the evening of September 11, 87 percent of all Americans—nine out of ten people under age fifty—told Gallup interviewers that the events of September 11 were the "most tragic news event of their lifetimes." Six months later, in March 2002, that percentage had changed only a little (to 80 percent). Fifty-five percent of respondents believed that Americans had permanently changed the way they live. But only about a quarter of Americans believed that September 11 caused permanent changes in their own *personal* lives; most said they were back to "life as usual." Gallup points out that these differences between broad social indicators (things happening "out there") and local or personal ones are not an uncommon finding.

Compared to poll results conducted immediately after the terrorist attacks on September 11, Americans six months later were doing dramatically less praying, crying, and flag flying. A September 14, 2001, poll showed that 77 percent of Americans said they were showing more affection for loved ones than normal. By a March 2002 survey, that number had dropped to 48 percent.[5]

Without the vantage point of time and history, it's impossible to say that the terrorist attacks on September 11, 2001, were a watershed event in our collective life. Philosopher René Descartes once wrote about the impossibility of drawing accurate conclusions while in the midst of a maelstrom: "It is as if I had suddenly fallen into a deep whirlpool; I am so tossed about that I can neither touch bottom with my foot, nor swim up to the top."

Until we can touch bottom or swim to the top of the whirlpool we're in, we can only guess at whether we have undergone true collective change or whether we are in a brief moment in time in which we seem to be pulling together in new ways and momentarily feel a greater sense of community and belongingness. Of course, measuring community spirit, social capital, and belongingness is not an easy task. But some early data and observations suggest the rather disheartening possibility that the changes we've seen may not endure, and before too long it will be back to business as usual.

When you take the numerous post–9/11 studies and surveys into account, it's clear that what has most clearly changed are our images, rhetoric, and gestures. Although surveys suggest that we now say we feel less social isolation and that we trust and care more about our friends and neighbors, we are even less likely now to have them over for a visit. Instead we've "cocooned" in front of our TV sets. After September 11, television viewing increased from the average 2.9 hours a day to 3.4 hours.

Increased interest in public affairs and community involvement has not been translated into joining a club, volunteering in the community, or bringing a dish of lasagna to an elderly neighbor. We underwent a swift and radical appreciation of how we could each contribute to the common good and how much we needed one another but, unfortunately, this new spirit of community didn't last very long.

A New Paradigm

Our American culture is one of many that prizes individualism over community. The debate about this dichotomy—between whether it is the individual or the collective that is the primary constituent of society—has occupied the attention of social scientists, philosophers, and scholars from the time humans first climbed down from the trees, walked on two feet, and said, "Hey, it's clear that we need each other, but how are we going to get along here?"

Throughout time and history, most preindustrial, non-Western cultures have organized their social relationships so as to meet the need for human community and safe harbors and often at the expense of individualism. These indigenous cultures—often called "high context" by sociologists and anthropologists—cherish the preservation of group harmony and strive to enhance feelings of interconnection by establishing social norms and mores that precisely encourage this kind of human social interaction. In contrast, "low context" cultures are those—like our own—that value individualism, often at the expense of collective feelings of belongingness.

Cultures like Native American and African tribes, the Maori of New Zealand, the Aboriginal people of Australia, and other collective societies are often revered for their high levels of social capital, especially as we struggle with our own society and its failures to provide norms and values that facilitate this critical cultural context. In their excellent book, *Call to Connection: Bringing Sacred Tribal Values into Modern Life*, authors Carole Kammen and Jodi Gold describe the nostalgia many of us feel when we think of the present social context of our lives: "Many of us feel tribe in the stirrings of our souls, connecting us with our ancient ancestors who lived in villages, and who depended on one another for growing and gathering food. They engaged in rituals to celebrate new life, to mourn the dead, to welcome the springtime, and to honor the spirits of life. Although we can never go back to that simpler way of life, we can once again embrace the values of the tribe, wherein we honor each other and the natural forces that support life."[6]

Unlike our own individualistic society, collective cultures provide a social context of values and norms that facilitate bonding and attachment between their members. For example, the ancient Hawaiian practice of *hanai* is one in which a child is raised not by his/her birth parents but by another family that is part of the extended kinship network in which blood relationships were recognized and honored extending even beyond what, in modern terms, would be considered to be thirteenth or fourteenth cousins. Birth parents continued to be involved in the child's life but he/she took the name and primary relationship of the adopted family.

Hanai brings new meaning to the idea that "it takes a village to raise a child," and this culturally prescribed practice of adoption all but guaranteed peaceful and close relationships. After all, one would be unlikely to go to war against others who were rearing, educating, and loving one's own offspring.

Conflicts in the ancient Hawaiian society were resolved through a process of reconciliation and redemption called *ho'oponopono*—a family problem-solving conference led by an elder or a respected outsider in which a problem was met with prayer, discussion, confession of guilt, restitution, and forgiveness. Perhaps sharing a relatively small island with limited resources isolated in the middle of the big blue sea led the Hawaiian people to these enlightened conflict resolution processes and social capital formation based on interdependence and interrelatedness. They simply had no choice. They had to get along and depend on one another.

Like the ancient Hawaiians, the present-day Canela people of South America hold harmony and peace as the supreme values for their society. The Canela live in the central grasslands of Brazil in much the same ways as their ancestors have for thousands of years, in a culture where peace and sharing are central to community life. About a thousand people live in thatched houses two or three deep with each family home connected to a central plaza by its own path. From overhead, the entire village resembles a giant wagon wheel with paths from individual homes leading to a wide circle of cleared area, the center of their communal life.

Anthropologist William Crocker of the Smithsonian Institution's National Museum of Natural History first began studying the Canela people in 1957. In his 1994 book documenting his research, Dr. Crocker described what he observed during the more than sixty-five months he spent living with the Canela tribe. "Above the age of 12 years of age, everybody in the tribe knows everybody else . . . the circle is the paradigm for village life. As we consider around-the-circle as well as across-the-circle bonds, we see that the kinship system constructs an intimate net which allows some flexibility, but which weaves many connections holding the tribe together."[7]

The Canela practice intricate bonding rituals and conflict resolution skills that they call "mending ways." The social cohesion of these people is both a cause and result of their relative isolation from modern Brazilian society in spite of their contact with "outsiders" for more than two hundred years. The Canela people maintain intimate bonds to their community through an elaborate system of kinship, rituals such as "Wild Boar Day" and the "Annual Fish Festival," twice-a-day tribal meetings, festivals, and, surprisingly, an extensive practice of extramarital sex that is consistent with the Canela value of sharing and generosity. Yes, that's right. Though these sexual relationships must follow very specific rules of ceremonial conduct, the Canela's extramarital system—in which women have sequential sex or private trysts with many male members of the tribe—is an important aspect of their social bonding. Sharing is expected; stinginess, sexual jealousy, and possessiveness are suppressed.

But before the most sexually adventuresome among us rush to book a flight to Brazil, it's important to point out that the extramarital system among the Canela is intended to heighten their sense of community and connection, and not for individual sexual experimentation. Dr. Crocker writes, "The sexual abilities of all members of the tribe are generally known through 'gossip' or conversation. Thus the Canela know each other with an intimacy almost unimaginable by us."[8] Extramarital sex is just one of the cultural structures that keeps the Canela united and allows them to retain their traditional cultural identity. In spite of powerful pressures from the modern world surrounding them, and while most other indigenous tribes have splintered apart and lost their identities over the past two centuries, the Canela have not only survived but they have prospered.

So, should we all form our villages into wheels and begin a sleepover schedule with our neighbors? I don't think so, but the Canela and other tribal cultures have a sense of connection and community that can show us a lot about what is possible and what different choices we make, and priorities we show, in our own society. It's true, as Kammen and Gold have pointed out, that we can never go back to those ancient social structures, but we can find ways to integrate some of their values about the importance of belongingness into our own modern culture. Because to be part of a tribe, as indigenous peoples have taught, is to know that you belong. Social structures encourage—sometimes dictate—that all members of the group experience both an internal feeling of belongingness and an external sense of community. In collectively oriented cultures and countries that honor the group, "to be" is to belong and "to belong" is to be. Whether defined as a family, a collective, a tribe, or a clan, to live in one of these societies means to belong to a strong, dependent, and cohesive group that becomes the source of one's identity, embraces and protects its members, and demands loyalty in return.

In these societies there is an expectation of civic engagement and the formation of families and communities are designed to produce high levels of cooperation, interdependence, social capital, and group success. They intuitively echo a comment widely attributed to writer Herman Melville: "We cannot live for ourselves alone. Our lives are connected by a thousand invisible threads, and along these sympathetic fibers, our actions run as causes and return to us as results."

Unlike the ancient Hawaiians, the Canela tribe, and other collective societies, America—and most industrialized Western societies—looks to rugged John Wayne cowboys, risk-taking pioneers, self-reliant revolutionaries, and high-flying entrepreneurs for models of how one should live in society.

Few modern Americans would be content to live with the rules and regulations that indigenous societies impose on their members. Instead, we prefer self-determination, independence, and freedom to tight-knit communities where acceptable behaviors are determined by group consensus. We are, after all, a nation founded on rebellion against authority we deemed as unfair and unnecessarily controlling. In a democracy, dissension and debate are a welcome and necessary part of the political and social process and an impetus to positive change.

Our cultural mantra honors individual liberty over external authority and competition over cooperation. We may talk about how much we admire teamwork (there is no "I" in "team"), but we mostly honor and reinforce our best sales rep, the season MVP, the Oscar winner, and the gold medalist, not the team he/she represents. Our society encourages the realization of our unique potential: individual achievement, personal responsibility, freethinking, self-expression, and personal choice over self-sacrifice in the service of the tribe. We expect our members to take care of themselves, "to pull his own weight," and our ties to others are, understandably, looser and less intimate than in collective societies. And while individualistic societies hold honorable and important values, I think they are like broccoli. Broccoli? Broccoli is an excellent source of nutrients and a third of a pound of broccoli contains more vitamin C than 240 apples! Broccoli contains no fat and is a desirable part of a healthy diet, but no matter how great broccoli may be for us, if that's all we eat, we'll get sick in no time.

Our desirable values of individualism and self-sufficiency are best lived when they're balanced by commitment to one another and recognition of the importance of our relationships. When taken too far, an emphasis on the individual undermines our sense of community and feelings of belongingness. When the individual is absolutely and singularly venerated, social capital becomes less valuable and our communities suffer.

We have a great deal to learn from indigenous people and collective societies that live close to nature and to one another. These cultures are strong in the places where our own is weak and offer us important ways of looking at the world, especially as we embark on the task of creating our own vibrant relationships and increasing social capital in our own society. But it's best not to romanticize other cultures and, viewing them through rose-colored glasses, believe that they hold all the answers to all the challenges of our own modern life. Everything of substance casts a shadow and there is a definite shadow to tribal communities that are closed off from the rest of the world.

In spite of the many advantages of belongingness and social connection in societies that value community life over individualism, there are distinct and dangerous downsides.

The strong sense of belongingness in tribal cultures, when not modulated by a healthy respect for individuality and diversity, can easily translate into an "us" versus "them" mentality: a closed system that allows no one new to enter and rigidly controls those who are "inside." Either you are one of us or you are against us. Patriotism deteriorates into jingoism. Rules and regulations, deference to authority, hierarchical power structures usually based on age and gender, and group consensus determine behaviors that are acceptable and those that are not. Nonconformity and rebellion are not generally well tolerated. And usually, the punishment for failing to conform to collective expectations is both harsh and complete. For all the advantages in social capital and the feelings of belongingness among its members, tribalism—in its worst expression—is a closed society that fragments, polarizes, and excludes.

In many ways, gangs, Nazism, and terrorist groups like Al-Qaeda (which in Arabic literally means "the base") are infamous examples of strong communities high in social capital and feelings of belongingness. These organizations represent the very worst aspects of a high-context society in which the individual is entirely embedded in the collective. Members of these groups unquestioningly accept and obey rules and commandments given to them by those in authority. Their members fervently believe in their collective philosophy. They are actively involved in these beliefs and feel a strong affiliation to, trust in, and loyalty for each other. Their sense of connection is so strong, in fact, that they are willing to die—literally die—to defend the beliefs and the agenda of the collective. Those who hold diverse values or are perceived to be different—"outsiders"—are often despised and deserve to be intimidated or eliminated by whatever fanatical means necessary. This is the ultimate and evil "we" versus "them" social structure.

More than six years before the Al-Qaeda strike on U.S. soil, commuters on Tokyo's subway system suffered their own horrifying attack by domestic terrorists. On March 20, 1995, members of a fanatic religious cult called Aum Shinrikyo (members changed the name to Aleph in 2000) that promised a fast track to salvation produced a toxic nerve gas, dumped it in soft-drink containers and lunch boxes, and put their deadly packages near the exit doors of subway cars. When the subway cars came to a stop, each of ten terrorists stabbed a bag with the pointed end of an umbrella and ran to a waiting car or taxi. The deadly gas sarin was released on three underground subway lines simultaneously and during the busy morning rush hour. Commuters nearest the sarin gas began to cough and foam at the mouth, their nervous systems began to shut down—sarin disrupts the normal communication between nerve cells—their pupils dilated until they couldn't see. Some experienced seizures, loss of feeling in their limbs, heart palpitations, and for some, cardiac and cardiopulmonary arrest. The gas attack killed twelve people and injured more than five thousand.

Our open world of democracy and globalization is one that is messy, incomplete, sometimes even bordering on chaotic. Unlike fanatics who can be happy to have all their questions clearly answered by someone in authority, in open systems we have free will and the power to make our own decisions. And yet, out-of-balance individualism casts its own shadow as well. Without the complementary effects of community and collective responsibility, we are in danger of evolving into a culture of isolated narcissists—a world ceaselessly echoing the refrain "Me, me, me"—accompanied by all the concomitant individual and collective suffering that comes with bowling alone.

What should be clear to us by now is that both ruthless collectivism and rugged individualism are unbalanced and destructive to human life. Either one in its extreme form fails to provide the kind of society that allows human beings to flourish in their individual achievements and freedoms while nestled in the loving embrace of community, social responsibility, and safe harbors.

It helps to imagine each of these excessive dualities—collectivism and individualism—as anchoring the endpoints of a continuum. In their pure forms, each poses enormous danger for human beings. But by imagining this continuum, it is easy to see that there are many other options, many points at which veneration of the individual and of the community exist in different proportions. And, as in all dualities, the wise strive to "hold the tension of the opposites," to integrate and balance opposing forces as we walk in both worlds. The ancient Chinese symbol of the yin-yang makes this complex idea of integrating opposites crystal clear with elegant simplicity.

From the ancient Taoist tradition, the yin-yang (also known as the tai-chi symbol) refers to the two primal and cosmic forces of the universe. The integration of these forces into a single emblem graphically illustrates how the whole is comprised of polar opposites that—when combined—create harmony and balance. Yin is the passive, feminine force and is associated with the unconscious, intuition, emotion, and relatedness. Yang is the active, masculine force that is associated with consciousness, logic, reason, and individuality. Let me make this clear: references to "masculine" and "feminine" do not refer to gender. All males and females have both masculine and feminine energies, aspects of consciousness, and personality features. The yin-yang symbol describes this graphically. Each lobe of the circle contains a spot of the opposite color, reminding us that every half of a dualistic pair contains something of its opposite within its heart. The yin-yang symbol reminds us that it is only when there is equilibrium between these pairs of dependent opposites can there be wholeness and harmony. This integration of opposites is desirable in all things—unconscious and conscious processes, spirit and matter, light and shadow, head and heart—and is applicable to each of us as individuals and our culture as well.

Yin-yang and "feminine-masculine" are shorthand ways of describing these polar opposites—referred to as eros-logos by the Greeks, or right brain–left brain functioning by neuroscientists.

Yin	Yang
Feminine	Masculine
Passive	Active
Dark	Light
Eros	Logos
Right Brain	Left Brain
Moon	Sun
"Shady Side of the Mountain"	"Sunny Side of the Mountain"
Yielding	Aggressive
Unconscious	Conscious
Emotion	Reason
Relatedness, Communalism	Individualism, Separatism
Open Systems	Closed Systems

Our modern American individualistic society is far more overloaded with yang energy than it is in collective cultures—like the Canela and the ancient Hawaiians—that value harmony and group success. Clearly, we are a nation that emphasizes analytical, logical, and rational thinking rather than intuition. As evidenced by all the data that attest to our stunning lack of social capital, we are not a society that values emotional, deeply connected ways of relating to one another. The yin—the feminine energy—in both men and women and our society at large is viewed as inferior, and is undervalued and underdeveloped. Thus, we set great store in thinking over feeling, reason over intuition, goal achievement over process, science over art, and independence over connectedness.

When the masculine/yang force dominates, societies tend toward competition without compassion, power without mercy, reason without love, and a lack of respect for emotion, nature, and unity. Without the attenuating and balancing properties of the feminine/yin, our culture and our own fractured psyches have become deeply entrenched in the endless self-centered pursuits of power and resources—greed and materialism in its most out-of-control expression. Psychologist Carl Jung once wrote that there were two basic forces in life: the will to love and the will to power. The more you have of one, the less you have of the other. In *Psychological Reflections*, Jung wrote: "Where love reigns, there is no will to power; and where the will to power is paramount, love is lacking. The one is but the shadow of the other."[9] Not surprisingly, in societies in which the will to power prevails, love is in short supply.

If you imagine the masculine/yang and feminine/yin as balancing two sides of a scale, it's easy to make a case for the fact that over the last five millennia on our planet, the scales have dangerously tipped in the direction of the masculine. Without the integration of the complementary feminine yin, the supremacy of the masculine *yang* has led us to modern societies in which domination (in both its patriarchal and, less commonly, matriarchal forms) rather than partnership has become the norm.

In her landmark book *The Chalice and the Blade*, historian and scholar Riane Eisler proposed that under the great surface diversity of human cultures lie two basic models of society: the *"dominator* model"—in which social relationships are *ranked* by hierarchical power structures in which every relationship must have a one-up and a one-down member, and the *"partnership* model"—in which social relations are based on the principle of *linking* rather than ranking. Eisler asked essential and provoking questions about the shape of our modern societies: "Why do we hunt and persecute each other? Why is our world so full of man's infamous inhumanity to man—and to women? How can human beings be so brutal to our own kind? What is it that chronically tilts us toward cruelty rather than kindness, toward war rather than peace, toward destruction rather than actualization?"[10]

Drawing on the anthropological and archaeological records, Eisler presents a powerful case that the answers to these questions can be found in the denigration and denial of the feminine/yin and the unconstrained reverence we place on the masculine/yang. The roots of our present global crisis—lack of belongingness to one another and to the earth itself—can be tracked to fundamental shifts in prehistory that brought huge changes in social structure and technology. "This was the shift in emphasis from technologies that sustain and enhance life to the technologies symbolized by the Blade: technologies designed to destroy and dominate."[11] We've been on a five-thousand-year-old path of bloody history in which the unrestricted and idealized power of the masculine/yang has created a kind of metaphorical and global testosterone poisoning. Eisler and others have proclaimed that we are now at a crossroads and that our central task is to organize our society and communities into ones that support and cherish the survival of the species and the development of our unique potential. A partnership-based society where the masculine and feminine are in equilibrium—where the individual and the collective can both be treasured and where cooperation and mutual respect, not power hierarchies, prevail—offers our greatest hope for the future.

The *I Ching*—the Chinese *Book of Changes*—describes the proper balance of yin and yang forces quite simply: "One yin, one yang. That is the Tao."[12] Harmony and balance cannot exist without both parts—both yin-feminine-relatedness and yang-masculine-individuality. Everything has both yin and yang in it and through their exquisite dance—the tension and resolution of opposing energies—comes change and new life.

On the sides of the cave wall in the Greek temple to Apollo in Delphi from which the oracle delivered her wisdom are written ancient words of sage advice. One urges us to "Know thyself." The other says simply, "Nothing to excess." It seems to me that what is needed is a paradigm shift—a new state of mind that reflects "both/and," not "either/or" thinking. This will be neither an excess of the yin nor the yang, but rather a third thing—a transcendent combination of and respect for individualism *and* community. Virtue will lie in "the middle way" as we struggle to reunite the needs of individuals within the context of community. We have just such an opportunity to reunite this ancient duality, to marry the masculine and feminine, the yin and the yang, and bring them into harmony and equilibrium.

Honoring the Wake-Up Call

If we're wise, we will honor the horrific wake-up call we've been given. We'll use our newly discovered vulnerability—learned at such a heartbreaking cost—to draw together with respect and compassion and make it stick. We'll embrace the spirit of what happened in those awful moments and days after the terrorist attacks to open our circles wide, to recognize our common bond with all humanity. We'll remain conscious of the illusion of separateness that had permeated our lives, and we'll reach out for one another instead of holding on to that false and dangerous perception that we can live as separate, disconnected selves. We'll miss this newfound and palpable sense of community when it is not present and we'll strive to rediscover and nourish it.

Vietnamese poet Thich Nhat Hanh has used the term *interbeing* to describe the real, primal, and spiritual connections between each of us, our human family, and with life itself. Interbeing is the impenetrable web of being, a single life thread that weaves everything together whether we recognize them or not.

If we are wise, we'll live with a deep appreciation of just how intimately we are connected as we live this human life, and we will hold tight to one another. We will never forget how it feels to be part of something larger than our own little lives and how comforting it is to know we're not alone.

We've seen just how critical our need is for connection and belonging. If we are to truly awaken, we'll remember just how much our human species needs one another. Remember, infants die without warm and loving relationships, and so will we. Each of us must individually find our way to our own connections, but collectively we must reevaluate the cultural and civic institutions that create containers for all of us in which we will thrive or perish. And we'll have to walk the walk and not just talk the talk. Those values we prize will have to become everyday actions. And the situation is urgent. We can no longer afford the disconnects between what we say we believe about living a meaningful life and how we behave. We can no longer afford the luxury of saying that we are compassionate without demonstrating kindness, saying that we are a united people without embracing each other, or believing ourselves to be patriotic without being willing to sacrifice for our freedoms, beliefs, and one another. We'll have to live with this new consciousness at the top of our minds and expressed in the particulars of everyday life as we forge a new way of living together.

We have an unparalleled and soul-searing opportunity to rethink our values and priorities and draw from our vast knowledge about how human beings can learn to live together with a respect for the full dignity of the individual while at the same time revering our human needs for one another and for safe harbors for everyone. Together, we can awaken the ancient stirrings of our souls and re-create our lives and our communities in ways that allow love to flourish. Each of us can encourage our human potential and all of our chances for living a full, rich life by remembering that we all share a single web of existence and that separateness is a dangerous illusion. We'll take a hard and honest look at our own life and relationships. We'll assess where we are strong and where we need to work harder to build the kind of fertile safe harbor of friends, family, and community that will provide a container for our own psychological and spiritual growth.

I am optimistic about our human resiliency, intelligence, and—above all—the power of our collective consciousness to courageously change our direction and move toward the fulfillment of our need for one another. We've seen the instinctive stirrings of love and connection in the hours and days after the tragedy of September 11 as we reached out to help one another. Our bodies, psyches, and souls have endured barren times of isolation and disconnection. But now we can listen anew to the yearnings of our hearts to belong to a tribe that sustains and nurtures us. As a society, we've been given a powerful and horrific wake-up call. The future world we create will be of our own design. And, I am certain, this new world will emerge in small fits and starts, beginning with each of us in our own individual lives and neighborhoods. The nineteenth-century German poet and philosopher Johann Wolfgang von Goethe reminded us of the power that each individual has to change the world, when he wrote: "Let everyone sweep in front of his own door and the whole world will be clean." That old saying, "If it is to be, it will begin with me," has never felt more prophetic.

I once read a story about the futility of attempting to make large-scale changes in the world without making changes in one's life. Each of us has the power to change ourselves and, in so doing, like tossing a rock into smooth water, our actions ripple out in every direction. The ultimate truth to the maxim "Think globally, act locally" begins with the very personal changes each of us makes in his/her own life. There is wisdom in the story about an old man who is pondering his life: "When I was a young man, I wanted to change the world. I found it was difficult to change the world, so I tried to change my nation. When I found I couldn't change the nation, I began to focus on my town. I couldn't change the town, and as an older man I tried to change my family. Now as an old man, I realize the only thing I can change is myself, and suddenly I realized that if long ago I had changed myself, I could have made an impact on my family. My family and I could have made an impact on our town. Their impact could have changed the nation, and I could indeed have changed the world."

Connections foster connections. But how do we start with ourselves, and how do we begin so boldly, beginning now? We start, of course, by acknowledging our need for connection and community and remembering—not just in our minds but in our hearts and in every cell of our bodies—just how much we need one another and that love, intimacy, and connection are at the root of what allows us to be vibrantly and passionately alive.

Next, we must honestly assess our own situation—the nature and quality of our connections, the strength of our own safe harbor. We ask: "Do I have a web of connections that nurtures and sustains me?" If not, what are the differences between where you are and where you would like to be? It is this "disconnect"—the difference between the real and the ideal—that offers the opportunity for the greatest change and growth. What are your personal goals for enhanced connections? Remember, goals can only be realized when they are specific and achievable. To say "I want to have more friends, more connections in my life, and feel more loved" is blurry and unrefined, no more of a helpful road map to Los Angeles from New York than "Go west, young man." What does that really mean? What road do you take? Where do you begin? More important, how will you ever know if you've achieved that goal? Instead of pondering cosmic ideals, look at your life and imagine the real differences you want to see. Your goals at first might seem simple: "I want to fill our backyard with friends and neighbors for a barbecue"; "I want at least one friend I can call at three in the morning when my life hits the fan"; "I want to know at least five of my neighbors by Christmas"; or "I'd like to participate in a community or civic group at least once a week." But, as in all things, big outcomes result from small, sometimes almost imperceptible, changes if these are only viewed in isolation. Remember, there is truth in the ancient Chinese adage, "A journey of a thousand miles begins with a single step."

We have to understand our own obstacles, the roadblocks that have prevented us from sailing ourselves home to a safe harbor of loving connections and relationships. What are yours? Are you too busy, too shy, or too isolated? Do you have the interpersonal skills and the psychological well-being to create and maintain truly intimate relationships, but not the time required to nourish them? Or is your belief that it is only the lack of time or energy for relationships an unconscious rationalization for other, deeper, reasons that keep you from intimate and meaningful attachments? This journey to connection will require courageous and sincere self-assessment, tempered, I hope, by the wisdom that there is no greater psychological or spiritual task in life than to "know thyself" and with the assurance that you can change. This point bears repeating: regardless of the reasons for your loneliness or disconnection, you can change. Your birthright as a human being is to live with the attachments of the heart that our species requires. The resources you need to accomplish this are already within you waiting for you to wake up and claim them. Life is about change and you can be about change. Henri Frédéric Amiel—a nineteenth-century Swiss writer best known for his journal of self-analysis—understood the dynamic relationship between change and life itself when he wrote: "So long as a person is capable of self-renewal, they are a living being."

Let's explore and implement a *personal* paradigm shift. We need only to open our hearts, reestablish and really live our priorities by removing roadblocks and sharpening our natural human skills for attachment and bonding.

Let's begin it now.

FOUR

A Thousand Words for Snow: A Model
for Understanding Our Relationships

> Nobody has ever measured, not even the poets,
> how much the heart can hold.
>
> —*Zelda Fitzgerald*

Ralph Waldo Emerson wrote a treatise on friendship in 1841 that still has the capacity to stir the soul. In his essay, Emerson captures the sacredness of friendship by describing it as a gift from God and a "masterpiece of nature." He writes: "I do not wish to treat friendships daintily, but with the roughest courage. When they are real, they are not glass threads or frostwork, but the solidest things we know."[1]

My friend Judy deeply understood the truth in Emerson's words shortly after she was diagnosed with breast cancer in her mid-forties. Her doctors were encouraging and optimistic about a full recovery following a lumpectomy of the tumor. She would need to follow this surgery, however, with chemotherapy and radiation treatments. Judy lives in a small town in North Carolina and would have to travel about two hours to Norfolk, Virginia, to receive treatments. She knew that the trip to the cancer center would be fine but had concerns about the two-hour drive home; she had been cautioned that radiation therapy might leave her feeling exhausted and nauseous for at least a few days afterward. Within hours of learning of the situation, more than a dozen friends and family members were in Judy's living room with a calendar and their work schedules. Quickly and efficiently this group of people who love Judy had worked out a system of drivers so that she could be chauffeured to each and every treatment session. At the Norfolk end, where I was living at the time, Judy's friends made sure that there was always a free guest room on her treatment days in case the travel—even with a chauffeur—proved to be too taxing. We stocked our refrigerators with ice pops and our cupboards with tea, bouillion, and saltines—all good food products for someone who may be sick to her stomach. Judy was deeply touched by the overwhelming outpouring of love and support that she received. One of her friends, surprised by her reaction, asked simply, "What did you expect us to do, Judy? We're your friends, your family." Judy had experienced the power of loving connection at a time when she needed it more than ever.

I was looking forward to a long weekend at a friend's beach cottage to celebrate my fiftieth birthday. I was confused when my partner, Nancy, drove past Margaret's little flattop cottage and headed south. "I thought we might need more room," she said simply. We needed more room for just our dog, Dorothy, and the two of us? But Nancy had made a good decision. Unbeknown to me, and for many months, Nancy and my friends had planned a knockout birthday party ("Exactly how many times do you think you're going to turn fifty?" they said later). That old salt-worn cottage—now decorated with pink and purple balloons, crepe paper, and tables filled with a feast of food and drink—quickly filled up with friends and family from all the stages of my life—from new friends of a few months to old ones I've known since I was a kid. The main room and deck of our cottage was packed with older relatives and friends, contemporaries and their children, familiar faces that are burned into my psyche from the sheer longevity of our relationships, and new ones that expressed the beginnings of what—I hope—will be friendships that go the distance. A table brimmed with flowers, gifts, and cards from cousins, aunts, uncles, and friends who weren't able to make the trip to this strip of beach off the coast of North Carolina. I remembered something that a professor had once told me about merging groups of people from different parts of your life: "You may like chocolate and you may like horseradish, but it's unlikely you'll enjoy them together." He was wrong. It was a delicious mix. That old beach cottage was filled with laughter, dancing, and singing. A karaoke microphone and speaker served as an impromptu podium for telling stories about me—a modest roast of a compassionate sort. The photographs from my fiftieth birthday party give evidence to the many blessings in my life, tangible evidence of the relationships that have contained me for all time. One photo shows people who knew me from the day I was born and fed me and cradled me in their arms. Another photo pictures those who remember the bell-bottoms we wore, the folk songs we sang so earnestly, and the conviction we held, in 1971, that we would change the world. These are people who, collectively, have witnessed and participated in all the many changes I've known these past fifty years. How did this happen? Where did they come from? Where do they all fit in this experience I call my life? Surely there are important differences between these people who make up my tribe and those I know only casually—those who will forget me and I them if our circumstances change or we were to move to distant neighborhoods. These relationships to me are significantly different than those I have with people who I may casually refer to as "friends" but really know nothing about. How do we know what constitutes our web of secure connectedness, our safe harbor?

The following model is my humble attempt to draw distinctions between the different kinds of relationships in our lives, and clarifies the nature and fluidity of those distinctions in one important aspect of a safe harbor: friendship. Friendships offer unique opportunities to form intimate connections. Some of us are blessed by a loving and close family of origin. And there are lots of things we can do to nurture them tenderly and bring these relationships even closer. We don't pick our families (they are connections of chance), but we do choose our family of friends. Thus, with friends we have greater creative latitude to build the kind of container that offers support and comfort when our life takes a difficult turn or celebrates our milestones and victories. You can call this web of connections anything you want—a clan, a tribe, a family. But regardless of what you call it, you need one.

We can imagine all of our relationships—including our friendships—as if they radiate out around our lives. Think of these distinctions—the rings—in this model as being like semipermeable membranes. That is to say, people can move in closer or move farther away from the center, depending upon circumstances and the level of connectedness they have to you. I should emphasize that this model is a representation of the true nature of human relationships in the same ways the notation system in music attempts to represent the sound of the song or an atlas defines the territory you are traveling. These are all clumsy attempts to offer information, new insights, and can be of some use so long as we don't fall into the trap of believing that the map and the territory are really one and the same.

Before I offer any more details about this model, let me very directly reveal my assumptions:

1. Everyone needs a variety of people and relationships in their lives.
2. Relationships are not static; they change, as do our lives and needs.
3. It is the inner circle of relationships—those with whom we are connected by the heart—that constitute our "tribe" or true safety net. These are the relationships that serve as our containers for emotional and spiritual growth.
4. With the possible exception of biological family, most relationships do not begin within this inner circle. We draw from the outer circles of relationship—with time and conscious effort—to build and form our "tribe."
5. What we really need is a sense of belonging to a tribe. What we really need are powerful attachments of the heart.

The arbitrary distinctions that I've drawn in this model are for illustration. In truth, life is more complex than this—or any—model can describe. The great web of being is unlikely to be as practical or linear as this model presents. As drawn, the model fails to integrate the swirling, dynamic, holographic, quantum fields that constitute what we call reality. The minute you begin to impose form—a rigidity of structure—on something as ethereal and nonlinear as the deep order of quantum interconnectedness, you lose the point completely. So instead see the lines between sections of this model as purely arbitrary and, rather than representing discrete boundaries, as a simple attempt to describe certain features of relationships in reference to their intimacy and closeness to you. Relationships change and merge as constant waves on a seamless fabric.

Also, one might argue that it seems a bit narcissistic to think that you (or I or any one person) truly belong at the center of everything. I admit this seems a bit like the ancient belief that the sun and planets revolve around the earth—a rather egotistical belief that, of course, has been proven to be flat-out wrong! Nevertheless, I hope you'll accept these two substantial flaws and use this model as a simple schematic illustration for instructional purposes that will help you to better understand the structure of your own human connections.

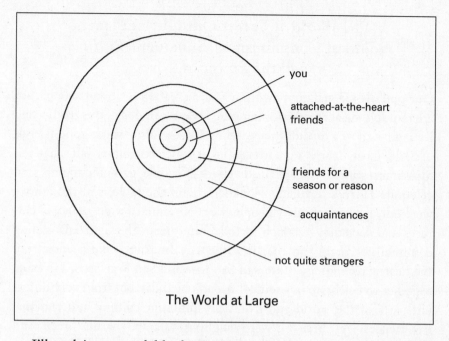

The World at Large

I'll explain my model by beginning at the outermost field and work inward toward the center in describing qualities of relationships that, if we are willing to work hard to remove obstacles and make our relationships a priority in life, will culminate in a safe harbor. After describing some of the characteristics of each relationship type, I'm going to ask you to personalize this concept by reflecting on your own life and, in a very practical way, better understand your connections.

The outermost field—The World at Large—is the vast well from which all of us will draw our small portion of particular relationships, the macrocosm from which the microcosm of our relationships will be formed. The everyday reality of our unique human experience takes place in an ineffable universe, but it is this enormous context that holds the potential for all our connections and bonds. Twentieth-century Jewish philosopher and theologian Martin Buber wrote about the sacredness of I-Thou relations—the ways in which human beings may welcome and actively love one another, drawing real and specific relationships from an unfathomable cosmos. "The world is not comprehensible, but it is embraceable: through the embracing of one of its beings," he wrote. To passionately seek our own deepest connections requires turning toward the wider community of human beings to whom we are already intimately and spiritually connected.

The World at Large: Our Global Planet, Nonlocal Consciousness, Subatomic Particles, and the Power of Love

Our options for making new friends and creating a vibrant safe harbor are multiplying at an astonishing rate. I was reminded of this truth when I was invited to a birthday party while I was visiting some good friends in Santa Cruz. It was a great evening at a nice restaurant but what was most interesting to me was the diversity of people, gathered together, to celebrate Harry's birthday. I looked around the table, and though we were only a group of thirty people, we represented a wide variety of cultures and societies. A bunch of folks came from the tight-knit sailing community around Santa Cruz. Others at the party were friends from the nearby technology centers of San Jose and San Francisco. We came together to celebrate our mutual friend's birthday but from very different parts of the world and from very different cultural and personal experiences. Yet, here we were laughing, talking, sharing bread, and passing bottles of wine from one end of the table to the other. I sat next to Shin, a young Chinese man who lives and works in Japan and who was making wonderful and witty conversation in English with his deft use of a high-technology handheld Chinese/Japanese/English translating device. He opened his wallet and, like proud fathers the world over, showed me photographs of his two beautiful little daughters. Harry and Carol are from England and own a frame shop in town, David is from Belfast and works as a senior executive for a Fortune 100 company, and there were others from Mexico, South America, India, and Germany, not to mention the rest of us who hailed from every compass point of North America.

The next week, I hopped on a plane with my business partner, Andrea, and headed to Acapulco for a conference about business and consciousness. There I spent a week studying, learning, and interacting with people from sixty-one countries including my friends Onye Onyemaechi, an Igbo drummer and dancer from Nigeria with an M.B.A. from Boston College; Luisah Teish, a Yoruba ceremonialist; Brooke Medicine Eagle, a Native American writer and scholar; Victor Sanchez, a Mexican researcher who has studied and lived with Toltec shamans of central Mexico; and Elaine Gaudet, an organizational development consultant from Ontario.

When I returned home—not to a large metropolitan melting pot like New York or Los Angeles, by the way—to my small town on the North Carolina coast, I ran into my good British friend who was raised in Zimbabwe as I waited in a long line at the post office with neighbors from Mexico, Peru, Vietnam, and China. I overheard a fascinating conversation between two twenty-somethings as they communicated with only a passing knowledge of the other's language. The young man I recognized as being from a family whose roots run deep in this part of North Carolina. The very attractive young woman with him smiled and flirted while they both struggled with her English/Russian phrase book, but I could tell by the way they looked at each other that love was in the air and they were having no problem with finding ways to overcome their language differences. To the young and enraptured, there is absolutely no communication barrier in translating: "Would you like to go to the beach with me later?" or waxing eloquent about the finer points of surfing.

Later, I sat down at my computer and Instant Messaged (IM'd) an acquaintance in Chicago, one in upstate New York (both just happened to be on-line), while I fielded a quick phone call from a friend in Arizona and read e-mails detailing their trip to Portugal from my father and stepmother, one expounding on family gossip from my cousin in New Jersey, a funny poem from an Irish writer friend, a history of how the Brehony clan in Australia were all originally deported there from Irish prisons from a distant relative (we think) who lives in Sydney, and a fabulous seafood recipe for preparing orange roughy from a carpenter in New Zealand with whom I correspond regularly but have never met. In fact, except for my father, stepmother, and cousin, I've never met any of these people whom I count as friends of a sort and, if they are not a true safe harbor, then at least they provide welcoming ports of call and offer the possibility of relationship.

The world has gotten smaller. Our technology has provided opportunities for travel and communication that were unheard of even one generation ago. When I was growing up, my parents had no computer and only a single black telephone hanging on the kitchen wall. Before that, I fondly remember my grandparents' "party line." Many households—sometimes as many as six or more—shared the same telephone line and the phones of every subscriber would ring whenever one of them received a call. Some highly advanced communities offered the amazing technology—for the time—called "coded ringing," which caused the different subscriber phones to chime with a distinctive ring—one long; one long, one short; two shorts ("You don't need to get that call, honey girl," my grandmother would call out. "Two shorts, that's for the Kieleys down the street"). As a child, I thought it was great sport to listen in on other people's conversations, something that is illegal today unless you are in possession of a federal warrant. "Is that you listening in, Kathleen?" "Oh no, Mrs. O'Shea," I'd lie. "It's not me, ma'am." Click.

Today, I don't have to caution a neighborhood kid to stay off my line when I'm making a phone call. Instead, I have a home phone line, a home office number, a work number, and a cell phone number, not to mention a DSL line for my computer and a digital pager. I'm surrounded by an electronic force field that allows me to stay connected to just about anyone who wants to reach me.

Whether we call it the information age, postindustrial society, or globalization, it's clear that the world has entered a new era that is driving ancient stirrings. From the moment our species first slung themselves down from the trees to walk across that golden savannah looking for food, we claimed our place as a mobile species. We humans are risk takers, willing to leave the safety of home and daring to explore new frontiers and improve the quality of our lives in the process. Early in the last century, my great-aunt Margaret Geraghty, then eighteen years old and on her own, packed up one small suitcase and sailed across the ocean from County Galway in Ireland. She was equipped only with $65 and a burning drive to live a better life and to help her sisters do the same thing. She worked hard and sent money back across the pond. A year later my paternal grandmother, Mary, sailed into New York harbor to sign her name on the register at Ellis Island. Together they saved money for two more one-way passages across the Atlantic and brought their younger sisters, Nora and Kate, to the United States. Today, millions of families follow that same dream: working hard, saving money, sending it home, bringing loved ones to the opportunity and promise that is America. We are a nation of immigrants and today technology has exacerbated our natural human wanderlust and caused our universe to shrink. Our range of contacts—potential friends, neighbors, and colleagues—is almost infinite.

Open systems—since they are dynamic and constantly evolving—will delight in our changing world by both recognizing our common humanity and honoring our superficial cultural and ethnic differences as expressions of our human creativity and the Divine manifestation of the life force. Open systems integrate new realities, import new energy, and bounce back to equilibrium. We're in the midst of such a new reality right now: a cultural paradigm shift. Our world is changing. We are experiencing directly and personally our metaphysical interconnectedness in which every sentient being and all people of every culture, race, and religion can recognize how we are alike instead of focusing on ways in which we differ. In today's world, with our unparalleled potential for relationship, it has become easier to recognize and appreciate that the appearance of separation between people—the world divided into "self" and "others"—is, as the Dalai Lama so aptly put it, an illusion and "an exaggeration."[2]

I'm an optimist, not naive. I realize that the blending and merging of cultures will be challenging—there are bound to be points of friction—and will require a new consciousness, a new appreciation of our common humanity and what we can learn from one another. We can also learn a lot about peace and community by remembering the words of Buddha: "Knowing that you will all die, how can you possibly quarrel?" But, frankly, I'm over the pedantic musings of critics and social theorists who expound on the menace of multiculturalism and the loss of our "American identity." Get over it. This "melting pot" *is* our American identity and always has been.

By celebrating our diverse heritage and the unity that it offers, we can better remember what many of us have overlooked and what was echoed in the haunting words of poet and novelist G. K. Chesterton at the beginning of the century: "Among all the strange things that men have forgotten, the most universal and catastrophic lapse of memory is that by which they have forgotten that they are living on a star."[3]

Our human integration is not just a metaphysical concept, as so elegantly described by Chesterton. When this idea has reached the level of bureaucratic policy, something powerful and real is afoot. For example, for the first time the decennial census in the year 2000 no longer required respondents to fit into neat and distinct racial and ethnic boxes: white, black, Hispanic, Asian, or Native American. Instead, the survey allowed people to check as many races as apply. That's a good idea because the number of interracial marriages—not to mention intercultural unions—in the United States has quadrupled since 1960 and continues to rise. In the 2000 census, twenty-four out of every thousand respondents said they were multiracial. A study by veteran demographer Barry Edmonston for the National Research Council of the American Academy of Sciences suggests that by the year 2050, 21 percent of the U.S. population will be of mixed racial or ethnic ancestry.[4] Even now, in Sacramento, California, America's most integrated city, two of every ten babies born are multiracial—an increase of more than 40 percent since 1982. The parents of schoolkids in Sacramento represent a wide variety of human cultures and speak more than seventy native languages.[5]

Golfer Tiger Woods, known best for his explosive swing, dead-on putting, and irrepressible smile, will appreciate this new freedom to declare his heritage. Tiger refers to himself as "caublinasian"—a word he made up that represents his combination of Caucasian, black, Indian, and Asian ancestry. With a father whose heritage includes European, African, and Native American blood and a mother from Thailand, Tiger said, in a 1996 media statement to reporters, that he would comment on his racial background this one and only time. In his press release, Tiger emphasized his pride in his multicultural heritage but stressed this point: "The bottom line is that I am an American . . . and proud of it. . . . Now, with your cooperation, I hope I can just be a golfer and a human being."

Closed systems will find the newfound interpersonal contact and relationships of multiculturalism to be dangerous, noxious, because they are unable to import this new energy of interconnection. The tendency of closed systems is to give off energy that can never be retrieved—they exist in a state of entropy. Ultimately, these closed cultural systems lose all available energy. They wind down until they eventually explode, collapse, or deteriorate into a state of inert uniformity. When talking about living systems or human cultures, closed systems in a profound state of equilibrium are like sitting in a stifling room without opening the windows. There's no fresh air in there, no new energy, no dynamic exchange with the environment. These systems, in the course of human evolution, have flat-lined. They're dead.

No longer able to isolate and protect themselves by physical geography—mountains and oceans are easily traversed with planes, ships, and the ubiquitous digital signals of cell phones and the Internet—these closed cultural systems allow no exchange of liberating energy that would revive and invigorate them. Instead of welcoming the stranger, closed systems will respond—have responded—with knee-jerk negativity and intolerance as they futilely search for ways to prevent "them" from becoming "us." These philosophies are old wineskins ready to burst, as we have seen by the violent and frenzied attempts these closed systems use to contain their provincial worldview and cultural/religious isolation. More than twenty years ago, even before our technology had exploded into what we now know as the digital revolution, futurist Alvin Toffler wrote about the panicked resistance of some to widespread cultural change. "A new civilization is emerging in our lives and blind men everywhere are trying to suppress it. This new civilization brings with it new family styles; changed ways of working, loving, living; a new economy; new political conflicts; and beyond all this an altered consciousness as well. Pieces of this new civilization exist today. Millions are already attuning their lives to the rhythms of tomorrow. Others, terrified of the future, are engaged in a desperate, futile flight into the past and are trying to restore the dying world that gave them birth."[6]

Today, telephones and computers, with their exquisite interconnectivity, can digitally transmit the file that contains a photograph of my new baby cousin or instructions about how to make a "dirty" bomb. High-speed jet travel can propel a family to a happy reunion on the other side of the globe or terrorists into the side of a skyscraper. Both our security and our future depend upon the consciousness that we apply to our evolving world. One thing is for sure: the genie of technology and our heightened contact with one another is not going back into the bottle. We cannot unknow what we already know. What can change—must change—is our human ability to responsibly use our advanced tools in ways that will sustain and nurture life on our planet and bring us closer together instead of blowing us apart. Our individual and collective choices will determine whether we will enter into a dawn of new awakening or a horrifying dark night of the soul.

In many ways, we are victims of what prominent sociologist William F. Ogburn in 1922 first referred to as "cultural lag." That is, advancements in our technology and material culture have a tendency to move ahead at a fast—logarithmic—pace, while the nonmaterial culture and the norms and values necessary to govern them tend to proceed more slowly—at an arithmetic pace. We are a radically transforming society and, yet, many of us hold on to stubborn but outdated behaviors and philosophies such as the illusion of separateness. Our personal lives and cultural systems are straining to keep up with our evolving technological world and with the integration of what we know about the true nature of reality.

We now know that we are living in a universe in which our connections more closely resemble the dynamic, intricate, and fluid connectedness of subatomic particles rather than the stiff stuff of fragmented and solid matter taught by the seventeenth-century reductionism of Newtonian physics, a concept that we so carefully replicated out of Tinkertoys in eighth-grade science classes. In the subatomic world, physicists have seen a level of connectedness among what originally appeared to be discrete parts, widely separated in time and space. At some level that we cannot discern through reason or our senses alone, there is an implicate order in the universe in which each of our lives is an integrated wave in this unbroken wholeness. We may know this in our hearts, but modern science is giving us more than just a dazzling and dynamic metaphor to understand the ways in which we are connected to one another. Both theoretical physics and empirical experiments that investigate fields of consciousness are giving proof to the ancient and spiritual idea that we are all part of the same One.

For nearly thirty years, the Institute of Noetic Sciences (IONS)—founded by NASA Apollo 14 astronaut Edgar Mitchell—has been at the forefront of research on consciousness and human potential by applying the rigorous process of science to investigating these ethereal concepts.[7] In February 1971, navy captain Dr. Edgar Mitchell—the sixth man to take that bouncy walk on the moon—experienced an overwhelming and profound sensation while hurtling back home to Earth through indigo space. Mitchell was struck with the realization that he, his fellow astronauts, the blue, jewel-like planet Earth he could see through the tiny capsule window, and the universe itself were all part of a deliberate, universal process and that *everything* was in some way conscious and deeply connected.[8]

Mitchell has spent his life in the pursuit of science. He holds a doctor of science degree in aeronautical engineering from MIT. He was a test pilot and U.S. naval officer, after all, not someone given to fuzzy thinking or elaborate New Age twaddle. And yet, this man of science experienced an epiphany not unlike those of the mystics of every religious persuasion. He described his personal paradigm shift in his 1996 book, *The Way of the Explorer*: "I have often likened that experience to a game of pick-up sticks; within a few days my beliefs about life were thrown into the air and scattered about. It has taken me twenty years to pick up those sticks and make some kind of sense of it all."[9]

Mitchell is describing a fundamental shift in awareness. With unexpected suddenness his most closely held beliefs about the nature of reality transcended the myopic and narrow-minded realm that logic alone conveys when not touched by the numinous and an appreciation of the mystery of life. And that's how the expansion of consciousness works, I think. It's sudden, blinding, and calls into question everything that seemed to make sense in our well-ordered ideas about the nature of reality and the universe. It's the cartoon character with a lightbulb drawn over his head shouting, "Eureka!"

A good metaphor for this sudden flash of insight—this new consciousness—can be found in poster shops and bookstores in shopping malls around the world. You've probably seen computer-generated pictures, called stereograms, though they're more often referred to as "Magic Eyes" after the company most known for designing them. Their colorful, wild, wallpaper-like repetitive graphics contain an underlying three-dimensional picture. Some people discern the image almost immediately while others throw up their hands in frustration and disbelief that there is anything more there than meets their eyes. Like suddenly seeing an image in a stereogram, consciousness emerges when we allow ourselves to look beyond the limits of our normal perceptions. Once you have seen the hidden image, it is easy to see it again. What we now know becomes part of the experience of consciousness. And the image of the stereogram is a good metaphor. What is real has always been there, right before our eyes. It was a shift in our own perception, not a change in the thing itself, that allowed us to see anew.

With what we now know about the wacky world of subatomic particles, that true nature of matter, and the human mind, it is misleading to believe that our individual or collective consciousness is inexorably connected to matter. Our sensory-based assumptions are that mind/consciousness must be located at a certain place in space and time. In Western thinking the location of mind is in the brain. But to anticipate finding consciousness there would be like taking apart a television set expecting to find "the program." It's not in there. You can wrestle every cathode ray tube, tuner, circuit board, and gizmo out of that device but you will not find a single *M*A*S*H* rerun or the local news. The signal is not there—it came from elsewhere. Your television set simply had the right electronics to receive the signal. Likewise, you can dissect a human brain but you will never find mind or consciousness.

Psychologist Carl Jung, writing at a time when quantum mechanics was in its infancy in the 1920s, suspected that the psychological nature of consciousness was decidedly not restricted to the brain. He was convinced that some nontemporal, nonspatial aspect of ourselves exists beyond the limitations of the world as we perceive it through our five senses. "There are indications that at least a part of the psyche is not subject to the laws of time and space," he wrote. "The psyche at times functions outside the spatio-temporal law of causality."[10] Jung's opinion was echoed in the philosophy of the French Jesuit priest, scientist, and visionary Pierre Teilhard de Chardin. Teilhard described a noosphere, or layer of intelligence enveloping the earth, and believed that mankind's evolutionary destiny was to fulfill our cosmic role of unity and connectedness through mutual, universal integration as we soar to higher and higher levels of consciousness. We will evolve, he believed, toward "The Omega Point" where this coalescence of consciousness will lead human beings to a new state of peace and unity. We will not do this alone; rather, we will do it together. In *The Phenomenon of Man*, he wrote: "The outcome of the world, the gates of the future, the entry into the super-human—these are not thrown open to a few of the privileged nor to one chosen people to the exclusion of all others. They will open only to an advance of *all together*, in a direction in which *all together* can join and find completion in a spiritual renovation of the earth."[11]

To Teilhard, a developed human being was one who had crossed the threshold to a new mode of thinking in which he has achieved some degree of conscious integration—integration of the self with the outer world, with others, with nature, with the cosmos itself: "Throughout time, humanity had lived (and many still do) in a narrow world, unaware of the true dimensions of time and space." To Teilhard and others, the great promise comes with experiencing our interconnections—our interbeing with one another and with Divine Intelligence—and in so doing we will never again feel alone. "The day will come when," Teilhard wrote, "after harnessing the winds, the tides, and gravitation, we shall harness for God the energies of love. And on that day, for the second time in the history of the world, man will have discovered fire."[12]

Like the philosophies of Jung and Teilhard, the discovery of subatomic particles and even a cursory understanding of their madcap world along with studies of human consciousness suggest that consciousness is nonlocal and, like quantum particles/energy, does not exist in any one place in spacetime.

A full discussion of the nature of mind—of consciousness—and how that relates to our human interconnectedness is beyond the scope of this book. But I read a study related to something that occurred at the moment of the terrorist attacks on the U.S. on September 11 that seemed to me to describe a startling truth about just how connected our consciousnesses may be. The Global Consciousness Project is an international effort involving researchers from several countries and institutions, including scientists working with IONS and the Princeton Engineering Anomalies Research (PEARS) at Princeton University. This project is designed to register resonance and coherence in the mental domain of the world and to explore whether the construct of interconnected consciousness can be scientifically validated through objective measurement. They designed an experiment that attempts to capture new knowledge about global consciousness—kind of like a collective EEG. Since 1998, the Global Consciousness Project has been studying thirty-seven Random Event Generating (REG) machines. These devices usually produce a continuous sequence of completely unpredictable numbers that can be recorded in computer files. These REG machines are attached to computers running software that simply collects a two-hundred-bit sample once per second and sends the data over the Internet to a server, where it is archived and analyzed at a lab at Princeton University in New Jersey.

Think of these devices as if they are "flipping" virtual coins, where each REG flips about two hundred coins at a time. In just the same statistical way as if you were tossing a penny, you would expect the results to be fifty-fifty: half the time you would come up with heads and half the time you would flip tails. If you flipped two hundred coins, you would roughly expect that one hundred times you would get heads. Experiments have shown that human consciousness can make the string of numbers slightly nonrandom when people intend to do so. That would be like affecting the outcome of a coin toss by focusing your attention on it. Now, it's unlikely that you could affect the outcome of a single toss (sorry, football team captains who want to win the toss so they can receive the ball on kickoff). But over time, by focusing your attention, you might be able to alter the outcome of a number of tosses, say, changing the outcomes of a "heads" appearing—rather than "tails"—to 135 times out of 200.

Most interestingly, the data gathered suggest that not only individuals, but the focus of world attention, can alter the predictable outcomes of these REGs when there is a special state of coherent group consciousness. For example, these machines generated a noticeable fluctuation in the numbers they were generating during the funeral of Princess Diana, the Winter Olympics in Nagano, Japan, and the sinking of Russia's Kursk submarine in August 2000. The difference is very small, but statistical analysis demonstrates that this correlation of the REG behavior with something about consciousness is real. It is as if our wishes or our shared emotions about significant events create a magnet for our shared attention—a cohesive consciousness—that could change the expected fifty-fifty odds of a coin flip ever so slightly.

It turns out that this small effect of consciousness on the electronic REG isn't diminished by distance or shielding, so it apparently isn't brought about by something physical like temperature changes, or sound waves, or electromagnetic radiation. Instead it seems that information is the important thing. The data collected by the Global Consciousness Project is changed from an expected *random* condition to a slightly *structured* condition, detectable by statistical tests. Such structure implies that the numbers are not completely unpredictable and that we can expect to see trends or patterns that should not appear in truly random data.

On September 11, 2001, the Global Consciousness Project's REG machines were continuously pumping out random numbers as they always do when all thirty-seven of these machines placed around the world—North America, Europe, Asia, India, Africa, the Middle East, South America, and New Zealand—suddenly dropped their random number generation and moved significantly in the same direction. As the whole world stopped and watched in horror and disbelief, an initial statistical spike registered an unmistakable and profound response on these REGs immediately after the collapse of the first tower of the World Trade Center. The numbers were still elevated from their normal randomness six hours later and remained that way during most of September 11, 12, and 13, 2001.

A. S. Berman, a reporter for *USA Today*, interviewed project member Dean Radin at IONS headquarters in Petaluma, California, about these startling results. Radin and other members of the Global Consciousness Project are hesitant to draw conclusions and are wary of publicity because attention to their study can affect random-number generation and skew results. Radin would only say that it was too early to tell what their data mean but that, "If you had not known September 11th was unusual, you would've settled on September 11th as being an unusual day solely on the basis of those results."[13] Is it possible that these findings—using insensate electronic random generators—manifest the ancient idea that we are all interconnected and that what we feel and think has effects on others, everywhere in the world?

In his careful and considered review of the data, Roger Nelson, director of the Global Consciousness Project and research coordinator of PEARS at Princeton, described these outcomes in an elegance of language that, to me, was unexpected from a man whose work revolves around generating random numbers and then applying chi-square analyses to them. He wrote: "We experience the world with beautiful immediacy, and with a quality of direct participation that seems completely natural. And yet it is quite magical. We take meaning from music, we know our loved ones from afar, and we leap in thought to the stars. Sometimes we sense that we have dissolved ourselves into a group or a larger whole. And we always have prayed as if it mattered. The mind's reach remains a mystery in scientific terms, but research on the extraordinary range of consciousness indicates that we may have direct communication links with each other, and that our intentions can have effects in the world despite physical barriers and separations. We are compelled by good evidence to accept correlations that we cannot yet explain. It appears that consciousness may sometimes produce something that resembles, at least metaphorically, a nonlocal field of meaningful information."[14]

Like me, you may find the evidence for universal connectedness emerging from scientific research—like the Global Consciousness Project—and quantum mechanics to be mind-numbingly complex. You might even have thought, as I once did, that leptons, quarks, charms, and neutrinos were some newly discovered dwarfs that bunked with Snow White and the other seven, rather than names for the curious energy/particles at the heart of atoms. But it is not necessary to be a rocket scientist in order to understand the intricate connectivity that defines our universe. One only has to look to the world's great spiritual traditions that have preached the same truth about the ways in which we are all part of the same cosmic order and, thus, all intimately connected to one another and to a divine intelligence, whether that be called the Creator, the Divine, the "I AM," the Great Spirit, "thou art That," the Great Mother, the Great Father, Jah, Tao, or God by a hundred different names. This is the Perennial Philosophy—*Philosophia Perennis*. The phrase, originally coined by the German philosopher Leibniz, refers to the immemorial and universal metaphysic that places man in a ground of being that is fully connected one to another and to a relationship—a similarity to or identification with a higher power. This is the spiritual reality that grounds our being and our lives. But, perhaps because we exist within it, we don't have the perspective to apprehend it in the more direct and familiar ways in which our senses seem to give information about the true nature of reality. We're rather like the fish in this Zen teaching story:

Two fish meet in a stream. "How have you been?" one asks the other. "You won't believe what happened to me. I had a close one. I saw a tasty tidbit floating overhead so I snapped it up. The next thing I know, I'm in this whole other world. I've got a piece of hard, shiny stuff hooked into my mouth and I'm hanging by a string. It was awful. I couldn't breathe. I was suffocating! Then this giant creature grabs me, takes the hard shiny thing out of my mouth, and throws me back into the water. Man, that was a close one." "Water? What water? What are you talking about?" asks the other fish.

Like this perplexed fish in the teaching story, we don't have the perspective to easily see what surrounds us, what we are immersed in. And yet, coming to the awareness of our interconnections with one another and with a higher power, whether by faith or by mystical experience, is what every spiritual tradition and religion teaches. In his remarkable book *The Perennial Philosophy*, Aldous Huxley observed: "For as all exponents of the Perennial Philosophy have constantly insisted, man's obsessive consciousness of, and insistence on being, a separate self is the final and most formidable obstacle to the intuitive knowledge of God. To be a self is, for them, the original sin, and to die to self, in feeling, will, and intellect, is the final and all-inclusive virtue."[15]

"*Mitakye oyasin,*" pray the Lakota. In the Sioux language these words mean "we are all related," and it elegantly sums up the belief in an underlying unified universe in which everything—that which is seen and that which cannot be seen—is connected. In a letter to U.S. president Franklin Pierce in 1855, Chief Seattle of the Suquamish tribe of the American northwest expressed the Perennial Philosophy in language that is often quoted by environmentally conscious organizations that recognize that the interconnectedness of all life necessarily includes the earth itself. His words are so elegant and profound that they bear repeating here: "This we know: The Earth does not belong to man, man belongs to the Earth. All things are connected like to blood that connects us all. Man did not weave the web of life; he is merely a strand in it. Whatever he does to the web, he does to himself."[16]

Hindus greet others with prayerful hands, a deep bow, and the word "*namaste*"—"The Divine in me recognizes the Divine in you." Buddhism teaches that clinging to the sense of a personal existence separate from the great web of being is to be locked up in a world of maya—of illusion—and that ignorance of this is the root of all evil. The Taoist writings remind us, "Do not ask whether the Principle is in this or in that; it is in all beings."

The word we most commonly use to describe the experience of our interconnection is *love*. Bede Griffiths, a Roman Catholic monk who lived for more than thirty-five years in an ashram in India, defines the power of love as being the force that attracts protons and electrons to circle around the nucleus of an atom or planets to orbit the sun. Near the end of his life, Griffiths wrote, "Every human being has in his heart this desire to love and be loved. It is the very structure of his being. It is

built into the cells of his body and is the deepest instinct of his soul . . .
the ultimate Mystery of being, the ultimate Truth, is Love. This is the
essential structure of reality. When Dante spoke of the 'love which
moves the sun and other stars,' he was not using a metaphor, he was
describing the nature of reality."[17]

It's not necessary to be conversant with the world's spiritual traditions
or armed with an understanding of quantum physics, able to conjure up
a unified theory, get a grip on Heisenberg's uncertainty principle, or
appreciate what happened to Schroedinger's cat in order to grasp the
idea that connectivity—and the potential for connectivity—is the organizing principle of an orderly universe. Indeed, what we have learned
about the nature of matter and reality from our relatively recent view of
the subatomic world is weird even to the people who study it. "Anyone
who is not shocked by quantum theory has not understood it," wrote
Danish physicist Niels Bohr, who must have been among the first to
be stunned by what he saw since he won the 1922 Nobel Prize for
physics for his work on the structure of atoms. Austrian physicist Erwin
Schroedinger took an even more phobic approach in describing quantum physics: "I don't like it and I'm sorry I ever had anything to do
with it."[18]

But whether we like it or not, whether we would be more content to
see the nature of reality as more stable, solid, predictable, and our own
lives as more separate, that is no longer possible. While this concept
may be mind-boggling, it offers both a metaphysical and spiritual reality
that gives us unlimited potential to discover and create our safe harbors.
Unlimited potential, that is, for open systems. Ask yourself: "Am I an
open or closed system?" Do you only allow yourself to feel close to
people who are like you, people who are ethnically, religiously, or racially
the same as you? If so, you are cutting off a vast opportunity to make new
friends. By going beneath the surface of these superficial human qualities
to the deeper layers of shared values and shared interests, you will find a
new world of connections and friendships waiting for you. To feel alone
or isolated in our interconnected world—with its virtually unlimited
opportunities for connection and its 6 billion human inhabitants—is
either a choice, a failure to prioritize the need for close relationships and
live those values in everyday life, or the result of psychological or spiritual wounds that prevent such relationships from materializing. What is

most important to remember is that more and more opportunities for relationships await us in the web of universal connections.

Beyond Metaphysics—The Everyday Particulars

Recognizing the deep and pure connections between all of us is, perhaps, enough of a safe harbor for mystics and contemplative hermits. I have no questions about our own deep universal interconnections and every spiritual tradition teaches about the power of love of God and humanity. This is the essence of agape—a Divine and selfless love that is transformed into love of our neighbors. It is Buddhist prayers for all sentient beings. And for those who descend the mountain of metaphysics to find real human contact, it should be clear that there is great truth in the idea that more and more relationships are in store for us, out there in the vast web of universal connections. But what does that mean for our everyday life?

In some deeply interior place, in moments of quiet reflection or prayer, we can easily recognize the exquisite interconnectedness of our life with all that is, if we will only open our minds and hearts to that truth. The evidence is all around us and it is healing and comforting. I also love the idea of snagging someone from that great web of being and bringing him/her into my real world, like a carpenter in New Zealand with whom to share seafood recipes. It's true that this relationship makes only a small deposit in my personal social capital account. It is not meaningless, by any means, but it feels more like connection in the abstract. Sharing that seafood meal with another person, to me, feels so much more fulfilling and satisfying. I want friends in my life and I want my friend right there: flesh and blood, sitting in my kitchen, enjoying the orange roughy and a big salad, and getting to know each other.

I think most people would agree that the quality of life is measured not in the abstract but in the minute particulars of our everyday experience. We are incomplete if our sense of connection and oneness with others remains always in the transcendental realm of spirit: "Yes, the world is filled with love and I am part of a great unified whole—a wave on the fabric of the connected universe." Completeness comes by bringing this spiritual reality down to earth, down to the specific.

Whom do you call to share your scrumptious orange roughy dinner?

Is this a relationship that grows over time and can you count on that person not only to share your meal but to be there when you need help or to break out the champagne for your victories? What does this relationship feel like? How do we best understand the truth about our relationships and cull them from the abstract? How do we identify and nurture the specific relationships that create our safe harbors from all the universal possibilities and, most important, how do we make that happen?

Acquaintances and Friends for a Season or Reason

I've heard it said that Native American tribes living in the cold regions of North America have a thousand words for snow. This is probably something of an exaggeration, although scholars have noted that the Yupik Eskimo language has at least a dozen very specific words that differentiate between properties of snow, such as falling snow, drifting particles of snow, fallen snow, the crust of fallen snow, and fallen snow floating on water. Precision in language means something if you have to deal with snow on a daily basis and your life depends on whether your dogsled or snowmobile must navigate through *aniu* (snow on the ground) or *qanisqineq* (snow floating on water).

Whether a thousand words for snow is literally true or something of a legend is a question best left to linguists, but what is clear is that all cultures evolve words and language that describe what needs to be communicated.

So why do we have just a single word for *friend*? Why do we expect one word to describe relationships as distinct as someone we play tennis with occasionally to another we would die for and whose presence in our life gives meaning, love, and rich emotional experience? Our language reflects our failure to appreciate the varying levels of intimacy and connection we need in our lives and the different kinds of friendships that provide that container. In comparison, think about the specific language system we use to describe members of our extended families. We can chart out and designate even very remote relatives on a genealogical chart, but we clumsily grope for words to describe the nature of our closest friendships.

Despite the academic differences between kin and friends, sometimes the definitions of who is a friend and who is a member of the family can be blurry and imprecise. My aunt Franny was at every family wedding, baptism, funeral, and Christmas dinner that I can remember. Like the fictional Auntie Mame, the extroverted Franny is front and center in hundreds of fragile and fading photographs documenting the life of my family that crowd into boxes in my attic. Here, dancing the jitterbug with a martini and cigarette holder and belting out the tune she taught my cousins, brother, and me to sing with gusto—"Aba daba daba daba daba daba dab, said the monkey to the chimp." There, holding my grandmother's hand on the first Easter after my uncle Jimmy, my grandmother's youngest son, was killed in an army helicopter crash. Franny sitting at my grandparents' dining-room table in countless photographs of countless birthday parties and celebrations and funerals. I was quite a bit older when I discovered that Franny didn't make up the "Aba Daba Honeymoon" song herself. She never actually claimed to have written it but neither did she dissuade us of that idea when we asked. I learned that Arthur Fields and Walter Donovan wrote it in 1914. It wasn't until I was older still when I finally figured out that Franny wasn't related to me at all. She was a friend who by the sheer power of love and connection had become one of the family. Anthropologists and sociologists use the term fictive kin to describe the kinds of friends who become part of an extended family network though they are not related by blood, marriage, or adoption. When Franny died, we grieved for the loss of our sweet and funny aunt and we had never even heard of the idea of fictive kin.

But regardless of what we call the close relationships in our lives, the research is clear: the presence of friends in life grants great psychological well-being, physical health, and longevity. Yet, despite the importance we say we attach to friendship (type the word *friend* into the Google search engine on the Internet and choose among 34 million hits), we know very little about how and why friendships are formed or ways to differentiate between various types of friendship.

Friendship is a relationship form that we declare to be of tremendous importance, and yet our culture doesn't honor these relationships in the way it does relationships among family members. Wedding ceremonies, witnessed by friends and consecrated with the sacred, define and publicly declare the creation of a specific family relationship. Formal friendship rituals—in which two people pledge unconditional loyalty and devotion—are unheard-of among contemporary Americans but are not in the least uncommon in other societies. These are not marriage ceremonies—they are public commitments of friendship. For example, traditional Native American tribes have "blood brother" ceremonies. Polynesians, rural Thai societies, and some African cultures have one rite for marriage and another bang-up celebration when platonic friends pledge their mutual allegiance. The children of the Bangwa people of the eastern highlands of West Cameroon are given a best friend—an *eshua ga*—by their parents, and in a custom much like an arranged marriage, these two assume lifelong commitments and obligations to each other.[19] In native Hawaii, the commitment of *pili hoaloha* (devoted friends) was a time of feasting and sacred ceremony. Some of these rituals granted legal powers and responsibilities for friends. Even some Western cultures offer rituals to publicly acknowledge and mark the evolution of a friendship. In Switzerland and Germany, a small ceremony termed *Duzen* ("to address informally") changes the nature of a friendship from a more formal one to one that is on "a first-name basis." The ritual calls for two friends, each holding a glass of beer or wine, to get physically close by entwining their arms, and to toast and drink up after making a promise of eternal brotherhood with the word *Bruderschaft*. When this little ceremony is over, the friends will have become a relationship that, rather than using the more formal mode of address *Sie* (Hey, Herr Schmidt!), they will now use *du* (Hey, Fritz!) when interacting. Our culture offers no such clear-cut commitment to our friends.

In addition to language problems we have to overcome in order to adequately describe friendships, there's precious little agreement about what constitutes a friendship in the first place. Sociologists make two indisputable assumptions about friendship: (1) it is a voluntary relationship that is not institutionalized and lies outside legal and formal control; and (2) friends are not related by blood. But after that cursory definition, the rest is up for grabs. What causes some people to become dear while others will always inhabit the outer edges of our lives? We'll travel miles and miles—spend money and time to get there—to be in the company of our close friends while we merely wave to our neighbor next door as we drive by, a far more convenient relationship to nurture if proximity were the only factor involved in determining our safe harbors. What is it that makes a friendship?

It seems to me that if you were to ask a thousand people what it is that makes someone a friend, you would hear hundreds of different answers. Still there are some common themes. Most people will agree that close friends, beyond their contributions as companions, are a source of self-esteem, affection, and good times. Close friends help us see and realize potential in ourselves that we may not see by ourselves. Together, good friends create a synergy that neither could have achieved alone. The writer Anaïs Nin wrote about how good friends have the power to change our world: "Each friend represents a world in us, a world possibly not born until they arrive, and it is only by this meeting that a new world is born."

Sociologist Jan Yager notes that most definitions of friendship evolve from those qualities that are most sought in a friend. When asked what constitutes a friendship, most respondents detail desirable and ideal attributes of the relationship, "such as commitment, self-disclosure, trust, honesty, and commonality."[20] In a study Dr. Yager conducted with college students, almost everyone agreed that *trust* and *honesty* were essential for friendship, followed by *faithfulness*, *loyalty*, and *being a good listener. Having ideas in common* and *love* were mentioned by more than half. Only a few subjects said that *attractiveness, age, intelligence*, or *being a good talker* mattered.[21] Studies show that women tend to value self-revelation, nurturance, emotional support, and intimacy in friendships—they want to know and be known. Men tend to regard common interests—the opportunity to do things together—as central to the major friendships in their lives. Children usually cite sharing and a lack of teasing as the prerequisites for those they call their friends. Older people often speak of the longevity of their relationships, permanence, and common life experiences as being central to their definition of friendship. Shared values are of greater importance for deep friendships than are shared interests. And some friends like to discuss their relationship—talk about why and how they're friends. Others, like writer C. S. Lewis, observed that real friends rarely talk about their friendship.

Our life takes place in the vast potential interconnections in the world at large. It is filled with people we may care about in a spiritual and metaphysical way—but the vast majority of these other human beings are unlikely to ever enter into our scheme of reference in any real, tangible, or personal way. And then there are people in your life who have emerged from the world at large and are "not quite strangers."

"Not quite strangers" is the place on this model where all nonfamilial friendships and connections begin. This is where form is wrested from the great web of being. Suddenly, there is the possibility of a real live relationship. Individuals move through the (hypothetical) membrane of the World at Large and into your frame of reference in a regular and consistent way. If there are enough reasons or the chemistry is right (there can be "love at first sight" with relationships other than that of lovers), that person will move closer to the center and become an acquaintance. Carl Jung wrote, "The meeting of two personalities is like the contact of two chemical substances; if there is any reaction, both of them are transformed."[22] We've all experienced that to some extent or other. We can know one person for years and have had hundreds of conversations, yet we are not really close. But another walks into our lives and, suddenly, there is a feeling of comfort, as if you are old friends. This newly discovered affinity may begin with a bang or progress more slowly, but some kind of mutual chemistry is evident, spurring you to become friends. In his *Symposium*, Plato retold a famous myth that teaches that in the beginning human beings were two selves in one body but Zeus cut them in half. Since that time, the legend says, human beings have frantically searched endlessly for their missing half. When we find that other half, it's as if we have always known each other. We respond to each other, not as strangers, but with a sacred recognition. Some friendships seem to begin that way.

Other people—for a variety of reasons—do not strike us in this deep and powerful way and will always remain in the layer called "not quite strangers." These relationships offer only a little in the way of real connection but, likewise, they extract only a little of your time and energy. Think about the bank teller you see every week, but don't remember her name and, unless she's wearing a name tag or you live in quite a small town where everyone knows everyone else, you've never ever known her name. Still, you talk about the weather or your deposit, but not much more than that. A "not quite stranger" is the produce manager at your supermarket. You see him fairly frequently and may even have a conversation about how the tomatoes that are available in the winter are hardly worth eating compared to the succulent, vine-ripened ones you ate last July. The relationship is superficial and replaceable. You could have an almost identical conversation with his assistant when the produce manager is in the back of the store checking in boxes of bananas.

Your conversation, if you even have one, and your self-disclosure will depend entirely upon the roles both of you play. Talking about the quality of winter tomatoes with a produce manager would be considered acceptable social behavior. Talking about how your cruel ex-husband would never let you eat tomatoes in your salad is not.

In general, we don't expect that people we come to know in a certain role will become our close friends or the source of our love and support so long as they remain exclusively in that role. Still, they are not quite strangers; they form a part of the fabric of our lives that brings consistency and stability. Many, perhaps most, people will remain in the outer layer of "not quite strangers," while we become closer to others who we then begin to think of as "acquaintances."

That bank teller and produce manager may appear at your local PTA meeting. No longer in the social role in which you first encountered them, you now realize that they have children in your kid's school and they, like you, want to be involved in decisions that affect the elementary school in your community. Under these circumstances, your relationships have an opportunity to grow and expand. Now, when you see them at the bank or the grocery store, you have a whole new area of conversation and potential connection. "Are you going to the PTA meeting on Wednesday night? I'm glad that the school board is telling us more about how the Standards of Learning (SOLs) are going to affect the fourth grade." Things are blossoming here. As you get to know these people, you may discover that you like them a lot. You're on the same wavelength—the same values—as far as PTA issues are concerned. You love her sense of humor. He shares your hobby. You had no idea that he, like you, is a collector of antique Pez dispensers and memorabilia,[23] a point that came up while talking about whether or not candy machines will be placed in the cafeteria at your daughter's school. Now, after the PTA meeting, you get together with him for a cup of coffee and talk Pez. You have discovered a common interest and passion. Writer C. S. Lewis said that friendship is born when one person says to another, "What! You, too? I thought I was the only one!"

If there is mutual interest, the two of you begin to have longer conversations, meet for coffee, and call each other with news about your shared hobby. You chat about how you, in a moment of extraordinary good fortune, found an ultra-rare Pez-Pal Admiral dispenser on eBay and then you discover that you're both planning to attend the Pezamania convention in Cleveland in July. By taking the time for conversation, you find that you share more than just idle chatter about the abysmal state of winter tomatoes. You've become visible while attending your PTA meeting and making contact with the produce manager—even if only by recognizing and greeting him as someone you know, at least a little. By opening up about your hobby, the two of you realize that you share an interest. You've taken the relationship out of the produce aisle and into the coffee shop—thereby changing the basis of the relationship—and you've made an investment of some time in getting more closely acquainted. The relationship may stay at this level forever. You might always talk about Pez collecting when you run into each other at the grocery store. You may still occasionally meet for coffee after PTA meetings to discuss your hobby, but that's about the extent of it. But if you begin to recognize that there is compatibility, shared values that embrace more than just your shared interest, and if you have fun together, this relationship can become closer than a mere acquaintance-ship in your life. If there is mutuality—you both desire to deepen the relationship—then there is a good chance that you will become "Friends for a Season or a Reason."

Friends for a season or a reason are transactional—based on shared interests or circumstances rather than on shared values or the deep mutual desire for connection that characterize enduring friendships. At the very least, all of our connections offer the opportunity to learn and to grow. Our experiences, even with casual friends of a season or a reason, stick to us and we to them. No stranger comes to our lives purely by chance. In the world of spirit, there is a reason for every encounter. The company we keep throughout our lives shapes us, molds us, and teaches us, and all true connections have value regardless of their ultimate outcome. Friends for a season or reason can be satisfying relationships on a lot of levels, you may learn a great deal from these friends, they fill your life with new activities and fun, they leave an imprint on your soul. And you may even discover that they become close, attached-at-the heart friends over time. Often we're too impatient. We expect intimacy to come at our behest and not in its own time. Our fast-paced world has encouraged us to expect things when we want them. Can't afford it quite yet? Charge it! No time to cook? Where's the nearest drive-through?

We want intimacy as quickly and with the ubiquitous availability of fast-food French fries. Many of us are not prepared for the sacred, gestational process that intimacy requires. Aristotle once cautioned, "The wish for friendship develops rapidly, but friendship does not." Several research studies about friendship back him up and suggest that it takes three years or more for a relationship with an acquaintance or friend for a season or reason to transform into a tried-and-true friendship.[24]

Most of our lives are surrounded by relationships of the friends-for-a-season-or-reason variety, and it's my observation that when many people talk about their "friends," they are talking about these kinds of relationships. These are the people you play tennis with once in a while, the mother of your daughter's best grade-school friend, the guy at the office who takes you fishing at his cabin a few times a year. These relationships hold potential for something more—something deeper and more connected. But unless they evolve into attached-at-the-heart friends, the relationships are likely to end when the season or a reason no longer exists. Most of our lives have many such relationships; fast friends under the initial circumstances, then all but forgotten over time. Do you have relationships that felt close but then—let's say—you moved to another state. For the first year, you exchanged birthday cards, maybe even traveled to visit one another. But over time, you can barely remember their names ("Honey, what was that woman's name I used to play tennis with when we lived in Austin? Remember, she was so nice, her daughter went to school with Stephanie, and she had a wicked backhand.")

The failure to understand the nature of these friendships and to hold irrational expectations—when they are misperceived as being a stronger connection than they really are—can cause heartbreak when the relationship tries to outlive its context. In her memoir about friendship, author Beth Kephart describes the true nature of these oftentimes transient relationships that at one time felt close: "There are dozens, maybe hundreds, maybe thousands of people with whom we go shoulder to shoulder every day. In our communities, our schools, our churches, our jobs. . . . People who live some part of their lives in parallel to some part of ours, whom we adopt as we move along. We adopt them, and we name them: colleague, companion, confidante, associate, sidekick, patron, confrere, even *friend*. We adopt them and celebrate them and claim they're part of us, and all of the sudden, they're gone. . . . Too many are merely serial, convenient, a way station, a passing through. We get jumbled together, we look sideways, we promise and then the framework starts to crumble. Those whom we thought of as friends become strangers, so incidental that we barely remember, if indeed we do remember, how or why or even when they were part of us."[25]

When I began to write this book, I had several long conversations with my friend Ken, because I think he knows a lot about the importance of friendships. He and his second wife, Ruth, live on Ocracoke Island—twenty-three miles off the coast of North Carolina and accessible only by plane or boat. Ken and Ruth speak often of the importance of their "tribe," their close friends in protecting, surrounding, and loving them on this tiny, fragile bit of sand sticking out in the Atlantic Ocean. Ken wrote me a beautiful e-mail about the changes he discovered in his life after divorce. What he thought to be lifelong friendships disappeared with his marriage—unfortunately, a not uncommon experience. Last February Ken wrote, "I know that one of the hardest parts of dissolving my marriage was the redefining, or the outright loss, of the people who had served as my containers. Some old ones are still in place, some new ones have come into my life, but it is different. I had to rethink all that I held as solid. The loss of community was an unexpected passenger on my voyage to divorce."[26]

Elizabeth came to my office in tears because she was going through a hard time in her marriage and felt isolated and unsupported by her friends. She was especially disappointed in her group of women friends from her office. They had been a fun bunch, going to impromptu happy hours on Friday nights after work, hanging out together at company functions like the annual picnic and holiday party, and celebrating one another's birthdays with lunch at a nice restaurant, small gifts, and a big cake. Elizabeth had taken a job at a new company on the other side of the city at precisely the time she and her husband separated. She expected her women friends to be there for her, to talk about what was going on in her life, and to offer support and advice. Instead, she discovered that she had very little contact with them. In spite of the fact that they all lived relatively close by, no one made the effort to connect with her and her invitations to get together were always met with "I'd love to, but I'm really busy right now." Because Elizabeth was not available for spontaneous happy hours and no longer contained by the structure of working for the same company, the friendships fizzled. There had been no *Duzen* ritual, no commitment to *pili hoaloha* or other ceremony clearly defining these relationships, but Elizabeth expected them to be more intimate and connected than they in fact were. Her women coworkers were friends for a reason—the reason being the shared work environment; when that reason was gone, so were her friends.

Sometimes the circumstances under which friendships originate can be predictive of long-term connections. Some shared experiences are so profound—so life-changing and heart-opening—that relationships forged in these refiners' fires cut right to the chase. There is a Chinese proverb that informs, "You may forget those you have laughed with but you will never forget those you have cried with."

Kate's best friend William was dying more than ten years ago. This was an extremely painful time for her but her grief and suffering were cushioned by the companionship of William's other friends. Though she had only met them in the weeks before William's health went downhill quickly, Kate feels that this profound experience—saying good-bye to a beloved friend—cut through all the usual slow build and time required to form deep connections with people she met. "In the course of two weeks, we faced a life-changing experience together," she told me. "We were saying good-bye to someone we loved, each in our own ways. We talked about our relationship to William and told stories that made us laugh and cry. In spite of all my grief at this time, something good and important happened over the two weeks that I spent with William before he died. His friends became my friends, and even in the first few days we knew more about each other than friends I've had for years. In some ways, I don't have that much in common with them, except that we love each other." Almost a decade later, Kate remains in close touch with these people and says she feels that "they are my family."

A small article that I read in *Time* magazine almost a year after the terrorist attacks on 9/11 described the power of shared suffering to create deep relationships, a clear sense of tribe, among people who began as strangers. I was moved when I read about the friendship between a woman from Long Island whose sister had perished at the World Trade Center on 9/11 and the widow of a man who was killed in the Oklahoma

City bombing in 1995. They have shared unspeakable tragedies. What courage it takes to open one's broken heart so completely. Cathy Ann Marchese-Collins had prayed that somehow her younger sister had escaped from the 102nd floor of the North Tower. But her hope disappeared when police officers came to her parents' home to report that DNA analysis had confirmed the identification of her sister's body parts from the World Trade Center rubble. Overwhelmed by this savage news, Cathy Ann called the woman she has been talking with every week for the past year. Her friend was someone who, like no other, could understand not only the loss of a beloved family member but the horrors of identifying their bodies through DNA, the morgues, and the memorials. Diane Leonard's husband, Don, was killed in Oklahoma City. She was sent by the Red Cross to offer help to the grieving families in New York and understood what was ahead of them just as she had learned from a widow of the 1988 Pan Am 103 bombing. The two women talk weekly for hours. "It's amazing to me how quickly you can talk to someone you don't even know," Diane told *Time* reporter Amanda Ripley. "The wonderful thing about talking to her is that she knows. She just knows," said Cathy Ann.[27]

Some reasons and seasons are more simply more powerful than others in opening the heart to the process that allows for intimacy, trust, and connectedness to emerge.

Acquaintance relationships are closer than "not quite strangers," and "friends for a season or reason" are closer than that, but neither is as intimate as "attached-at-the-heart friends." With the possible exception of those we meet under difficult and painful circumstances, we generally reveal little of our inner selves to our season and reason friends and even less to our acquaintances. Neither constitutes the truly significant relationships in our lives. When we see an acquaintance and ask, "Hey, how are you doing?" we rarely really want to know. It's not that we're insincere, but we've just adopted our culture's shorthand greeting that could easily be exchanged with, "How's it goin'?" (we don't want to know that either) or, more simply, "Hello!" (we expect a friendly hello back). We can accept a casual, nonintimate, nondisclosive response to this question. We ask, "How are you doing?" He says, "Great, I get off at four for a weekend of fishing." That's not very revealing information and our level of comfort remains high. But for the most part and without some explanation, we would be stunned and awkward if an acquaintance began reciting a litany of his real-life problems in response to our off-hand greeting of "How are you doing?" "Terrible," he says as he pushes the cart of fresh vegetables down the aisle, following you as you shop for some salad fixings. "My wife just left me because we've had such a rotten sexual relationship since her mother moved in with us. And then there are my kids. Things haven't been right since they turned into teenagers. Billy's dating someone I can't stand and Wendy is anorexic." This degree of intimacy and disclosure coming from an acquaintance would cause us to finish our shopping in a hurry and all the while we'd wonder about this guy's social skills, appropriateness, and emotional intelligence. After all, didn't he know we were really just saying "Hi"? On the other hand, the kind of disclosure I've just recited would be perfectly acceptable, even expected, between close friends.

We expect disclosure and intimacy from our friends and if they, time after time, brushed off our sincere question about how they were doing, we'd find that our level of closeness would never increase. It would be hard to consider them as being true friends of the heart.

Attached-at-the-Heart Friends

When the philosophers and poets offer their stirring comments on friendship in its purest and most meaningful form, they are talking about attached-at-the-heart friends. They are waxing eloquent about the real deal. "My friends are my estate," wrote Emily Dickinson. "What is a friend?" Aristotle asked and answered, "A single soul dwelling in two bodies." The Greek playwright Euripides lauded the value of friendship and told us a bit about how he must have felt about his family when he wrote, "One loyal friend is worth ten thousand relatives." "Friend, our relationship is this," wrote the thirteenth-century Sufi mystic Rumi, "that wherever you put your foot, you feel me in the firmness under you." And in a rare moment of sharp and concise prose, the usually long-winded Charles Dickens simply said, "Friendship? Yes, please."

Attached-at-the-heart friends are the people we expect to be in our lives forever—the true basis for a secure and safe harbor. We expect clarity in the relationship and absolute assurance that our friend will be there when we need her. In fact, it's not so much that she is there but the belief, the certainty, in our own hearts that we can count on her.

With good friends, we cherish each other, we know that we can love and be loved with confidence and that, regardless of how our lives might change, we'll be connected throughout all time. We are not just friends in spots but also friends in the very essence of our being, knowing that we're there for each other through thick and thin. Beyond the lofty definitions provided by scribes and poets, there is easiness in attached-at-the-heart friendships. Our good friends help themselves to a glass of iced tea from our refrigerator without asking, they flop on our bed as we're putting on our makeup in the master bath, and they often know what we need from them long before we even know what we need to ask of them. They know when we need to talk, when we need to share our deepest feelings, and when we need the powerful presence of their silence as they stand by ready to help when the time is right. Attached-at-the-heart friends experience a fluidity of roles: one day you're the one who needs advice and comfort and the next day you're the one giving these to your friend. These are the relationships we count on in our lives, knowing that our attached-at-the-heart friends are there for us—and we for them—in good times and in bad. They are the first ones we call when we've had a stroke of good fortune and the first ones we seek when life has thrown us one of its inevitable difficulties.

As you read this, think about whom you could call (and who would call you) at three in the morning. It's not that this question defines our closest friendship, but the answer is a good barometer of a deep level of friendship. So ask yourself, "If my life were falling apart, who after being awakened by my frantic middle-of-the-night phone call would say, 'I am listening and I want you to tell me everything'"?

We learn to love openly and purely with our friends. Not love, in the abstract, but love at its most authentic, forged not in the quiet reflections of spirit but in the down-and-dirty crucible of relationship and soul. These are relationships that are always being re-formed, growing and changing.

I believe that friendship and love are closely related and was always touched by an old proverb that teaches that the verb "to love" in Persian means "to have a friend": "I love you" translated literally is "I have you as a friend." But the truth is that the words "friend" and "love" are closely related in most languages: the Latin *amicus*, "friend," and *amo*, "I love"; the Greek *philos*, "friend," and *phileo*, "to love." In English, we have to go back a millennium before we see the verb "to love" related to the word "friend," but, if you look hard enough, it's there: the old English word for "friend" was simply the present participle of the verb *freon*, "to love."[28]

The Celts have a beautiful concept of friendship that is stated in the words *anam cara*. *Anam* is the Gaelic word for "soul" and *cara* is the word for "friend," so the phrase, translated literally, is "soul friend." These are attached-at-the-heart friends in their purest and most magical form. These are friends to whom you can reveal everything—nothing is held back, and the relationship is one of absolute belongingness. In the shelter of these deep and enduring relationships we may glimpse the sacred and eternal depths within our own human soul. With an *anam cara*, you can share your innermost self, your mind, and your whole heart. Irish poet John O'Donohue describes an *anam cara* as a relationship in which "your friendship cuts across all convention, morality, and category. You were joined in an ancient and eternal way with the 'friend of your soul.' The Celtic understanding did not see limitations of space or time on the soul. The soul is a divine light that flows into you and into your Other. This art of belonging awakened and fostered a deep and special companionship."[29]

Friends not only love us, but also reflect back with gentle honesty, spurred on by a deep desire to know us not because they must, but because they want to. We're bonded, not by blood, but by the sheer power of unconditional love. Compassionate and trustworthy mirrors, friends are our containers for psychological and spiritual growth as they satisfy our earliest and lifelong yearning for attachment. We are connected to these friends by a resilient web of intimacy, trust, and love. We can be goofy in front of them but they still love us. We can make bad choices and they help us pick up the pieces. They've heard our stories, know our history, but can listen each time those stories matter as if they've never heard them before. We're better people in the safe harbor of our attached-at-the-heart friends. These kinds of friends are magical and, as Emerson has declared, "the masterpiece of nature."

Our true friends love us and stand by us, no matter what. The loyalty and nonjudgment that seem to characterize true friendship have the power to allow us to be real, to be ourselves, and to remove the editing that we so often use when we're with people we don't know or trust nearly as well.

It is perhaps in true friendship that we have the clearest glimpse of our own authentic Self beneath the persona and posturing—the mask—that we so often use as a shield in other relationships.

Fritz Tubach and Bernie Rosner met by coincidence—a strange twist of fate—during the summer of 1983. It turns out that their wives had been friends in high school in Los Angeles but had lost contact for more than twenty years. One day, not unlike any other, the two women ran into each other in a local drugstore. During this chance meeting, they learned that each had married a European man about fifteen years older than she whose first wife had died of cancer and left children without a mother. Thinking that this was an interesting coincidence, Sally (Fritz's wife) and Susan (Bernie's wife) decided to gather all four of them for dinner. That's when Susan and Sally discovered that they lived in the same neighborhood—less than five blocks away from each other in this affluent northern California suburb. It seemed that the couples would have a lot in common. Bernie, the general counsel for the Safeway Corporation in Oakland, and Fritz, professor emeritus of German at the University of California at Berkeley, and their wives had common interests in good food and wine, tennis, travel, culture, and contemporary affairs. Still, Fritz was apprehensive about the upcoming evening with his wife's old schoolmate and her husband. He had learned through Sally that Bernie is a Jewish Hungarian-born survivor of Auschwitz. Fritz, on the other hand, is the son of a German Nazi officer.

In their book *An Uncommon Friendship*, Fritz recalls his anxiety—his fear of ghosts—as he and Sally drove to the Rosners' home for the first time: "This dinner for four could be attended by uninvited guests—any of the dead members of his family or of mine. Perhaps my distant uncle, who had been an SS officer in charge of a refugee camp near Würzberg and hanged by the surviving inmates at the end of the war, might appear. Or perhaps my own father in his Nazi Party uniform would join us for dinner, or my host's father and mother as they emerged from the ashes of the crematorium."[30]

The complex chemistry required for all four members of two couples to become friends was just right. Everyone had a wonderful time together. Fritz remarked that the hours passed quickly during that mild summer evening as they sipped cognac and watched a sampling of Bernie's video collection of grand opera. The Rosners had a big-screen

TV and tuned in the most beautiful arias of Mozart and Verdi. "Classical music enveloped the living room as we listened to excerpts from Strauss's *Der Rosenkavalier*. Who, at our age, would not be touched by the Marschallin's musing on time as a wondrous thing—'*Die Zeit ist ein sonderbar' Ding.*' Wouldn't it be best for both of us to just surround our pasts with the detached glow of great music?" Fritz mused. The friendship clicked and soon the two couples developed a pleasant, if superficial, suburban friendship. The two men could talk about their parallel early years while each was growing up in a small European village. But they avoided the moment when these parallels ended one day in the spring of 1944 when the SS and their Hungarian Nazi henchmen arrived in Bernie's village of Tab, and deported the twelve-year-old Bernie, his family, and the other Jewish inhabitants to Auschwitz. At the same time, Fritz was a member of the *Jungvolk*—the boys' division of the Nazi Youth Movement—and was slated to become a member of the Hitler Youth on his thirteenth birthday. His father—an active member of the Nazi Party since 1933 and a counterintelligence officer on the German General Staff—and the rest of his family survived the war. Bernie was the only survivor of his.

The subject seemed too hard to broach, too impossible to weave into their casual friendship of common interests, music, tennis, and discussions of philosophy and European literature. "Bernie and I were caught for more than a decade between our European pasts and our American present, and neither early childhood memories nor the many things we now had in common were enough to bridge the divide that had existed between us during the years when Hitler was in power," Fritz wrote.

In 1989, during dessert at one of their many dinners together, the Rosners mentioned that they were planning to visit Hungary and Bernie's village, Tab, the following summer, and invited the Tubachs to join them. For the most part, they were typical American tourists, snapping photographs, enjoying fine meals, and sightseeing. Bernie animatedly talked about the Hungarian countryside he remembered from his early youth. While in Tab, Bernie gazed toward some run-down brick buildings dominated by a tall chimney near a stand of trees. He raised his hand to shade his eyes from the bright sunlight and said, "That's the brickyard. That's where the horrors began." Fritz writes that Bernie's fleeting remark hung there in the summer heat but that it was the beginning of a different course for their friendship—a deepening of a journey that has taken them far beyond the one-day trip to his native village and far beyond the casual friendship that marked the beginning of their relationship.

Their friendship and the book of memoirs they have written together that documents it, they say, is proof that our shared common humanity just might have a chance at changing the world and ourselves. Their stories show just how we can build both personal and collective bridges between us and that deep and meaningful relationships can be forged from the most unlikely sources. As an epigraph for their book Bernie and Fritz chose a line from German-American political scientist Hannah Arendt, whose analysis of the banality of evil as she documented the Nuremberg trials is an unforgettable work. Arendt wrote, "We humanize what is going on in the world and in ourselves only by speaking of it, and in the course of speaking of it, we learn to be human."[31]

Cathy Lewis, my cohost for our public radio program *The Art of Living*, and I interviewed Fritz and Bernie for an episode of our show. Now both retired and in their seventies, the closeness of their friendship is evident in the way these men finish each other's sentences, laugh at each other, and urge the other to tell this story or that one. Like old and happily married couples, there is ease, unselfconsciousness, in the way these two men talk to and about each other—a level of comfort that comes only with true intimacy and closeness. What began as a pleasant—if superficial—friendship has transformed into one of deep understanding and mutual respect. Theirs is a friendship that is nurtured by trust in each other, and the seasoning and nuances of intimacy that can only happen when relationships are given the time and attention to ripen. We asked each of them, Bernie and Fritz, if writing their memoir was difficult. They both acknowledged that the most painful parts were in opening up to themselves—reliving heart-wrenching memories of their painful pasts—and spoke about the ache of remembering. But, they were quick to point out, there was no friction or tension between them as they dredged through the past. Instead, they helped each other through it, learning from each other, and giving comfort and help. Why would there be problems between them even as they came to terms with such a horrific history, they wanted to know? "After all," they both said, "we're friends."

Like Fritz and Bernie, attached-at-the-heart friendships can flourish across age, race, ethnicity, and history. To get to the heart of what true connection really is—a haven in a troubled and often chaotic world—we have to know what we need. We have to be hungry for relationships that will go the distance with deep attachment and love. Attached-at-the-heart friends are about fully understanding how much stronger we are together than alone. They're about sharing experiences, sharing our lives, and emerging through all the twists and turns of outrageous fortune with a genuine belief in the power and longevity of our relationship. It's not enough to have folks in our lives with whom we play tennis and then forget when we exchange our backhand for a baby carriage, our collection of Pez dispensers for an array of Beanie Babies.

The relationships in our lives are not static. Things change. Some relationships come to an end and bitterness and resentment may replace what was earlier affection and belongingness. But our inner circle—our safe harbor—transcends all the events of our lives. There are moments of insight when we know that we can live better than we are, when we are convinced that we are hungry for something important. "There are seasons in human affairs, of inward and outward revolution, when new depths seem to be broken up in the soul, when new wants are unfolded in multitudes, and a new and undefined good is thirsted for," wrote nineteenth-century essayist William Ellery Channing.[32]

As in everything, the most crucial step in getting what we need is to recognize and understand the goal. And the goal goes beyond feeling one's connection to the world at large, but to pull from that realm of potential relationships a web of people who are connected to us by the strong fibers of love, mutual caring, respect, commitment, and trust. This is how we weave our web of security and attachment. And it is within the protection of our dearest relationships that we can most certainly become our true selves, and move toward psychological and spiritual maturity.

So what is the state of your safe harbor? Remember that even those of us in loving marriages or partnerships need the kind of attached-at-the-heart friends I've been describing.

It can be instructive to take a look at your own sphere of relationships. Where are you strong and where do your relationships need shoring up? Take the model reprinted below and make it personal.

Spend a few minutes reflecting on your own friendships, then take a pen or pencil and mark on this model the specific details of your safe harbor. Write down names of friends—and family members—in your life and assign them, as best and honestly as you can, to one of these various categories of relationship.

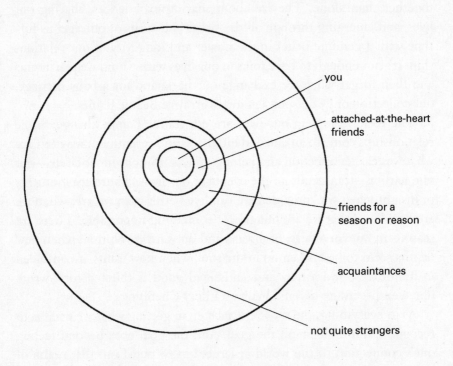

you

attached-at-the-heart friends

friends for a season or reason

acquaintances

not quite strangers

The World at Large

Carefully study what you've written down here. Do your relationships pile up in one category while others are relatively empty? Is your life filled with acquaintances or friends for a reason or season? Who resides in that inner circle of attached-at-the-heart friends? Do they really belong there? Are these healthy relationships that honor and nurture you? Can you be yourself with those friends? What can you do to make these relationships even stronger? Do you have friendships that have drifted, become stagnant because of lack of time and nurturance? Are you out of touch with people who used to be good friends?

The goal is to move people from the outer rings to the inner. Remember, these are semipermeable membranes and you have the power to change the nature of your relationships. Love and our ancient and enduring need for connection are the forces that move strangers closer to our hearts.

Fritz and Bernie started out as casual suburban friends enjoying dinner, opera, and cognac together. Their relationship might have stayed right there—friends for a season or reason—but there was something in each of them that wanted to know the other. The desire for a deeper level of friendship was strong enough that each had to gather the courage to traverse difficult terrain if they were to make this happen. Would your life be enriched by one of your acquaintances or season-or-reason friends moving closer to your center? If yes, then who are they? Right now, honestly list those friends you would call at three in the morning with the full assurance that they will be there for you, they will care, they will love you and help you through whatever tragedy caused that late-night phone call. Who among your friends do you believe knows that you would welcome such a call from them if they were in need? Do *they* know it or do you just hope they know it? Which relationships hold unrealized potential? What friend for a season or reason can be cultivated to become something more than that? Who do you need/want to spend more time with? Who do you want to know better? With the exception of those lucky enough to be born into a strong and close family, this is the process by which we build our families of the heart. People can move closer to center from the outer rings of this model. Who is there in your life—from the produce department at the supermarket, from the parents of your kid's schoolmates, from your workplace, your church, your neighborhood—that can move closer to your heart? You are already rich in potential connections. How will you actualize these and bring out their potential? After you've filled in the model with the various kinds of friends in your life, take a moment to reflect on the following questions. I recommend that you actually take out a piece of paper and write down your answers to each of the questions in the following box:

Family and Friends

1. Are you emotionally close to your family of origin? Do you feel connected to them?
2. Are you emotionally close to your friends? Do you feel connected to them?
3. If yes, how often do you talk with these family members or friends? Spend time with them? How often do you communicate (by e-mail, phone, fax)?
4. Is there anyone in your family of origin among your friends that you have a grudge against or have stopped talking to?
5. Name the friends you feel you could call at three in the morning and they would welcome the chance to help you.
6. Which friends could count on you to help them at three in the morning? Who would call you?
7. When did you last spend time with (if local) or talk with (if living outside your area) the people listed in #4 above?
8. Why are you close to your best friends? Describe the qualities of those relationships that cause them to be closer than other "friends."
9. Have your friendships stood the test of time or have they deteriorated or ended when circumstances changed?
10. How would you like your connections to change?

Community

1. Draw a map of the street where you live (if you live in an apartment, draw your floor or the adjacent floors). Name the people who live in each of these houses (or apartments). Write down three things that you know about each of them.
2. What are the issues that concern the members of your community?
3. When was the last time you attended a community or neighborhood meeting or volunteered to contribute something to them?
4. What skill or talent do you possess that could add to the social capital and connections in your community?
5. How would you like your community to change in the future? What will you do to make that happen?

In our transient society it isn't always easy to keep and nurture the close friendships and family relationships that we so clearly need. Most of us know far more about losing friends when they move or our circumstances change than we do about how to make these relationships last a lifetime. But we can change that. Change begins when we can see the next step and take it. And even at this very moment, your world is filled with possibilities for grace and for the love of good friends.

Ask yourself if there is someone hanging around in those outer orbits of family and friends who wants to come in. How would your life be changed if this person were a true friend of the heart? We all have the power to show hospitality and to welcome another into our most intimate fold. True connections of the heart are within reach and, once attained, are enduring.

I was thinking about this question—of moving from stranger to close friend—several months ago when a barnyard goose found her way to the small lake behind our house. We don't have a clue how or why she ended up here but think that maybe someone abandoned her. We took a picture of her and compared it with photos we found on the Internet and learned that she's of a species called Toulouse. We named her "Toulouse Goose" for, well, obvious reasons. For months my friends and I watched the wild Canada geese who live on this lake run her off. They'd bend their heads low to the water, mouth open, pink tongue flying, and try to ram her. Not exactly a warm "Hi, howdedo?" The Canada geese would fly at poor Toulouse, angrily honking, until she jumped off the dock or flew away. As nesting season approached, the Canada geese ramped up their efforts to get rid of this intruder. Toulouse swam alone on the lake and honked throughout the night. Her sound was a mournful, plaintive wail that made us all sad. We feed all the geese but have a special concern for Toulouse—the "ugly duckling," the goose without a home.

But in spite of being so clearly unwelcome, Toulouse held her ground. She just wouldn't let the other geese run her off. She'd stay by the edge of the flock, but I watched her move closer every day. Slowly but surely, she began to swim closer to the others.

Then one night, a flotilla of Canada geese and their goslings streamed across the smooth lake. There in the middle of the flock swam Toulouse. She'd found her home—no, she made her home—and her mournful wails no longer pierce the night.

I carry the image of Toulouse with me now—a reminder of the importance of perseverance and of how, by welcoming a stranger, we make a friend.

In the best of all possible worlds, we are all surrounded by loving relationships. In the following chapters we'll talk about the attitudes, skills, and priorities required to bring the world at large into your range of acquaintances, then into the realm of friends for a season or reason, and finally, importantly, into the attachments of your heart. And it is here that love awakens and throws light across the darkness of loneliness and disconnection. Once you've started your journey toward a true safe harbor, you will never want to stop. You'll be hungry for the ongoing shelter of loving and being loved.

If, like Charles Dickens, you answer the question of friendship with a simple "Yes, please," then recognize your own power to change your life and begin it now.

PART II

A Map to Connection

Introduction

> No one can cheat you out of ultimate success but yourself.
>
> —*Ralph Waldo Emerson*

It's easy to get into a rut and feel overwhelmed with all of our commitments and responsibilities. Instead of believing that people create their present and future, it can easily seem that our destiny is set—has been set—by our past. Old, outdated, often inaccurate images of ourselves determine our reality: "That's just the way I am," or "I can't change that," we might think. Before change is possible, it is necessary to release old attitudes and behaviors that keep us from our truest, most actualized self. Our spiritual and psychological growth relies on our ability to leave behind what is not working for us and courageously embark on a new path. In order to grow and change, it is necessary to let go of our unconscious acceptance that we are not entitled to a life rich in connections and love. Some of us will have to make major shifts in feelings about our own lovability and our human need and right to have deep, rich relationships. Others will have to learn to live our priorities in new ways, remembering that no one on their deathbed ever wishes for more money, cars, or status. They wish instead for deeper connections and more time to spend with those they love. Given the world we live in, where connection requires a new consciousness, we'll have to work hard to create our tribe and unlearn the ways we've been living before we can learn new and vibrant ways of being in the world. We may have to empty our cup before new insights and realities can fill us up.

Zen teachings emphasize the importance of "beginner's mind" or *shoshin*. Beginner's mind is innocent of preconceptions, judgments, and ancient scripts. It's about being present to explore and open to new possibilities. It's the mind that sees the world through the eyes of a little child filled with curiosity and wonder. There's a Zen teaching story that I love that illuminates this point:

A rather arrogant professor went to visit a Zen master. While the master quietly served tea, the professor talked about Zen. The master poured the cup to the brim and then kept pouring and pouring the tea. Soon, tea splashed over the sides of the cup, onto the table, and all over the floor. The professor watched the overflowing cup until he couldn't stand it anymore. "Enough! It's too full!" he yelled. "No more will go in!" "You are like this cup," the master said. "How can I show you Zen unless you first empty your cup?"

Another way to look at this is that we may think we have singular or personal limitations that prevent us from making friends and building our connections. Do you agree that we can get stuck by our preconceived notions about what we can achieve in life? Let me give you an example. The other day, I ran into an old friend I hadn't seen for a while. I couldn't believe how fit and trim she looked. I told her she was looking great and she said she'd been training to run in a marathon to raise money for breast cancer research. What? This is a woman who used to think that a remote control was the greatest invention in the modern world because now she didn't have to walk two steps to change the channel.

"I realized how stuck I had been in my image of myself," she said. "And then I heard a story about gnats." "Okay, gnats," I said. "If you keep gnats in a Mason jar they'll jump as high as they can to get out. But the top stops them. After just a little while, you can take off the top but they won't jump any farther than that. They learned how far they could go." This is the way elephants are trained in India, I remembered. Trainers teach baby elephants to stay by tying one of their legs to a short rope and attaching it to a stake in the ground. At first the baby elephant pulls and pulls against his restraint, but to no avail. No matter what he does, he can't get away. When the elephant is grown, all a trainer needs to do is tie a small rope—attached to nothing—around the elephant's leg and he is now held to the spot, not by a stake but by his own beliefs.

Are you like a gnat or an elephant, seeing limitations that are really only in your own mind? How do those limitations keep you from developing close and intimate relationships with friends and family?

In the following sections of the book, I've identified some of the elements or human dimensions that affect our ability to have, keep, and nurture strong friendships. By giving some thought to these and exploring the exercises that accompany them, you can, in a sense, lift the lid off the Mason jar of your own expectations of yourself. You can see if the rope that binds you is in fact tied to anything solid, or if it is just a self-imposed constraint. You can stretch a bit, try new ways, and bring new consciousness to your own circle of friends and harbor of support.

On your journey questions will arise: How will I go about changing? Where will I find the time and energy to nurture my friendships and relationships? Why don't I feel the closeness and support of other people, anyway?

In some ways, those who are truly isolated and lonely may have greater incentives to change. Psychological pain is a great motivator. For most of us, though, our lives are okay. Perhaps, we don't have the vital presence of attached-at-the-heart friends that touch our souls and surround us with their love, but we get along. We have marriages, partnerships, and families that meet many of our needs for connection. The truly isolated may feel depressed but the rest of us are just cloaked by ennui—a boredom or vague dissatisfaction with our lives. Because it doesn't hurt so badly, we may be more inclined to just let things roll on as they have been. I urge you not to do this. Keep in mind how much richer, happier, and more fulfilled your life will be when you are a part of a tribe, feel the love that comes from people who know you at a soul level, and are securely moored in your safe harbor. These connections will also improve your health and well-being. You'll live longer.

I've learned that there are two steps to making any change in ourselves. The first step is accepting our new insight and awareness. Only when we have understood the discrepancy between where we are and where we want to go—with our goals clearly set on our horizon—can we draw our map. The second step is to take action: to get up each day and honor these new priorities, this new agenda that will be reflected in our behavior. You can begin when you see the next step. Goethe once wrote, "Human beings, by change, renew, rejuvenate ourselves; otherwise we harden."

The following section offers specific reflections and doable exercises that can help you build strong human connections. I am not arrogant enough to believe that these are the only ways to get there. As you begin the process of deepening your relationships, I've no doubt that you will come up with your own fantastic and effective strategies. But these offer a starting place.

FIVE

Your Friendship Values

Use your good judgment at all times.
There will be no other rules.

—*Nordstrom's entire personnel manual*

As an organizational consultant, I've spent many hours with executives who want to help their companies live up to their fullest potential. You might think this is an enormously complex task, what with thousands of employees and issues relating to macro- and microeconomics, markets, management structures, feedback systems, globalization, technology, strategies, and tactics. But, in fact, the most enlightened executives and managers know that if they carefully define the core values of their organization, the rest falls into line. Think of these core values as being like the foundation of a building. Regardless of how complex the structure may be, if the foundation is solid and we build from that foundation, the building will be sound, able to withstand the elements, and, one hopes, beautiful. Values are the foundation upon which everything else relies.

Conscious organizations always begin by defining the core values that they live by. It's understood that the company cannot develop a vibrant mission, vision, culture, strategy, or action plan if the basic framework of core values is not in place. Core values set the direction for behavior. Our most deeply held values are the map to reaching our destination. Successful business executives understand what baseball player Yogi Berra meant when he said, "If you don't know where you're going, you'll end up somewhere else."

Values are qualities or traits that one considers to be essential and should reflect our priorities and deepest desires. Value statements are grounded in these principles and describe how they should be manifested or actualized in everyday life.

There are advantages to modeling our personal behavior after successful organizations. I'll leave out all those companies—like Enron, WorldCom, and Tyco—whose greedy CEOs strayed so far from their organization's core values and now must look forward to some time wearing orange jumpsuits.

Few of us spend any time reflecting on the values that we hold most dear. Here's a short exercise that can help you identify and clarify your own:

1. Find a quiet place, let your voice mail or answering machine handle your phone calls, and close your eyes. Breathe deeply, taking in air through your nose, then holding it for a moment and exhaling through your mouth. Do this a few times to relax. In your mind's eye, imagine the kind of friendships and connections you seek in your life. Let your imagination soar and take in specific details. Do you see yourself hosting a cookout for neighbors and friends? Do you see yourself as having a friend who is so close that he/she enters your house without knocking? Do you see your answering machine light indicating that there are calls and when you check messages there are several from friends asking you to get together with them? Do you want a friend who will be there for you even when your life is difficult? See that person racing through the night to get to your side when you're suffering. See yourself helping a friend in need. Find your own image, but make it personal and specific.

2. When you open your eyes, write down some of the images and ideas that came to you. Reflect on these and begin to pull some of the values from these scenarios. For example, if you imagined yourself as having the kind of friend who would do anything to be at your side when your life is in crisis, you might assign this behavior to the value of "Devotion" or "Reliability." Also, look at your own life. What are the values you live by right now?

Begin to think about the values that are important to you in your relationships. I'm going to suggest a number of values for you to consider as you look over your list, though I'm not saying that these are all of them or that they will be the ones you identified. Think of them as food for thought. But this exercise will give you a place to start thinking about your personal friendship values. Look at the following list and write each value (or at least the ones that appeal to you) on a separate index card. As you are engaged in this exercise, you may come up with some new words that represent values that are not included here. Write those words on separate cards as well. In their excellent book, *Co-active Coaching*, life coaches Laura Whitworth, Henry Kimsey-House, and Phil Sandahl suggest a question that will help you prioritize your values: "If you can only take ten values with you into a strange and possibly dangerous territory, which are the values you absolutely must have?"[1]

The friendship values and words to trigger your thinking cited below are simply ideas to get you started. It's most important that your values come from your own heart and experience, not from a "shopping list."

Some Suggested Friendship Values

Acceptance, Advice, Affection, Affinity, Assertive Self-Expression, Authenticity, Availability

Belongingness, Bonds, Boundaries

Camaraderie, Candor, Caring, Chemistry, Companionship, Compassion, Commitment, Common Interests, Common Values, Concern, Connection, Compliments, Community, Communication, Confidences, Conscious, Contact, Container, Conversations, Cooperation

Dependability, Depth, Devotion, Differences (celebration of), Diligence

Effort, Empathy, Emotional Intelligence, Emotional Support, Encouragement, Enthusiasm, Expression of Feelings

Familiarity, Faithfulness, Feelings, Forgiveness

Grace, Gentleness, Generosity, Genuineness, Giving and Gifts, Good Times/Bad Times, Grit

Helpfulness, Honesty, Humor

Interest, Interconnections, Interdependence, Integrity, Intentions, Initiation and Invitation, Intimacy

Joy, Just

Kindness, Kinship, "Know Thyself," Know and Be Known
Laughter, Lifelong, Listening, Love, Loyalty
Mindfulness, Mirror, Mutuality
Nonjudgmental, Nurturance
Openness
Patience, Playfulness
Quality
Realness, Receiving, Reliability, Respect
Safety, Self-acceptance, Self-disclosure, Self-knowledge,
    Self-responsibility, Shared History, Sharing, Sincerity, Social
    Capital, Social Skills, Supportive, Sympathetic
Tenderness, Thoughtfulness, Time, Tribe, Trust, Truthfulness
Unconditional Love, Understanding, Unity, Unselfishness
Values, Valuing the Friendship
Warmth, Wisdom
X-ray Vision (easier for a friend to see inside our personality than
    for us)
Youthful Exuberance
Zest

3. Now take your index cards and begin to sort them into two piles. Name the first pile "Must have" and the second one, "Not as important." This doesn't mean that these second-pile cards mean nothing to you, but rather they don't matter as much as those in the first pile. Continue to go through this experience until you have only eight (8) cards in the pile called "Must have." These are your core values—the ones that are the most meaningful to you and the ones that will direct your attention as you build your connections.

4. Look at the eight cards with your core values written on them. Now rate each on a 1- to 10-point scale in terms of how you are honoring or living these friendship values in your life. Use a scale where 1 = never and 10 = always. For example, if you say you value "Helpfulness," think about the last few weeks and write down all the times you were helpful to your friends. What are you learning about the ways you live these values?

5. For those values that are not getting much attention in your life, think of a specific action plan that will allow you to manifest them on a

regular basis. I recommend thinking of one short-term goal and one longer-term one. So, for example, if you have chosen "Helpfulness" as a core friendship value, then ask yourself what you might do to be more helpful to a friend. Remember, you don't have to wait to be asked to call a friend and offer to take her kids for an overnight so she and her husband can have a dinner out together. Your elderly neighbor may never ask for help, but the next time you are mowing the lawn, you can offer to do his, too. These are the ways that our values are put into practice.

6. Think about what it costs you not to honor your values in your life. Write down any obstacles that keep you from doing these things. Then write down an action plan to overcome these obstacles.

This short exercise can illuminate a great deal about your core friendship values and the ways you are (or are not) living them in your life. Attached-at-the-heart friends don't just magically appear in our lives. These relationships emerge from our specific and everyday behavior. It is a result of putting what we believe, our priorities, and our values into action. The more we really know about ourselves and our beliefs, the more effective we can be in developing the kind of relationships that contain our spiritual and psychological growth. When we are on that journey, we will live a rich and fulfilling life.

SIX

Know Thyself

> Love opens the door into everything, as far as I can see,
> including and perhaps most of all, the door into one's own
> secret, and often terrible and frightening, real self.

—*May Sarton*

Eleanor Roosevelt once said, "Friendship with oneself is all important because without it one cannot be friends with anybody else in the world." We may not like to hear that truth, but Eleanor was right.

The journey outward—toward the comfort and connection of deeply attached friends—begins at home. It begins with the Self. We need to look within, to the patterns and the tendencies that may be preventing us from building relationships that are truly intimate and last a lifetime. This self-searching is the most elemental aspect of making friends, and also the most difficult to put into practical terms. There is no "test" to know thyself; there are no shortcuts. But there is a way to begin, to become more conscious of the patterns that limit us and the aspects of our personality that sabotage our efforts to connect with others. Let me give you an example of this kind of self-limiting behavior.

Sharon kept striking out in making friends. She'd have a lunch date or two with some interesting woman she'd met in her apartment complex and then the relationship would fizzle. No friendship ever truly developed. Her neighbors would get together with her once or twice, but when she'd call to set up a follow-up lunch date or activity, they would politely put her off by claiming to be "too busy." They'd say they would call her back but they never did. To her credit, Sharon was trying hard to change her life, but she was consistently unsuccessful at turning acquaintances into friends.

She came to my therapy office depressed, lonely, and convinced that the world was rejecting and cold. "I don't know what else I can do," she said. "I try to make friends but people just aren't open. They're selfish and uninterested in anyone but themselves. Besides, I'm busy with my job and don't have time to work this hard to make friends."

As I got to know Sharon, it was clear to me that her belief that other people were only interested in themselves was a far-reaching and bitter projection.

When her neighbors failed to return her phone calls about getting together, Sharon decided they were selfish and interested in no one but themselves. In truth, Sharon was the one who was self-absorbed and myopically focused only on her own problems. She is wounded by a thorny childhood, has attachment issues, and carries those scars into every relationship in her life. She is extremely needy and ceaselessly recites a litany of her problems even to new acquaintances, much to their dismay. She overreacts to every slight with enormous feelings of rejection. If you were to ask her acquaintances to describe her, I'd bet they would say Sharon is "high maintenance."

Being raised in an abusive or severely impaired family restricts our growth and leaves us with psychological and spiritual wounds that inhibit or prevent the development of meaningful relationships.

Sharon doesn't seem to understand that friendships begin with a certain expectation for mutuality—a give and take. She cannot fathom the distinction that psychologist Erich Fromm described when he compared immature love as being "I love you because I need you," with mature love, which says, "I need you because I love you."

It's hard for people to love us unless we can also love them and Sharon is so impoverished in her ability to love that she has very little to offer. Once we're attached and in the context of a meaningful relationship, we are right to expect our friends to share our difficult times as well as our good ones. In many ways, this is a measure of the depth of the relationship. Actress Arlene Francis once made a comment that describes just how this works. "Trouble is a sieve through which we sift our acquaintances. Those too big to pass through are our friends," she said.

But Sharon tried to put these acquaintances through her sieve before they even knew anything else about her, before a relationship was in place. They were not yet invested in spending time listening to her problems. If we liken the beginning of friendship to a dance in which each person moves delicately, finding their rhythm with each other until finally they are moving together, Sharon's dance was one of stomping all over her acquaintances' feet. In starting out on the dance of friendship, Sharon's intimate level of disclosure and discussion about her problems was not appropriate. Now, those women she asked to lunch might be very compassionate and feel bad that Sharon had such a difficult childhood, but it's asking a lot of people we barely know to get close to us when the experience of getting to know us is intense and aversive. We may not want to engage in an endless discourse of small talk as we get closer to people, but with the exception of the relationships that are birthed through a shared crisis or tragedy, this is the mundane way most friendships begin. Like all of us entering into a new relationship, we want to enjoy the process, laugh, and leave hungry for more contact, not return from the restaurant with a headache and exhausted from a ponderous lunch date with that woman who lives down the hall.

Sharon's perceived "lack of time to make friends" is really just an excuse. I'm not suggesting that she, like most of us, is not busy with work and other responsibilities, but that is not the reason that she is lonely. Until Sharon honestly looks at her own personality and how she comes off with others, it's unlikely that she will develop enduring friendships. She will always be lonely, which will reinforce her basic belief that she is unworthy of being loved. This will make her even more desperate for contact the next time she invites someone to lunch. She's on a merry-go-round, a vicious cycle that will never stop until she does some difficult and deep inner work.

I realize that Sharon may be an extreme example of someone who is having a difficult time in making and keeping friends, but her story raises important points for all of us. Many of us carry wounds or worldviews that interfere with healthy and intimate relationships with other people. Our emotional heritage colors our present reality and has a powerful impact on our ability to connect with others. Sharon has a severe inability to make friends. In filling out the friendship model in chapter 4, she would have a difficult time placing any names almost anyplace on the model. But most of us do have friends—our model would be filled with names of acquaintances and friends for a season or reason—but still, some of us have a harder time in bringing them into the center of our lives. We're fine until we realize that our lives lack the intimate attachments of really close friends. Let me give you an example.

To the casual observer, David seems to have lots of friends. He is cute, funny, and genial. Unlike Sharon, his social skills are well developed and he has more opportunities to do things with friends than he has time to do them. But he told me that he "doesn't really feel close" to anyone; as he described his relationships, it became clear that these were acquaintanceships and casual friends. In spite of his many activities with friends, he yearned for a deeper and more enduring emotional intimacy with them. As we discussed his emotional history, it became clear to both of us that, at age fifty, he was still carrying around his parents' views of the world.

Both of his parents came from large families and when they grew up, their entire social life consisted of interacting with each other. As each of the siblings married, there was usually a long period before that new person was fully "accepted" into the tribe. The subtle but unambiguous message Mom and Dad conveyed to David and his sister was: "You can trust family, but you can't trust anyone else." David's parents grew up and remained in the same small town where each of them had an abundance of siblings, so there was plenty of social capital in their lives. No one ever had to learn how to make new friends. Even as a child, David's first cousins were his only consistent playmates. His family's connections came ready-made from their families of origin. Without intending to, David's parents taught him that their family was a "closed system." But David's sister and cousins live more than a thousand miles from him. He lives in a large metropolitan area, and what worked for his parents in maintaining close connections with their relatives down the street wasn't working for him.

Think about your own family of origin. Was your family open to including new people in their sphere of relationships? Many people grew up in families with excellent social skills and a worldview that embraced others. As children, they grew up observing and learning from strong models for making friends and belonging to a neighborhood or community. Their memories are filled with gatherings, cookouts, and dinners with friends. Their mothers and fathers were active in the community and had friends of their own. Their fathers played golf with the guy down the street for forty years and their mothers wouldn't miss a Wednesday night bridge game with their cronies. These families encouraged their children to get out and meet other kids in the neighborhood and to bring them home for sleepovers or dinner.

But other families enforce powerful unspoken (or spoken) excluding factors such as: "No one is as smart as our family" or "We don't want to be friends with those people because they're not Italian, or Irish, or Catholic, or Latino, or Serbian, or Daughters of the American Revolution," or because they *are* one of those things. These old philosophies—if unexamined—might be affecting you now as you strive to build your connections.

One part of knowing thyself is understanding the ways we are influenced now by how we were raised. It can be difficult to look into our past. Many people avoid this because it can be painful and often they feel disloyal to their families if they were to honestly look at what they learned as they were growing up. "My mother never hugged me but I knew she loved me," one client said, then quickly and defensively added, "But she did the best she could." Of course she did. With few exceptions, most parents do give their children the best they can. But that doesn't mean that everything we learned as children is good for us now. The intention in looking at our emotional heritage is not to blame anyone for parental shortcomings or failures. Rather, it is to better understand ourselves and discover where old scripts are keeping us from the life and relationships that will serve us in our present reality. Call it your emotional heritage, call it your "psychosocial development," or call it— as my good friend Ruth does—"ancient shit," but whatever you call it, it's likely that you continue to carry with you the ways you learned to be in the world from your own family. Are any of these attitudes or behaviors holding you back from creating your own vital relationships now?

Take a moment to reflect on the messages about the importance of friends and connections that you received while growing up. For example, think about your specific early experiences. Was your mother or father particularly shy or lacking in social skills or opportunities to connect with others? Did your family have cookouts or gatherings with friends? Were birthdays celebrated with invitations to neighborhood children or did you simply share a cake after dinner with your own immediate family? Do you find yourself recapitulating these attitudes now? If yes, do they serve you?

1. Think about and describe the ways in which your family was connected (or not) as you were growing up. A good prompt for these memories might be to make a cup of tea and spend an hour looking through boxes or albums of old photographs of you and your family. What do you see in those pictures?

2. Do you find yourself continuing those family patterns in your present relationships? If the answer is yes, describe how these attitudes and behaviors make your life rich and full or keep you from the kind of relationships you would like to have.

3. Do you need to change anything about your attitudes with regard to your connections to other people? If so, what are they and what action plans can you put into motion to improve your connections?

It's possible to live our whole lives and know more about other people than we know about ourselves. But we cannot grow psychologically and spiritually until we plumb the depths of our own personality, our own unique Self. This self-knowing is a lifelong task. We don't just say, "Today I'm going to plumb the depths of my personality," and boom, we're finished. If we are to change and grow, first it's necessary to look into this underworld, to open the dark, unconscious parts of ourselves to the bright light of awareness.

The Iceberg

An iceberg is an apt metaphor for the relative proportions of our personality that we know and understand (what is conscious) and that which we know little about (what is unconscious). Consciousness is like the little tip of the iceberg that shows above the surface of the frigid water. It represents only 10 percent of the entire iceberg. About 90 percent of the mass of Arctic icebergs is submerged. Importantly, it is not the tip of the iceberg that sinks ships, for what we can see we can navigate around. It is the part of the iceberg under the surface of the water that creates danger in every aspect of our lives and especially in the delicate process of making friends. What we don't know about ourselves may be sinking our friend-*ships*.

Carl Jung referred to the part of the personality that we present to the outside world as the persona. The word comes from the Greek and refers to the masks that theater actors wore to designate a particular character. This is the social mask that we put on for others to see and is a primary way in which we adapt to society—it allows us to conform to the roles that we play in our relationships and culture. Responding to one another through the use of these social masks allows conversation and commerce to flow easily from one person to another. In the course of growing up, each of us creates a persona in order to adapt to the expectations of our parents, teachers, religion, and culture. We recognize that certain traits are desirable while others are not, and, from childhood on, we learn to integrate the "positive" traits into our persona: most of us want to be seen by others as caring, intelligent, honest, generous, courageous, loving, polite, and successful people.

The persona is a useful and necessary link that we develop between each other; it regulates our relationships, avoids the need for continuous explanations and social introductions, and allows us to function smoothly as a society. When we are interacting with strangers, acquaintances, and, mostly, friends, we are interacting almost entirely through our personas.

Think about your own persona. It will be a valuable use of your time to try some of these short exercises and reflect on these questions. Write your responses and thoughts in a journal or notebook.

1. How do you think other people perceive you?

2. List ten adjectives that you would use to describe your own personality. This will describe your persona.

3. Ask a casual friend and a close friend to list ten adjectives that describe your personality.

4. Are there discrepancies between the adjective lists written by your close friend, your casual friend, and yourself? If so, what are they? What do these lists teach you about yourself and the way you are perceived by others?

In the movie *Shrek*, the main character—an ogre—tries to describe the complexity of ogre psychology to his donkey friend. "Ogres are like onions," he says and explains that even ogres have multiple layers to their personalities. Ogres may appear to be ill-tempered monsters and mean on the surface, but underneath it all, Shrek says, they have tender feelings just like everyone else. Well, people are like ogres in that regard. We all have multiple layers to our personality, and below the surface, underneath many strata of that onion, lives the *shadow*.

Carl Jung first used the word *shadow* to describe the unconscious—largely unknown—parts of ourselves. Often we are clueless—totally unconscious—about the contents of our shadow, but sometimes we have inklings and vague feelings about what is down there. Sigmund Freud believed the unconscious to be a repository for only negative aspects of our personality. If you could see your own shadow, he said, you would find repressed desires, uncivilized impulses, and childhood fantasies and resentments. Characteristics like jealousy, lust, greed, and selfishness are banished to that dark place. On the other hand, Jung thought that the shadow holds everything—not just our less than desirable qualities, but everything that we think we're not, everything that is unlived in our lives. The shadow, then, is like a subpersonality operating beneath the radar of our conscious mind. If on the surface someone is gruff, underneath his or her persona lies an undeveloped and unexpressed sweetness. If we are rigid and unbending, we are likely to have a spontaneous, joy-loving part of our personality deeply hidden away in our shadow. So, to Jung there's gold in them thar' hills. A great deal of unrealized potential resides in the deepest layer of our psychological onion.

When we know someone well, we often understand our friend's shadow better than they understand it themselves. You've recognized another's shadow if you've ever said: "Oh, I know he always comes off like a know-it-all, but underneath, he's a nice but insecure person" or "She can be hard to get along with but, deep down, she's really a good person" or "He'll always help you out, but he's keeping score." Statements like those refer to the aspects of someone's personality that don't show so immediately on the surface. The closer we are to others, the more we know about them, the more we come to understand their "deep down selves." The fact that there are these other layers to personality explains why, underneath her whiny and difficult persona, Sharon is truly a caring person but, on first meeting, one only sees—and is turned off by—her self-absorption and neediness. The *shadow* explains why even ogres can be tender.

Knowing your own shadow allows you to incorporate it into your personality and stop projecting it onto others. Before Sharon became aware of what she was projecting on others, her behavior turned them off. As she became conscious of her most deeply held feelings, she was able to grieve for the tragedies in her childhood and stop desperately reciting them to everyone who would give her the time of day. As she healed, she discovered that she could invite an acquaintance to lunch and make small talk. She was able to slowly disclose more about her history and her feelings as the friendship developed. She also learned to listen to what this new friend had to say about her own life, and these interactions, in turn, helped her to grow. Today, Sharon has learned a lot more about the dance of friendship and has a number of good close friends. With the newfound confidence that these people give her, she continues to heal and build her own friendship not only with them, but also with herself. Her inner dialogue has changed. She no longer sees herself as a loser, unlovable and alone. The friendships would not—could not—have developed without Sharon's courage in looking at her own inner life.

Coming to self-acceptance does not mean believing that we are perfect. Perfection is an illusion and if you think you are perfect you have some bigger problems to deal with than can be addressed in this book. Instead, self-acceptance means that we learn to love ourselves while we strive toward our own fullest potential. Self-acceptance means being honest and gentle as we acknowledge and deal with our less-than-perfect onion. And David, by the way, just keeps growing and deepening his friendships. Having freed himself from the tyranny of how he was raised, his motto now is, "Put another potato in the pot! Everyone is welcome!"

The famous words of Socrates emphasize the importance of self-knowledge. "The unexamined life," he said, "is not worth living." Self-reflection is critical for psychological and spiritual growth. The fifteenth-century Catholic contemplative monk Thomas à Kempis understood the spiritual importance of self-knowledge and wrote in his gentle book *Imitation of Christ*, "A humble knowledge of thyself is a surer way to God than a deep search after learning."[1] And from the Tao Te Ching, "To know others is to be wise, to know oneself is to be enlightened."

Understanding our shadow is critical for relationships to deepen.

Why? Because our friends often know more about our shadow than we ourselves do. We may like to believe that we relate to our friends and family only through the persona—the self we present to the world. But as we get closer, we can see through that mask just as they can see through our own. Underneath our ordinary interactions with our friends, a dynamic self-dialogue ensues between different elements of each of our personalities.

But we can't change anything about our behavior or the unconscious projections we make on our friends until we become aware of our own inner life and how others perceive us.

Don't immediately assume that the *only* reason that you do not have deep and enduring friendships is that you don't have the time or energy to nurture the relationships that could sustain you. But for many of us, this is true. Most of us have the necessary psychological health to develop and maintain acquaintanceships and casual friends. We're pleasant to be with, helpful, fun, and easy to talk to—some of the basic prerequisites for any kind of relationship. But developing loving and attached-at-the-heart friends requires more than these simple social skills. These friendships are a journey of the soul and if these are to be truly intimate relationships, they must go deeper than relating exclusively on the basis of each of our social masks.

But for some of us, claiming a lack of time to fully nurture relationships is an excuse for other things. Ask yourself questions and spend a little time reflecting on your own personality. What are your motivations for friendship? Are you a good friend? What do you bring to the table of friendship? Do you love yourself enough to have good friends?

There are many ways to better understand your own shadow and none requires that you leave your ordinary world and spend the next year in an ashram doing nothing other than contemplating your life and relationships (though if you can afford the time to do this, it's not a bad idea!). Instead, discover your own shadow by carefully observing your own behavior. Introspection, dreams, and therapy or analysis can help you discover the inner layers of your onion. But you can start with the following simple exercises:

1. List five things about yourself that you think even your best friends don't know about you.

2. Ask your partner/spouse/best friend this one question: "What is my biggest flaw?"
3. What do others do that drives you crazy even though it doesn't directly affect you?
4. Take the ten adjectives you listed in the last exercise and now write down the opposite of each one. These words describe your shadow—the part of you wanting to be known. Notice that if you were to combine both the "positive" adjective and the "negative" one—you might find a new balance. (For example, if you included "generous" and the opposite is "selfish," this does not mean to become a selfish person. Rather, it means that you may not be taking good care of your own self-interests, and you should begin to do so.)

When I asked a casual friend to consider the above questions, he spent just a bit of time thinking about what others might not know about him. In reflecting on this question, he wrote that it took him a long time to trust people. Remember that we often have inklings, sometimes even well-formed ideas about what we are not revealing to others. When he asked me to guess what he had written, I immediately said, "You have trouble trusting people." "What!!?" he said. "I've never told you that." I'm not bragging here about how perceptive I am. He didn't have to tell me and I'll bet that every one of his friends and acquaintances knew after just a few interactions that he had issues with trust. His lack of trust was patently evident in his offhand comments about other people and in almost every aspect of his behavior.

As I've mentioned, self-growth is a lifelong journey and there are no shortcuts to knowing oneself. Social scientists, however, have some interesting constructs about ways of looking at aspects of our personality that affect friendships and our ability to connect with people. One of these is emotional intelligence—a set of interpersonal skills that bears directly on our abilities to initiate and nurture friendships.

Emotional Intelligence

Research suggests that more than 80 percent of success in life and relationships results from emotional intelligence rather than other kinds of intelligence. In other words, and *especially* in matters of human relationships, it takes more than just brains to succeed. In making and maintaining attachments of the heart, emotional intelligence, or EQ, matters more than IQ. Dealing effectively with people, understanding yourself, and being able to think about feelings are more highly predictive of success than being able to solve problems logically. Psychologists John D. Mayer of the University of New Hampshire and Peter Salovey of Yale were the first to use the term *emotional intelligence* in a series of academic articles in 1990 and 1993. But Daniel Goleman popularized the concept in 1995 with his bestselling book, *Emotional Intelligence: Why It Can Matter More than IQ*. In this book, he talks about the emphasis that our society has placed on logic and reason as a measure of intelligence, while it consistently overlooks the power of our emotions. He wrote: "Our humanity is most evident in our feelings . . . faith, hope, devotion, love—are missing entirely from the coldly cognitive view. Emotions enrich. A model of mind that leaves them out is impoverished."[2]

In spite of its popular discussion, emotional intelligence is a complex idea that is hard to define and even harder to measure. We still have a lot to learn about it. But most scholars would agree that EQ is a broad set of inter- and intrapersonal skills that have to do with identifying, using, understanding, and regulating emotions. EQ is the psychological competence to create positive outcomes in relationships with others and with yourself. People with high levels of EQ seem to have embraced the mantra to "know thyself" in ways that those without these skills have not. They understand and manage their own feelings and can also more accurately recognize and identify emotions in others. They're better at handling relationships.

Don't you think it's true that people who are able to project mutual trust, respect, rapport, and warmth to others are generally more effective and successful? The ability to express and control emotion, to communicate, and to show optimism, empathy, initiative, and sensitivity are important qualities for relationships. Ask yourself: How well do you recognize your own and others' feelings and how well do you manage those feelings? These abilities are the fundamentals of emotional intelligence. Emotional intelligence takes into account the issues of the heart as well as those of the head. And the good news is that EQ appears to be a skill that can be learned, practiced, and mastered. This is not to say that our inborn temperament plays no role whatsoever, but Goleman and others are clear on the fact that this is an intelligence that we acquire primarily after we're born and, unlike IQ, it is something that we can improve throughout our lives.

Perhaps the best way to understand your own emotional intelligence—or lack of it—is to carefully self-observe. Do you understand your feelings? Are you good at identifying others' feelings? Can you manage your emotions? For example, if you are furious with a friend, do you scream and yell at her or do you honestly and calmly talk about your feelings?

In spite of the plethora of Internet-based tests and inventories that purport to measure EQ, it is difficult to quantify. Still, we can learn about ourselves by reflecting on the questions that some of these inventories have included to help us understand our own levels of emotional intelligence. For those so inclined, you may go on-line to http://www.utne.com/interact/eig.html where you can take this test and have it easily scored.

Emotional intelligence can be seen as a subset of a larger universe of social skills. Social skills include all the ways we communicate and relate to one another: how we give, receive, and interpret social messages. The social skills necessary for social inclusion, making friends, and keeping them are numerous and, for the most part, learned. We learn these social skills by the models we observe, and through conditioning—behaviors that are reinforced will be repeated and those that are punished will drop from our repertoire. Because social skills are learned, impairments in them may result from inappropriate or a lack of healthy models, the failure for learning opportunities, or emotional problems that interfere with social skills. To know thyself means being aware of the way others perceive us. Social skills are critical, especially at the early stages of a relationship when we are making conscious and unconscious decisions about who we will bring closer to the center of our lives. And the importance of effective social skills in initiating and maintaining relationships is the subject of the next chapter.

SEVEN

Social Skills

> Society is no comfort to one not sociable.
>
> —*William Shakespeare*

Scheduled to give a twenty-minute lecture to several hundred scientists, Grace was supremely cool, indifferent to her celebrity, and showed no signs of the public-speaking anxiety that plagued other presenters or the nervous anticipation of her handlers. To the contrary, she was a vision of loveliness as she smartly found her way through the crowded Shaw Conference Center in Edmonton, Alberta, ever mindful of the human need for personal space. Smiling appropriately while politely asking for directions, then following those to the letter and unable to use stairs or escalators, she took the elevator to the registration desk. Several people were already lined up to register, so she courteously tried to find the end of the line. Starting at the beginning and working her way back to the end of the queue, she unfortunately got a little pushy and didn't seem to notice Leslie Kaelbling from MIT, standing third in line. So Grace just butted her way in, pushed Leslie out of the way, and took her place. Later, many onlookers described this as the most "human" of her actions. With that little faux pas behind her, Grace waited patiently in line as the people in front of her moved forward. She smiled and asked the registrar for a name tag and for the fancy bag of freebies given at conventions. "One of those nifty bags would be handy," she said with a demure smile. Later, her flawlessly delivered presentation was met with a loud ovation—the crowd went wild. "Thanks for coming," she yelled over the enthusiastic crowd. "See you next year in Acapulco!"[1]

Meet Grace, the social robot. Designed by a group of researchers from several universities and colleges (Carnegie Mellon, Northwestern, and Swarthmore), the Naval Research Laboratory, and Metrica, Inc., Grace (**G**raduate **R**obot **A**ttending a **C**onferenc**E**) is a B21R mobile robot that uses a scanning laser range finder, a stereo camera head on a pan-tilt unit, and a single color camera with pan-tilt-zoom capability. She can speak using her high-quality speech synthesizer and recognize responses using her microphone and speech recognition software. Carnegie Mellon computer scientist and project coordinator Reid Simmons solicited drama students to teach Grace how to act more human so that people would feel comfortable with her and noted that Grace was designed to be female because her mostly male engineers believed that women communicate better. Though, as journalist Judy Lin of the Associated Press put it, six-foot-tall, three-hundred-pound Grace is "not much of a woman. . . . She has no arms or legs. Instead, the barrel-shaped torso, sheathed with solar panels and black plastic bumper guards, rolls on wheels. The robot's feminine attributes are limited to a voice that sounds like an automated telephone operator and a heart-shaped cartoon face, which captivates passers-by with its big blue eyes and high cheekbones."[2] On July 31, 2002, Grace made her debut at the American Association for Artificial Intelligence (AAAI) national meeting. With some basic human social skills under her belt, her designers are refining Grace to be better able to recognize people and ask appropriate questions. In short, they're teaching Grace to schmooze for next year's robot challenge in Mexico.

What is so interesting about Grace, beyond the brilliant hardware and software engineering that created her, is the acknowledgment that human beings live in a context of certain social behaviors that make one acceptable to others and that, for the most part, these are learned rather than innate. To me, Grace is also a cause for celebration. If a bundle of wires, tubes, gizmos, and software can be taught to have social skills, then there's great hope for even the most socially unskillful among us.

Social skills are requirements for all interpersonal relationships. In building connections we need to be able to gain entry to a group or make at least a superficial connection with another. In order to develop attached-at-the-heart friends, we must have the skills to nurture and sustain those relationships. Social skills can be thought of as learned behaviors that achieve positive responses from others.

In most cultures, and as Grace the robot found out, smiling at others and asking polite questions are good. Butting in line and shoving someone out of the way is not. Beyond those, there are certainly huge cultural differences between the specific social skills that are expected by members of that society. For example, just consider personal space. Personal space is that invisible psychological boundary around our body that we consider to be "ours" and protect from all but our closest friends and loved ones. The specific spatial distance for what is acceptable personal space varies wildly from culture to culture. A number of years ago, I gave a weeklong workshop on communication skills to women from the developing world. All of them were physicians, nurses, or health-care workers from around the world and you would think that the common experience of improving health care to so many people in need would have been a powerful bridge between the participants. But there were conflicts and hurt feelings from the beginning. The women from Asia did not like their South American counterparts. "They're pushy. They're rude," they told me. The South American women didn't like the Asian women any better: "They're unfriendly. I can't get close to any of them."

What these women were experiencing was not at all what I experienced. I found the women from South America to be suitably assertive and not the least aggressive. By and large, the Asian women were soft-spoken but quite friendly. But the cultural differences in nonverbal behaviors and especially in what was considered to be "acceptable" amounts of personal space were so different between the Asian and South American women that each drew her own conclusions from those differences. The South American women stood closer during face-to-face interactions and made more direct eye contact. Unlike their Asian counterparts, they often touched the listener's arm when they were speaking. They used more and broader hand gestures when making a point.

My experience in conducting this workshop reminded me of an old story about Edward T. Hall, an anthropologist at Northwestern University who worked for the State Department in the 1950s, training diplomats in cultural differences. The story, as I have heard it, is about a British diplomat and an Arab diplomat speaking at a conference. The

Arab kept moving toward him, while the man from England kept back-ing away to establish the distance at which he was most comfortable. The results were comical—the Brit kept backing away and the Arab kept chasing him around the room.[3]

There are multiple verbal and nonverbal social behaviors, norms, gestures, expressions, rituals, values, and standards of etiquette that we use to gauge, and often judge, others. Remember, too, that changes in culture can exist between people in different regions of the country and even from different families living in the same neighborhood. I've seen people get off on the wrong foot in a relationship because one comes from a "touchy feely" family and physically touched the arm of a new friend as they've talked or hugged them good-bye. I've watched that person recoil and later tell me that she thought that person was "too familiar" or "overbearing."

You don't have to be traveling to far-off lands or, like the robot Grace, presenting a lecture to hundreds of curious scientists to require a mod-icum of social skills that grease the way to any relationship. A few weeks ago, I casually watched a man I know at a gathering of neighbors. I know that he is a good person and has some interesting and well-thought-out opinions on a variety of intriguing subjects. But he sat in a chair apart from the crowd, arms folded over his chest, and a sour expression on his face. Everything about his demeanor and body language said, "Don't you dare come over here and talk with me." So, of course, no one did.

A full discussion of social skills could fill many books—and there are lots of excellent resources on this subject. I'm going to address only a few of these that directly affect our abilities to make and nurture friends. When we better understand how others perceive us—the messages that we communicate—we take a big step toward self-awareness.

Our social skills consist of four interrelated components: behavioral (what you are doing, and this includes both verbal and nonverbal aspects of behavior), cognitive (what you are thinking), emotional (how you are feeling), and physiological (what your body is doing). As you explore your own personality and the ways you easily or not so easily make friends, and nurture them through the concentric rings of closeness shown on the model, consider some of these following elements of your social skills.

Behavioral Aspects of Social Skills

Verbal Skills

Can you make small talk? You may not want to spend the whole of a relationship chatting about the weather or the outcome of the last football game, but small talk builds rapport and trust and is most often the first step into a social conversation and a potential relationship. We like to be around people who have interesting things to say and, at least at the outset of a relationship, show good judgment and can have a conversation that is not threatening. It will be obvious to most people with developed social skills that some topics for this initial conversation are appropriate while others are not. Appropriate: the weather, a shared experience (e.g., you saw your neighbor coming out of the same movie theater when you went to see *Chicago*), books, a new restaurant that opened in town, or current events that are not emotionally charged. Not appropriate: how much money you make and how much they do, when they first started going bald, or how vibrant their sexual relationship with their spouse is. Those deeper, more personal subjects may, in fact, enter into conversations between close friends but are not advisable subjects for a first meeting.

Even though small talk may be lightweight on the scale of important issues in life, it is the conduit through which strangers become acquaintances and acquaintances become friends. Small talk is far more about creating social bonds than it is to convey specific information.

How do you rate your small talk skills?

Think about some of your good friends. What did you talk about the very first time you met? I'll bet the subject wasn't at all like the deep conversations that you have today. How did that relationship progress from that first banal discussion, "Looks like rain," followed by her response "Yes, it does, doesn't it"?

Next time you're in a group of people, carefully observe someone who you believe has excellent social skills. Listen and watch. Is she doing things differently from the way you are? The best way to learn and improve your abilities—from social skills to playing golf—is to model your behavior after someone who does it better than you do.

Self-disclosure

One important aspect of our verbal social skills is self-disclosure. As a relationship evolves—like the exquisite and subtle dance it is—small talk gives way to greater and greater levels of self-disclosure. Do you open up and confide in those close to you? Can you express affection, concern, caring, and admiration? Can you be gently honest about your true feelings even when your friend may not like to hear what you have to say? True intimacy requires knowing and being known and that rests on our abilities to reveal our feelings and experiences appropriately to those close to us. Communication specialists talk about the "norm of reciprocity" when talking about self-disclosure. It doesn't have to be tit for tat, but we expect our friends to similarly disclose when we've taken the interpersonal risk to reveal our innermost thoughts and feelings. This back-and-forth of disclosure and feedback helps us understand one another and builds trust and intimacy.

Think about how comfortable you are with self-disclosure. Write down areas of your life and feelings that you willingly talk about. Are there areas that are simply "off-limits" even to your closest friends? If so, why? What is the price you pay by not allowing yourself this level of real intimacy with those who love you?

Me, Me, Me—the Song of Narcissism

Recently I sat on the beach reading quietly and listening in on the conversation of the three people near me (okay, you know from that story in the post office that I do these things). I began to count the number of times that they used the word *me* or *I*. I stopped at four hundred and, truly, I only listened in for about ten minutes. Each person seemed to be just waiting for a moment for the conversation to lag to add something about herself. Now, I've just talked about how important self-disclosure is, but this conversation seemed to revolve entirely around one-upmanship. Good social skills that result in positive and vibrant relationships rely on a true and heartfelt interest in other people as much, or more, than talking about oneself. Questions that express your interest in what your acquaintance feels or does are powerful ways to move a relationship to a deeper level and an important way to get to know someone else. Make sure your conversations—especially those with new acquaintances or new friends—reflect your interest in their lives as well as revealing some things about your own. Remember that the Greek myth of Narcissus was really about the separation and the avoidance of relationship for a futile—and tragic—absorption with the self. The character Narcissus was beloved by everyone but he scorned them and fell in love with his own self-reflection, thinking that it was someone else. He rejected the world and eventually died a solitary and lonely death. Constantly thinking and talking about your own life is a turnoff. Learn to ask questions of others. Express your interest by listening to what they have to say about their lives.

Listening Skills

The early-second-century Roman philosopher Epictetus once observed, "Nature gave us two ears and one tongue so we could listen twice as much as we speak." That's good advice, but given how difficult it is for many people to really listen, we seem to adhere more to an interpersonal style of "reloading" our next comment while another is talking. As writer Fran Lebowitz put it, "The opposite of talking is not listening. The opposite of talking is *waiting* to talk." Social science bears out this perception. Research has shown us that most people are indeed thinking about what we're going to say next while another person is talking. This "waiting to talk" instead of actively listening with an open mind and heart, wanting to learn more about our new acquaintance (even if it is only his opinion about the fabulous music in *Chicago*) is even more extreme when the subject of conversation is emotionally arousing. There's more about listening skills in a section to come, but for right now, just take a moment to respond to the following questions.

Observe your own listening skills today. Do you really hear what someone else is saying to you or are you thinking about what you're going to say next?

Jot down a few observations about yourself, then look around you. Just be like a fly on the wall as other people are talking to one another. What do you observe about their listening skills? Write down what you've observed.

Nonverbal Social Skills

There is an old adage that I've heard attributed to Ralph Waldo Emerson, Mark Twain, and at least a dozen others, but regardless of who coined the phrase, it's true: "Who you are speaks so loudly that I cannot hear what you are saying." Studies have shown that our nonverbal behavior communicates more than 90 percent of the messages we send out. We respond emotionally to nonverbal cues and make immediate interpersonal judgments based on these. "He's friendly," we think about an acquaintance who greets us with a smile and pleasant eye contact. "She's unfriendly," we say when our neighbor shuffles down her driveway, looking straight ahead, and gives us a nonchalant wave over her shoulder as she continues toward her mailbox. "She's nervous and shy," we think as a colleague blushes before she gives a presentation. The man at a nearby table at your favorite restaurant who raises his hand and sharply gives a "come here" sign to a waitress is rude.

I read a study that purported to identify more than eighty nonverbal elements of communication emanating from the face and head and another fifty-five produced from the body and limbs.[4] Some of these cues—like throat-clearing, face flushing, and eye blinks—are innate and inborn. Many other nonverbal behaviors are learned and are culturally based. For example, to Americans the "thumbs-up" signal is a positive gesture that communicates "okay" or "success." Pilots attempting to be "heard" over the roar of jet engines use this signal to the ground crew to say, "I'm ready. Let's go." But make that identical hand movement in the Middle East or Nigeria and you've just said something obscene. Using your thumbs up in Japan—where the thumb is seen as the "fifth digit"—to an attentive waiter will order you five of something. You thought you were simply "saying" that you liked the food and now, suddenly, you're struggling to down five plates of shrimp tempura.

I don't intend to address all of these nonverbal cues, but think about some of the most common ways we communicate with one another without ever saying a word: proximity or use of personal space, eye contact and length of gaze, voice qualities—including tone, pitch, rhythm, timbre, loudness, inflection—facial expressions, body language, posture and body orientation, gestures, and touch. Additionally, we nonverbally communicate a wealth of other information by our grooming habits, our choice in fashion, and the way we smell. Think about all the information you take in and judgments you make about someone else without a single word being spoken. What impressions or assumptions do you have about the fastidious businessman in his $1,800 Armani suit, the neighbor with a penchant for bow ties and suspenders, your coworker's 1950s beehive hairdo, or your teenager's tattoo and lip ring? You might think these characteristics are inconsequential stereotypes or, at best, superficial, but the fact is that we constantly react emotionally to these wordless messages at a gut level because they tell us something about who someone thinks they are and how they might relate to us.

There is compelling evidence that nonverbal signals are processed in the most ancient parts of the brain beneath the more recently evolved areas designed to recognize language—the brain stem, the basal ganglia, and the limbic system. So we perceive nonverbal information far below the level of conscious awareness. When we are interacting with another person, our senses are taking in and we are giving out tons of information long before either of us opens our mouth to speak.

When we communicate authentically, there is congruence between the words we say and our nonverbal behaviors. We expect this correspondence, and when there is a disconnection between those elements of communication, we tend to distrust the verbal message and "listen" instead to what the rest of our senses are telling us. When we're reading other people's "body language" it's important, of course, to take cultural differences into consideration. Really, that waiter in Tokyo was not a jerk because he brought you those five plates of shrimp tempura at your enthusiastic thumbs-up for the fine meal.

Think about how your nonverbal communication facilitates the way you connect to others. What does your body language communicate when you meet a new person or talk with an acquaintance?

What turns you off or turns you on about other people's nonverbal communications?

Look at your emotional reactions to people on the basis of how they come across to you and try to identify what it is about their appearance or what they are doing that caused you to feel the way you do.

Look at a photograph of yourself in a "typical" and candid situation. Don't pick a photo of the time you are dressed and posing like Elvis for your pal's Halloween party. Then try to look at yourself as a stranger might. What do you convey about your approachability, your openness to friendship, and your personality by your nonverbal signals?

What can you learn about yourself by the nonverbal signals you give to others?

Cognitive Aspects of Social Skills

What are you thinking when you meet new people? Do you anticipate that they will like you or do you fear that they will not? What we think more often than not determines real-life outcomes. Research has shown that people who have difficulty making new friends or reaching high levels of intimacy with others often have negative expectations for the outcome of relationships and their negative thinking sets other self-defeating behaviors in motion. They anticipate the worst possible conclusions—"She will never like me"—which then may become reality. Psychologist Albert Ellis, the founder of Rational Emotive Behavior Therapy (REBT), calls this process of exaggerating the worst possible outcomes "catastrophizing."

Our thoughts can be heard in the recesses of our minds and this inner dialogue or "negative self-talk" can stop us in our tracks on our way to making and nurturing connections. What we say to ourselves is a good indicator of one of our most important relationships—the relationship we have with ourselves.

So, listen to what you are thinking in social situations. Do you hear yourself saying, "I'm no good at talking with people" or "I don't have anything to say" or "My opinions are stupid"? I've talked with many people over the years who say the harshest, most mean-spirited things to themselves that they wouldn't, in their wildest dreams, think of saying to anyone else. They base these thoughts on half-truths, distortions, faulty logic, and ancient family scripts, and then overgeneralize them to other situations: "She will never like me" now becomes "No one will ever like me."

How can someone possibly relax and enjoy making a new friend with this turmoil and negativity going on inside their heads? Well, they can't. And, importantly, this inner dialogue both reflects and creates our emotional states. I think, therefore I am anxious/uncomfortable/a loser. What we think and then tell ourselves—the images we create in our own minds—has a profound effect on our life and relationships.

If we notice a high incidence of negative self-statements like the ones I've mentioned above, it's likely that we are holding on to self-defeating beliefs. Our thoughts and beliefs can make even the most benign situation stressful and uncomfortable. Our family, friends, culture, gender role, religious institutions, and education all contribute to our beliefs about the world around us and ourselves. Most of our beliefs are long-standing and firmly held. They become filters through which we view our life and the world at large. Many of these beliefs are positive, helping us to live fully and achieve our potential. Others keep us mired in the same old patterns that inhibit growth and change. But that is an erroneous conclusion. People can and do change by altering the way they look at things, by focusing on the present not the past, and by replacing self-defeating patterns with healthy beliefs and attitudes. One approach to revising our way of thinking about things is a technique called "cognitive restructuring." Cognitive restructuring is a fancy term for "changing the way you think." As such, cognitive restructuring relies on identifying irrational, self-defeating beliefs and replacing them with rational, positive, and true beliefs that will charge you with self-confidence and a desire to make your life what you want it to be. There are three basic steps in the process of cognitive restructuring: identifying your self-defeating beliefs, developing realistic alternatives, and systematically substituting more realistic beliefs for self-defeating ones.

1. **Identify your self-defeating belief(s).** This is not always easy but familiarity with some of your personal negative self-talk will help point the way.
2. **Develop a realistic alternative or counterbelief** by creating more rational beliefs about your qualities as a person and your desirability as a friend. Some common examples of self-defeating beliefs and each one's more realistic alternative are listed below. Take a moment to write down some of your self-defeating beliefs about your social skills and friendships and then create a more realistic alternative belief. Note that the realistic alternative should not be "pie in the sky" or overstated in a positive way. For example, if you hold a self-defeating belief that says, "I am worthless and unlovable. Everyone hates me," a realistic alternative might be "I am worthy of love and even though I

sometimes do unlovable things, many people care about me." To insert an inflated, untrue alternative or counterbelief like "I am the world's most lovable person and everyone is dying to meet me" is not the way to go. In that example, all I've done is replace one irrational belief with another.

Self-Defeating Belief	Realistic Alternative
One should be liked or approved of by everybody.	No one is liked by everyone. It's unrealistic to think that's possible.
To be worthwhile, one must be competent in everything.	One should not be expect to be perfect in all respects.
A person's present and future behavior is irreversibly dependent on significant past events.	People can and do change.
Individuals have little internal control over their personal happiness or misery.	We can exercise a great deal of control over our own happiness or make our misery worse.
It is easier to avoid situations that make me feel uncomfortable.	In the long run, it's better to face difficulties. They become easier with practice.
Only people who have been popular as children should expect to have lots of friends as adults.	There are many kinds of people in the world and many happy people with lots of friends were not popular as children.
People are mean-spirited and don't want to let newcomers into their crowd.	Many people love to embrace new friendships, and I would not want to hang out with people who were closed off to new experiences and new people.
I'm not a likable person and don't deserve to have close friends.	Everyone has positive qualities, and friendships and relationships are as important as air. I need them.

3. **Begin to systematically substitute the more realistic alternative for the self-defeating beliefs.** Practice telling yourself the alternative belief. Even if you can't always catch your negative self-statements or self-defeating beliefs, practice the alternative belief several times a day. Think of it as a little affirmation about your own power to make your life your own and to grow and change. You may find it helpful to write the realistic, positive belief on a little card to keep in your wallet or on notes that you stick on your bathroom mirror to remind you that you're in charge of changing your life.

The power of the mind is awesome. A steady dose of negative thoughts and images not only makes us feel bad but it alters our physiology. A single negative thought can change levels of corticosteroids and other stress hormones. On the other hand, our minds can work for us or against us at any given moment. Positive anticipation, imagery, and affirming visualizations (seeing yourself "win" in your mind's eye) can also affect your reality. To develop and integrate positive thinking does not mean that we are not aware of areas of personal development that need nurturance. It simply means that we have the power to seek and imagine positive outcomes. As Confucius said, "The more man meditates upon good thoughts, the better will be his world and the world at large."

I once read a study where sports psychologists used imagery to improve the free throw shooting ability of a basketball team. The researchers measured the percentage of free throws so that they had a good baseline measure for every member of the team. Then they divided the team into three groups. One group actually practiced shooting free throws on the court, the second group met together and talked about free throw shooting and strategies for improving, and the third group practiced shooting free throws in their minds. When the researchers took the players back out onto the court to measure if there had been any improvement, they found startling results. Both groups that practiced—either in reality or in their imaginations—scored a statistically significant higher percentage of free throws than did the group that just talked about this basketball skill. Even more surprising, there were no differences between the group that practiced on the court and the one that practiced in their heads. A follow-up study measuring muscle contractions during imaginal practice found small but significant muscle movements in the exact muscles that would have been used if these players were shooting free throws on the court.

Professional athletes and psychologists understand that we condition our minds by repetition and reinforcement. They know the power of mind to change behavior and that the images that fill our minds determine our performance. And the same concepts hold true for all behavior. You don't have to be a basketball player to benefit from creating and rehearsing positive images and the kind of positive self-talk that leads to your goal.

Just think about how constant negative messages about our lack of worthiness or our poor skills in initiating or maintaining relationships set in motion behaviors that will almost assuredly result in no friends. On the other hand, if we begin to think more positive thoughts, we fill our minds and our resulting actions with positive behaviors and mental images that will lead to improved free throw shooting or enduring friendships. We change our futures when we change our thinking; when we develop habits of positive thinking, we crowd out the old voices that told us we couldn't live the way we yearn to.

Our thoughts are a critical component of the social skills required for creating and maintaining healthy, vibrant relationships. The thoughts we communicate to ourselves control our feelings and our actions. An old proverb teaches the relationship between our initial thoughts and our destiny:

> Watch your thoughts; thoughts become actions
> Watch your actions; actions become habits
> Watch your habits; habits become character
> Watch your character; your character becomes your destiny.

Among the mind's most prodigious qualities is that it can be changed and transformed.

1. What kinds of beliefs and images do you hold about your ability to create and maintain friendships? Are these self-defeating or self-empowering? Now look at the more rational alternatives that you've listed in the exercise above. What specific action steps can you take today to begin to change these self-defeating patterns?

2. Keep a little notebook and pen with you as you go about your day tomorrow. Make a point to observe your own self-talk and self-defeating beliefs. What do you say to yourself? Do these opinions interfere with you relationships?

Remember that you can change your life and your relationships by taking responsibility for your behavior and beliefs. You can change your irrational, unhealthy beliefs into life-affirming, friendship-generating attitudes and actions.

Emotional and Physiological Aspects of Social Skills

When we are interacting with people, we are behaving—verbally and nonverbally—in certain ways, thinking certain thoughts, and feeling certain emotions. While all this is happening, our bodies are reacting to the thoughts and emotions we are experiencing and our physiology, in turn, amplifies our thoughts and feelings.

For many, meeting new people is exciting and interesting. The thought of making new friends and engaging in interesting conversation revs them up. But for many others, this experience of meeting strangers or initiating activities with someone they don't know well can be excruciating. Just the thought of this kind of social activity causes their heart and respiration rates to soar. They feel anxious and sick to their stomachs. The one situation that immediately comes to mind is giving a presentation or talking to a group of people. In survey after survey, the fear of public speaking (a kind of social skill) leads the list of most difficult situations. Interestingly, fear of death usually comes in second on lists of most feared situations.

Take a moment to reflect on your own level of physiological and emotional anxiety in the following situation: you've been invited to the home of a coworker you know only casually. She's having a cookout and expects about forty or fifty people to attend. Some will be people from your workplace but you've just taken this job so you don't know any of them very well. How do you feel as you head out the door to go to this social gathering? Rate your answer on a scale of 1 to 10, where 10 is "absolutely comfortable and excited to go" and 1 is "terrified and looking for ways to get out of it."

If your answer is less than a 7 (on this 10-point scale), reflect on what causes you discomfort. Do you feel anxious? If yes, does anxiety inhibit any other social relationships? Do you just feel that you don't know what to say to initiate or contribute to a conversation with an unfamiliar person?

The answers to these questions are important because they are ways of looking into yourself and making changes. For example, more than 7 percent of the U.S. population—about 15 million Americans—suffers from social anxiety or social phobia. Although these fears and anxiety can feel like an almost insurmountable problem at times, they can be greatly reduced by our learning anxiety management skills and gaining more experience in getting to know people. As we become more practiced and familiar with interacting with strangers and acquaintances, we get better at it—just like any other skill you can think of. If you suffer from debilitating anxiety or extreme shyness in social situations, you can benefit tremendously from working with a therapist or counselor who specializes in this problem. There are also a lot of good books and websites that offer advice, strategies, and support. One I particularly like is www.socialphobia.org.

If you are only moderately anxious in social situations, try to be aware of your breathing. Take deep breaths. Very often when people become anxious, they begin to hyperventilate and don't even realize they're doing it. Listen carefully to your own inner voice. Don't increase your anxiety by negative self-statements like "I don't have anything interesting to say" or "Oh, I know she can see how anxious I am" or "This is awful. How can I get out of here?" Instead, just listen and give yourself encouragement: "This person might become a new friend" or "I'm doing well here. This isn't so bad."

Let me take this opportunity to dispel any misconceptions about introverts and distinguish that mode of relating to the world from shyness or social anxiety. We all have both introverted and extroverted features to our personalities, though usually we present one or the other side to the world. Psychologist Carl Jung referred to these aspects of personality as "temperaments" or "types" that have to do with our major mode of psychological orientation to the world. Extroverts are oriented toward the outer world and gain energy from their interactions with others. They are seen as outgoing, sociable, candid, and they adapt easily to social situations. He or she is a "people person," someone who enjoys making new friends and is energized by spending time with others. Introverts, on the other hand, are more oriented toward the inner world of thoughts and reflections. Adjectives commonly used to describe introverts are "thoughtful," "quiet," and "introspective." Introverts are people who generally prefer communicating one-on-one or in small groups rather than big crowds. Though introverts and extroverts may both have excellent social skills, interacting with others charges up extroverts, whereas it takes energy for introverts to interrelate in social situations. It's not that introverts are "party poopers" but, rather, they can be easily pooped by the party.

You will not be surprised to learn that our American society is very extroverted. Research has shown that in the general American population about 75 percent of people describe themselves as extroverts and only 25 percent as introverts. Western societies, and particularly the United States, seem to reinforce the outgoing, gregarious, sociable temperament of the extrovert. People who enjoy spending time alone may be viewed as unfriendly, distant, or self-absorbed. This is not true for all cultures, however. Many Eastern cultures expect and reward more solitary, meditative pursuits. In these societies an extrovert might be seen as overbearing, loud, and hyperactive.

The main way we interact socially—whether in an extroverted or introverted way—Jung called our "superior function." The other he called the "inferior function"—not inferior as in "less than" but inferior as in not as fully developed. Extroversion and introversion can be thought of as representing end points on a continuum rather than discrete categories of behavior or attitude. No one is purely extroverted or introverted; we all embrace some elements of each interpersonal style.

Jung was very clear about the need to develop our "inferior functions" in order to become a whole and self-actualized person. The ideal personality is one that is comfortable with people and enjoys their company but also spends some time alone reflecting on inner life and engaging in solitary pursuits.

The Myers-Briggs Type Indicator (MBTI) is one commonly used psychological test that measures introversion and extroversion. The formal version of this inventory is a licensed product and must be administered by a certified professional. However, there are numerous and less scientific versions of this inventory all over the Internet. Go to a search engine and type in "Myers-Briggs" or "MBTI" and spend some time assessing your own relative amounts of introversion/extroversion. This can be a fun and enlightening exercise, especially if you do it with a friend. Compare yourselves on these measures. Are your differences ones that enrich your relationship or do they sometimes cause friction?

When I've taken these on-line tests, my score on a more formal MBTI shows what all my friends already know: I'm an extreme extrovert who has to work on developing my inferior introverted side. I do this by trying to stay mindful that I need some time alone and savoring my time with one-on-ones with close friends. But, in spite of the fact that I am an extrovert, many of my very best friends are introverts. We enjoy one another's company, trust one another, and communicate just fine. On the path to wholeness and psychological growth, we can learn a great deal from our friends who represent a different interpersonal "type" than our own predominant one.

And that leads me to my next point: our lives are enriched by close relationships with people who may see the world in ways vastly different from our own. As we continue to explore ways to develop our connections, we cannot overlook the power of accepting our friends for who they are and celebrating the differences between us as opportunities to learn about ourselves and connect with one another at a soul level.

EIGHT

Acceptance: Are You a Friend?

Should we all confess our sins to one another, we would
all laugh at one another for our lack of originality.

—*Kahlil Gibran*

Jennifer dearly loves her good friend Anna. They've been friends for
a long time and have seen each other through some of life's most difficult times, but their political views could not be more different and,
even though Jennifer is an extrovert herself, she told me that Anna
"talks all the time." Jennifer says that when Anna is driving her crazy,
she just thinks about her kind and generous heart, her wit and intelligence, and how much she means to her. She realizes that her friend's
compulsive long-windedness covers up some significant insecurity and
how hard she's worked to overcome a difficult past. Of those moments,
Jennifer says, "I remember that I, too, must have foibles that make her
want to pull her hair out. I remember that we are friends and that I love
her and the fact that she often is a chatterbox seems of no consequence
whatsoever."

The very people and things that annoy us most can be opportunities
for self-growth. When a friend bugs us, it is wise to remember that pearls
are the result of an irritation to an oyster. Most of us don't always
remember this when we're in the middle of one of those exasperating
moments. It can be difficult to see how something that is painful at worst
or annoying at best can be a seed for something good and beautiful.

So consider the pearl. Did you know that these gorgeous gems begin as an aggravation? A grain of sand finds its way into the oyster's shell. The oyster tries to get rid of the grain of sand but when it can't, it reduces the scratchy irritation by coating it with layers of calcium carbonate, the soft, iridescent mother-of-pearl material from its own shell. With that, the oyster begins to do one of the most beautiful things an oyster ever has a chance to do—it creates a pearl.

Friends who are different or have annoying habits can be like that grain of sand. Remember that in our friends' hearts and minds we have our own grain-of-sand qualities. But it is in the knowledge that our friends see beyond our persona—our public mask—and our flaws that we begin to feel the kind of validation that allows us to fully love ourselves. The growth of our self-esteem and knowledge of ourselves as being worthy of love come through the mirrors of our loving friends. They really know us, and they still love us.

Don't you want to be loved because of who you are and not just because you share a common interest or live in a particular neighborhood or are a convenient season-or-reason friend? I think we all do. Author Beth Kephart in her book *Into the Tangle of Friendship* talks about the power in this kind of friendship of the heart: "Unlikely friends allow each other to dream on, to rearrange or appropriate the world in ways those outside their circle can neither grasp nor affect. Differences may stack up tall around them—class, age, religion, race, gender—but something bigger than all that makes them safe and strong in each other's company."[1]

Similarities and Differences

A true and meaningful friendship means accepting your friends for who they are and celebrating not only the similarities but the differences between you.

Think about your closest friendships. How are your friends similar or different from you? Think about a specific friend and note ways in which you are alike and other ways in which you are very different.

Do you accept and celebrate the differences you have with your friends? Do they return these feelings to you? Are you loved in spite of yourself?

Have a conversation with your closest friend about accepting each other, faults and all. What do you learn when you bring those ideas out from the recesses of your own mind and heart and into the space between the two of you?

Are there people in your life who you've avoided getting to know because they seem too different from you? Can you imagine what it might be like to be friends with one of these people? Why do you resist a relationship with them?

Do the differences between you and your friends sometimes bug you? What do they do that bugs you? Do you understand why they engage in these behaviors? What can you learn about yourself from these annoyances?

The Futility of Seeking Perfection

There is a wonderful character in teaching stories from the Middle East—especially popular in Afghanistan, Turkey, and Iran. His name is Mullah Nasruddin, and in this simple story he illuminates the futility of seeking perfection.

This old Sufi tale tells of Nasruddin and his friend sitting in a café, drinking tea and talking about life and love.

"How come you never married, Nasruddin?" asked his friend.

"Well," said Nasruddin, "to tell you the truth, I spent my youth looking for the perfect woman. In Cairo I met a beautiful and intelligent woman with eyes like dark olives, but she was unkind. Then in Baghdad I met a woman who was a wonderful and generous soul, but we had no interests in common. One woman after another would seem just right, but there would always be something missing. Then one day I met her. She was beautiful, intelligent, generous, and kind. We had everything in common. In fact, she was perfect."

"Well," said the friend. "Why didn't you marry her?"

Nasruddin sipped his tea and sighed. "Well, it's a sad thing. It seems that she was looking for the perfect man."

We can look for perfection until the cows come home and we'll never find it. Instead, when we accept those friends we love—flaws and all—we can live a happy life and our relationship can flourish.

Do you expect perfection in your friends? Do they expect this from you?

Unconditional Love and Acceptance

Attached-at-the-heart friends offer, at least as far as is humanly possible, the power of unconditional love and acceptance. While we humans may wax eloquent about the spiritual requirement for unconditional love, it's a lot harder to put into practice than to talk about. When we feel judgmental or vehemently disagree, when our friends do things that make us want to scream, it's far too easy to allow the relationship to suffer. Unconditional love is the kind of love that writer G. K. Chesterton was talking about when he wrote, "Love means to love that which is unlovable; or it is no virtue at all." It's the kind of love that we always get from our four-legged friends but not often enough from our two-legged ones.

This kind of unconditional love without measure lives in our hearts and souls, not in the linear thinking of the brain that tells us to keep score, to make certain that we're getting what we need from our friends. Unconditional love and acceptance cannot be described in words; they must be experienced directly in the loving containers of our safe harbors. Perhaps this is why Paramahansa Yogananda, born at the turn of the century and a pioneer in bringing yoga to Western cultures, spoke of the power of unconditional love in the way he did: "The world as a whole has forgotten the real meaning of the word *love*. Love has been so abused and crucified by man that very few people know what true love is. Just as oil is present in every part of the olive, so love permeates every part of creation. But to define love is very difficult, for the same reason that words cannot fully describe the flavor of an orange. You have to taste the fruit to know its flavor. So with love."[2]

Do you feel that your friends accept you and love you for who you are, flaws and all?

Giving and Receiving

Love is a verb. We express the nature of our relationships by giving with a generous heart, not because we must, but because we want to. Friendship isn't easy—it takes its time and it takes its toll. There are responsibilities. Our friends need us—potato salad needs to be made for her party, he needs a ride to the airport and, by the way, his flight is at 5:30 A.M. But regardless of what we must do, we do it. This is the economy of true friendship, which is not about words that describe it but the actions that show it. Friendships require being there for one another, trusting, and demonstrating loyalty by going the distance no matter how difficult or inconvenient.

Paula had a momentary dilemma. Her good friend's mother had died suddenly and the funeral was being held in a town that was a four-hour drive away. The timing couldn't have been worse. It was the first week of school and her youngest was starting a new day-care program. She had an important business meeting in the afternoon. Her husband was out of town for his job and she couldn't even imagine how she would work out the details of her life to spend a day traveling back and forth for the funeral of a person she had never met. She would be in the car eight hours for the one-hour service. The brain says, "This is too much. You're busy. Send a card. Send flowers. Attending the funeral isn't a good investment of your time and energy." But the heart says, "This is your good friend and she is suffering. Your presence there does matter. Your being there will help her." And so Paula, because she understands friendship and expresses her love in real, tangible ways, solved the problems of child care and rescheduled the meeting. Her decision had been made the moment she heard the pain in her friend's voice sadly reporting that her mother had just died. Her friend later told her how important it was that she was there at her mother's funeral. "I don't know how I could have managed it without you," she said.

This decision to put the friendship ahead of other responsibilities and commitments was the right one. Safe harbors matter. For the rest of their lives, these women will remember that funeral. As sad an occasion as it was, it will always be a marker of the intimacy and love between them. It is now only six months after the fact and Paula can barely remember the subject of that important business meeting. True friends are there for you when they'd rather or need to be somewhere else.

My friend Mickey responded to my mini-survey about friendship and, as always, she had clear insights into this subject of the heart. She is a wise woman surrounded by a tribe of friends who stick together— through festivals and hurricanes—on tiny Ocracoke Island off the coast of North Carolina. She was praying Hail Mary's for me that I'd make a pressing deadline when she wrote, "A true friend is like a shiny red, yellow, or green apple. The stem is the connection, the seeds are the growth, the core is the unconditional love, the pulp is honesty, sharing, and trust. The skin is the holding together no matter what, the bonding. The stem or connection is sometimes instant. A flash of energy that feels familiar. The seeds or growth period can vary, years, months, or days. Friends grow together when each person nurtures the unconditional love. Pulp . . . be honest, share everything and, most importantly, trust. Skin holds it all together through thick and thin. Whatever it takes though the skin may be tough at times."[3]

The skin may be tough at times. When you've been attached-at-the-heart friends for lots of years, you've seen your share of good times and bad. When you open your heart to love and are loved, there is a lot of laughter and a lot of tears.

For some people, giving is easier than receiving. I've noticed this is an especially prominent theme for women. But when you see friendship as a two-way street, it's a bit selfish to refuse our friends the opportunity to do for us. The wonderful American writer Zora Neale Hurston once wrote, "There is nothing to make you like other human beings so much as doing things for them."

How open are you to receiving from your friends? Are you able to ask for help when you need it? Do you expect your friends to be there for you when you need something from them?

Write about a time when you really needed your friends and they were there for you. Then remind them about how important this was for you.

Think about a time when you put everything aside to be there when a friend needed you. Write it down.

Are there times when you weren't there for your friends because of time constraints or other responsibilities? Would you make that same decision today?

This discussion of giving and receiving brings me to the important issue of interpersonal boundaries, the subject of the following chapter.

NINE

Boundaries: Armor, Gelatin, and Semipermeable Membranes

> Love consists in this, that two solitudes protect,
> and touch, and salute each other.
>
> —*Rainer Maria Rilke*

We all want to be close to others—that's a natural human need and an incredibly important one. We've seen what happens when we are isolated or disconnected. We suffer psychologically, spiritually, and even physically. We don't live as long and we certainly don't live as well. The research is clear: even having one close friend extends our lives by decades.

But it is possible to be *too* close to others, when we can't tell where we end and they begin. We're too close when our self-esteem depends entirely on what others think of us, or when we don't allow ourselves to hold our own opinions or feel our own feelings. On the other hand, we may guard ourselves against intimacy with other people. We may be suspicious and distrustful and never open up to anyone. When that is the case, we are ensuring a lonely and isolated life.

The German philosopher Arthur Schopenhauer wrote about personal boundaries and the dilemma of intimacy as being like a bunch of porcupines on a cold winter's night. The quandary for porcupines, he said, was to find their optimal level of closeness and independence. They needed to be able to huddle together to benefit from their mutual warmth—aahhh—while not getting so close that they poke each other with their sharp quills—ouch! So here are these poor little creatures trapped in an endless cycle of painful engagement and cold, loveless isolation. Over and over, they come close, stab the hell out of each other, then jump back only to shiver and freeze.

It's unlikely that Schopenhauer actually observed real porcupines in the wild or he would have known that they don't strut around with their thirty thousand spiky quills sticking out just waiting to jab anything that brushes up against them. Really, they're rather sweet little rodents that are not known to attack anyone else and only get this pincushion defense going when they're in danger or scared. When they're not threatened, the quills lie down and I'll bet they can cuddle and huddle all they want. Nevertheless, Schopenhauer does raise a good point: healthy boundaries are vital to healthy relationships and they change and grow as a friendship deepens and becomes more emotionally intimate. Just as a physical boundary, like a gate, is designed to let some things in and keep some things out, interpersonal boundaries define our emotional space. Like Schopenhauer's porcupines, humans also need a balance between dependence and separateness.

I think there are three kinds of boundaries—two unhealthy and one excellent. The first unhealthy boundary is to be armored, distrusting, guarded, and letting no one in. The other unhealthy boundary is to be like gelatin—squishy and with no firm definition, no independent sense of self. But the excellent, healthy boundary is a concept we learned about in eighth-grade biology class. It's the way each cell of the body protects itself with a semipermeable membrane. This semipermeable membrane protects the cell from toxins but lets in nutrients. We can learn a lot from cells. We want to let in light, love, and connection but keep out the influence of toxic people, lest we lose our own unique personality in the service of a relationship.

Let me briefly describe each of these interpersonal boundaries in turn and give examples. But first, I must say that these types of interpersonal boundaries are really best conceptualized as a continuum of behaviors rather than discrete categories. We can imagine "Armor" on one end and "Gelatin" on the other and the healthy "Semipermeable Membrane" as somewhere in between. Also, we may employ a variety of healthy and unhealthy relationship styles with different people and at different times in our lives.

Armor

Jane is so armored and self-protecting that she practically clanks as she walks by. Truly, her interpersonal boundary is as rigid as if she were decked out in the gauntlets, greaves, cuirass, shield, and helmet of a medieval knight. She doesn't reveal her feelings or share her opinions about anything and has trouble getting close to people. She is closed, tight, and withholding of her feelings and spirit. Underneath this fortified persona beats the heart of a very fine person but, frankly, it's a great deal of work to try to reach her. Not surprisingly, Jane has few friends who are willing to put out the effort to get close to her. Because she is not well liked and doesn't really have a sense of belongingness, she has become even more suspicious of others' motives about wanting to know her, trusts even less, and doesn't seem to recognize the vicious cycle she's in. Because her superficial social skills are within the normal range, she can talk with people on the job and has a few other casual friends who share her interest in art. But she is uncontained in any emotionally nurturing way and once she leaves the art gallery opening where she's shared a glass of wine with her artist friends, she goes home alone to a life bereft of any meaningful relationships. Like David, whom I wrote about in an earlier chapter, Jane likes to blame her busy schedule for her lack of close friendships, but the truth is that even if she had all the time in the world, her psychological defenses would prevent her from deep and meaningful friendships.

A few years ago, Jane's elderly mother died. A neighbor read about her mother's death in the newspaper and came to the funeral home to express her sympathy and told Jane she was going to be home all week and, if Jane wanted, to come over for a cup of coffee. It might help just to know that there was someone to talk to. Jane thanked her, then gave a tight-lipped "I'm fine. I'm really fine." Jane refused this offer of connection and support. She was unwilling or unable to become engaged in a relationship. Jane's boundaries are too tight.

Gelatin

Unlike Jane, Beverly is an open book. She details all the events of her life to anyone who will listen, making absolutely no distinctions between a virtual stranger and a family member. If you were to take a job in Beverly's office, I've no doubt that, by lunchtime, there would be very little about her history or present situation that you wouldn't know. You would find her to be needy, tedious, and high maintenance, but you might feel guilty for feeling this way because Beverly will be so kind and generous to you. She'll give you inappropriate gifts—too intimate too early in the relationship to be accepted. Very often, Beverly is taken advantage of. She is not a rich woman but she's lent money to acquaintances who've never paid her back. And she becomes emeshed in the lives of people who don't always treat her very well.

She'll agree with every word you say but, rest assured, she will do the same with a colleague who holds a diametrically different opinion on whatever subject it is. It's as if she is so in need of pleasing others that she will go against her own values and beliefs in order to fit in and be liked. Because she is like a chameleon, many people describe Beverly as untrustworthy, though she certainly doesn't mean to be. It's as if she takes on the personality of whoever her friends are at the moment. Now, quite often, good friends will take up hobbies or interests when we introduce them to something—just as we might discover that we have an affinity for some activities they turn us on to. But Beverly doesn't seem to have an original thought or interest. She says yes when she really wants to say no. She is a walking poster-child for the real (not overly defined) behaviors of co-dependency. Her interpersonal boundaries are like gelatin—soft and pliable—and Beverly can't tell where she ends and another begins. Beverly's boundaries are too loose.

Semipermeable Membrane

Think of a semipermeable membrane as being something like a filter or a strainer. At the cellular level, some atoms flow through the membrane easily, while others are kept out. If you've ever made a cup of tea with loose tea leaves, you can appreciate the fact that a strainer lets through delicious tea-flavored water but keeps the leaves themselves far from your lips. And so it is with interpersonal boundaries. We want to let in the light of love and connection but, at the same time, resist toxic relationships and maintain a healthy sense of our own unique and independent self.

Sometimes it is necessary to keep certain people away from the deep core of our being. Some people may be toxic to our sense of self and to our own growth and development. I think this is rare. Most friendships have a great deal of unrealized potential. But we need to be protected by our semipermeable membrane. Some "friends" are toxic to us in exactly the same ways that certain chemicals or bacteria threaten the health and integrity of a cell. We don't have to be—shouldn't be—friends with people who do not treat us with kindness and respect. I'm not speaking here of a good friend who is going through a bad time and may be short or difficult to be with. We stand by those friends—in good times and bad. I'm talking instead about relationships that make us feel small, ones in which we are always the giver and there is no reciprocity in giving and taking, ones in which our friends encourage and reinforce self-destructive behaviors or attitudes. We cannot be friends with people who betray us and make no attempt to apologize or ask forgiveness. Remember that "friends" who constantly put others down behind their backs are very likely to be saying those kinds of things about you when you are not present. We cannot be friends with people who constantly wound us, do not treat us with dignity, abandon us when we need them most, are jealous of the good things we achieve, or keep us from our Creator-given right to growth and change.

As much as we may value friendship as an ideal, it is not healthy to maintain relationships with friends who are destructive or harmful to us. Beware of "friends" who are constantly critical or judgmental, ridicule you or put you down in front of others, or try to keep you from other friends or family. Friends who blame you for their problems, are jealous or possessive, force you to do things you don't want to do and are against your own values, or show violent behavior are giving you a big red flag that they are not good for you.

Before dismissing a friend, make certain that you have searched your own soul and understand how, if at all, you have contributed to the problems. Perhaps by working together you can resolve the issues that make the relationship an unhealthy friendship for you. But, if in the end you cannot work out the problems and do not feel you are being treated with dignity and respect, the friendship has to end. This is the power of the semipermeable membrane: it allows in the good and keeps out the bad.

In our interpersonal relationships, we can think of the "Armored" boundary as "turning against," the "Gelatin" boundary as "turning with," and the "Semipermeable Membrane" boundary as "turning toward" others. When we "turn against" others, we essentially stop any relationship from forming. We may operate at an acceptable level with relative strangers, perhaps even with our acquaintances or friends for a season or reason, but we have locked out the real McCoy of intimate friendships. By "turning with" our friends, we forget that it takes two to make a healthy relationship. We lose our sense of self, our own creativity, and the personality that complements that of our friends. It is only in "turning toward" one another that we discover the connections that we seek.

1. Draw a line across a piece of paper and label one end "Armor" and the other "Gelatin." Take a hard look at two of your most important relationships and think about the way you would describe the boundary in these relationships. Mark your paper to indicate your relative position on that scale in terms of these relationships. Do these boundaries feel healthy to you? Do they need to change? If so, how do they need to change?

2. In a journal, write a one-page story that begins with the following sentence: "Teresa was so close to her friends that she . . ." Let your imagination soar and let the story write itself. Don't start with any preconceived notions about whether or not Teresa's closeness to her friends is a good or bad thing. Just let the story come out. After writing it, take a short break and then go back and read it. Did you learn anything about how you view closeness? Does the character of Teresa reveal anything to you about your boundaries with others in your life?

3. Reflect on the boundaries that you have with your friends. Are there patterns in your relationships in terms of the kind of interpersonal boundary you construct?

4. Do your boundaries work for you? Are you certain that you're letting in the good and keeping out the bad?

5. Are there toxic "friendships" that need to end in your life? How will your life be different without those people in it? Will it be improved or not?

6. If you already realize that some of your relationships are toxic, what has prevented you from removing these people from your life?

In the next chapter, we'll look at the power of communication with our friends. In his landmark book *How to Win Friends and Influence People*, Dale Carnegie once observed: "There are four ways, and only four ways, in which we have contact with the world. We are evaluated and classified by these four contacts: what we do, how we look, what we say, and how we say it." In earlier sections we've looked at some of the social skills that impact on these ways of knowing each other. Now let's delve more deeply into the importance of communicating our feelings and thoughts clearly to our friends and avoiding mixed messages as we build our connections.

TEN

Communication Revolution

There is no pleasure to me without communication:
There is not so much as a sprightly thought comes
into my mind that it does not grieve me to have
produced alone, and that I have no one to tell it to.

—*Michel Eyquem de Montaigne*

Susan and Beth almost ended their friendship because of a failure to communicate. They were neighbors who discovered that they really liked each other and had lots of common interests. They were on the path to becoming more than just casual friends, but there were obstacles along the way. Susan was constantly feeling let down and disrespected by Beth. Beth would tell her she'd come over soon and then show up an hour later. In the meantime, Susan would put off doing things that needed to be done, waiting for her friend. This went on for months but Susan just held her tongue, even though her obvious body language and behavior made her annoyance clear to everyone. One day, while particularly stressed out from a bad day at work, Beth was, once again, late. When she finally arrived, Susan let Beth have it. "You're inconsiderate and arrogant. You think your needs are more important than mine. I'm tired of putting up with your irresponsibility," Susan yelled. "Oh yeah, well I'm tired of wondering what the hell I've done to tick you off. When I come over, you're always in a rotten mood and act like you're mad at me but you deny it." Door slams. Beth stalks off and that might have been the end of what could have been an important friendship in their lives. To their credit, the relationship had promise and they liked each other enough to try to solve the problem. They were angry but willing to try to salvage their friendship. As it turned out through some heartfelt and emotional conversations, it became clear to both of them that their conflict could be traced to one big misunderstanding: each had a different definition for the word *soon*.

Beth would tell Susan she would be over "soon," and in her parlance that meant, oh, an hour or so. To Susan *soon* meant in the next fifteen minutes. So she'd just wait for her friend, her anger and disappointment rising with each tick of the clock. By the time Beth got there, Susan was furious but lacked the assertive skills to express her feelings.

How can that be? you might think. How can two intelligent women sacrifice a relationship over something as petty as that? I assure you, it happens all the time. We don't need the intentional verbal gymnastics and linguistic hair-splitting of ex-president Bill Clinton to the Starr Commission ("It depends on what the meaning of the word 'is' is.") to discover just how imprecise our verbal communication can be. Miscommunication leads to misunderstanding and misunderstanding leads to hurt feelings and wounds our relationships. This scenario illuminates the old maxim that there is always someone who knows better than you what you meant by your message.

Just as using certain gestures in our part of the world may mean something very different in another, when we are not clear in our messages, things don't turn out as well as they could.

Everyone enters into a relationship with a complex array of communication skills (or lack thereof), style, expectations, strengths, weaknesses, and peccadilloes. When you add the complex variables of nonverbal expression and the underlying neural circuitry required for subtle movements and speech, it's a wonder that we communicate at all.

Communication theorists emphasize the complexity of human communication and note that when we communicate—even with simple statements or requests—there are at least six "people" involved: (1) who you think you are, (2) who you think the other person is, (3) who you think the other person thinks you are, (4) who the other person thinks he/she is, (5) who the other person thinks you are, and (6) who the other person thinks you think he/she is.[1]

In relationships, we communicate for a variety of reasons, including the need to gather information, to build a context of understanding, to establish our identities with one another, and to meet our very human need for inclusion and affection. Our relationships are improved beyond measure when we communicate from the heart, and that does not require a Ph.D. in linguistics, a mellifluous voice, or a vocabulary of a million words. What it does require is a willingness to open ourselves up and express our thoughts and feelings in ways that are emotionally authentic and to listen with a deep desire to know our friends.

Express Yourself

One of the most exquisite expressions of friendship and love that I can remember in my own life consisted of only two simple words. My mother was dying and my family had been at the hospital for two days. Around midnight my brother, aunts and uncles, my partner Nancy and I had returned to my parents' house to shower and, maybe, catch a few hours of sleep before returning in the early morning. Together we had prayed and said our good-byes to my mom and we wanted to give my father some quiet, alone time in these final hours with the woman he had loved for forty-seven years. Barely an hour later, the phone rang. It was my dad telling me that Mom had died. I hung up the phone. Nancy hugged me as I wept helplessly, and she said these two simple words with heartfelt compassion: "I know."

Sometimes our communication is as simple as that—one heart opening up to another with simplicity, compassion, and a minimum of words. Other times, we need to be very clear verbally about how we feel and what we need. This point is easy for me to remember ever since my "tribe" had a Thanksgiving Day gathering where we provided the turkey, dressing, and the place and everyone else brought a traditional dish to share. Leaving it up to fate and the best judgment of the group found us with the stuffed bird and twelve variations of sweet potato casserole. They were all delicious and quite different—some with pineapple, several with those tiny marshmallows on top, but our dinner might have been more balanced—adding, say, an apple pie for dessert— had we talked clearly and directly about who would bring what.

Remember also that our messages are better understood when our nonverbal behaviors are congruent with what we're saying and when our behavior backs up our spoken message. We're better understood when we avoid mixed messages.

So let's look at some typical areas of communication between friends and check in as to how well you do with these.

Self-disclosure

Intimacy between friends relies on reciprocal self-disclosure—the reveal-ing of private personal experiences and strongly held thoughts and feel-ings. One of the hallmarks of attached-at-the-heart friends is trust. Remember that trust is both the means to self-disclosure and its end product. Our level of self-disclosure is, in many ways, a barometer for the depth of our friendship: we disclose more personal, more controver-sial aspects of our self to those we trust the most, the people with whom we can allow ourselves to be open, vulnerable.

Can you—do you—talk with your friends about your feelings and opinions?

Does this feel comfortable or do you have to work at it? Are there certain areas that are easier to disclose than others? For example, can you express your thoughts and opinions more easily than you can express your feelings? If that is true for you, what stops you?

The Appendix contains an interesting and fun exercise that will help you offer feedback and disclose in a nonthreatening way. It's a variation on an exercise that my business partner, Andrea Bear, and I designed for our organizational consulting activities with our company, Full Poten-tial Organizations. I think you'll have an interesting time with it.

Clarity

Are you a clear communicator? Do you say what you mean? Do others understand what you are saying or does someone have to be a linguistic detective to follow your tracks? Just think about the vignette of Beth and Susan. If they had spent two seconds defining the word *soon*, their whole problem would have been solved without any conflict.

Assertiveness

Assertiveness can be defined as the straightforward and clear expression of thoughts, opinions, and feelings in direct, honest, and appropriate ways that are respectful of the dignity of another. From this definition, it should be clear that assertiveness can be contrasted with passive behav-ior (which does not express honestly or directly) and aggressive behavior (which does not respect the dignity of another). Unlike aggressive inter-personal behavior, assertive communications do not demean, humiliate, dominate, or degrade. You would think assertiveness would not be dif-ficult, but I'm afraid that many people have problems with this set of interpersonal communication skills. Assertive behaviors can be sub-divided into four general categories: (1) expressing positive feelings, (2) expressing negative feelings, (3) initiating activities or conversation, and (4) setting limits.

Reflect on your own behavior. Are any of these types of assertive skills difficult for you? Remember that some of these are situation-specific. Very few people are always assertive or always nonassertive. For example, you may have difficulty setting limits with your friends (you're the one up making potato salad at midnight because you couldn't say no) but have no problem at all with setting limits for your kids ("It's bedtime now, Joey, and I mean it!"). You may be perfectly comfortable in expressing positive feelings to a beloved friend but have trouble saying positive things to an acquaintance.

Spend a moment thinking about your comfort level and ability to communicate in these four areas of assertive behavior, then jot down sit-uations that are easy and those you need to work on. Remember that assertive communication is a learned skill that is improved with practice and that every behavior consists of verbal, nonverbal, affective (emo-tional and physiological), and cognitive components.

Let me specifically address the importance of initiating activities and offering invitations as powerful parts of the process of drawing casual friends and acquaintances into our deep core of relationships. Friends that become our tribe go beyond these kinds of "transactions" and are relationships that transcend a specific social context.

Our friendships grow through the shared experience and history of interacting outside the usual or original setting in which we met. We can contribute to that process by having contact across multiple set-tings, letting our friends know that we *want* to—not *have* to—spend time with them.

Are there people in your life that you would like to know in another context? For example, are there coworkers who might become close friends if you had opportunities for interactions outside the office? Make a list of some prospects and outline an action plan to bring them closer to you.

Areas of Assertive Behavior	Situations That Are Easy for You	Situations That Are Difficult for You
Expressing positive feelings—compliments, feelings of warmth or affection, caring, concern, admiration, affection		
Expressing negative feelings—delivering criticism, expressing anger or disappointment		
Initiating conversation or activities—include asking things for yourself in this category		
Setting limits—saying no, refusing requests		

Interpersonal communications that are respectful, open, and honest are necessary ingredients in building connections. All relationships that have depth and longevity must develop processes for dealing with conflict and disagreements. We've all heard about friendships that dissolve over matters that seem inconsequential in the larger scheme of things. When we are able to resolve conflict by honest discussion, flexibility, and compromise, we strengthen our friendship. By recognizing the intention behind our friend's behavior and learning the fine art of forgiveness, we grow psychologically and spiritually. So, rather than a conflict tearing us apart, it becomes part of the invisible connection that binds us to one another.

We expect more from close friends than we do from our acquaintances, but we are holding a self-defeating and irrational belief if we expect that even our best friends will never disappoint us or fail to know what we want. In fact, expecting them to anticipate our every need as if they are somehow magical mind readers is sometimes called the "myth of the good friend"—if he/she really loved me, then he/she would know exactly what I need. Unless you happen to be good friends with your own clone, there are bound to be differences of opinion, values, and attitudes.

It's important to let our friends know how we feel even when we must tell them something that we'd rather not. Our feelings don't dissolve into the ether just because we don't feel comfortable expressing them. Very often people who have a hard time expressing anger or disappointment bring them in the back door by expressing their feelings through nonverbal and passive-aggressive behavior—a deliberate but indirect attempt to express angry feelings: "No. Certainly I'm not angry with you. But, oh, by the way, I forgot to pick up the dress from the cleaners for that big presentation you have to do in ten minutes." Oops. What does this communicate?

Let's say your friend has done something that really bothered you—like Beth's "lateness" irritated Susan. This may not even be a big deal if you look at it event by event. But bad feelings accumulate if not discharged. Over time, we build up resentments until finally—like a dam bursting from one drop of water too much—we blow. We may say things that we don't really mean and we're likely to break all the good rules of feedback, such as focusing on the behavior, not the person, delivering our message with kindness, and being specific. Instead we express broad, angry messages that hurt feelings. We don't say, "Beth, it bothers me that you say you'll be over soon and then I wait an hour for you." Too often and sometimes because we're stressed out from other things that have nothing to do with the issue at hand, we say—in a loud and angry voice—"You're inconsiderate and arrogant." We may feel guilty for losing control and our friendship may take time to recover. By releasing our feelings as they come up in assertive and gentle ways, we don't get into that problem. It's advisable to remember what an old Russian proverb teaches: "Once a word goes out of your mouth, you can never swallow it again."

Think about a time that you blew up at a friend. Could you have handled it differently, better? What was the outcome—the impact—on the friendship? How can you avoid this in the future?

Take the questions above and reverse them and reflect on a time when a friend blew up at you and hurt your feelings. Did you and your friend resolve your conflict? Did you forgive or were you forgiven?

Advice and Truth

Mahatma Gandhi observed, "Whenever you have truth it must be given with love or the message and the messenger will be rejected." I don't know much more to say than that. Our good friends deserve our most honest feedback and truth—at least as we see it. And the truth is that we can be entirely supportive while taking the interpersonal risk required to tell our friend what he/she needs to know. Advice is best given by referring to yourself. Instead of saying, "You should or you must . . . ," try putting yourself in your friend's shoes. "If Jamie were my son, I might . . ." This is not a verbal manipulation but a subtle way of saying: "I recognize something that might need to be changed and I can imagine myself in your situation. And if I were, I would try this. . . ." Expressing empathy is especially powerful if you have, in fact, walked in your friend's shoes: "When my mother was dying, I felt . . ." Advice-giving without a self-reference can sometimes be heard as arrogant or as a know-it-all kind of mentality. Most often, you are not giving your friend any information that he/she has not already considered. When giving advice to a friend, be very aware of your own intentions. Is your primary goal to help your friend or convince him/her that you know more than he/she does? Don't insist that your friend take your advice and never, ever, say, "I told you so." Loving our friends means letting them follow their own path while we cheer them on. Sometimes, our very best friends will make decisions that we wouldn't think of doing in a million years.

More often than not, our friend already knows what he/she needs to do to solve a problem. Even more important than giving advice is learning to listen.

The Fine (and Lost) Art of Listening

There is a well-known and funny *Far Side* cartoon by Gary Larson that was run in newspapers around the country that shows in two panels "what we say to dogs" and "what our dogs hear." In the first panel, the dog's owner says, "Okay, Ginger, I've had it! You stay out of the garbage! Understand, Ginger? Stay out of the garbage or else!" In the second panel, a very contented-looking mutt hears, "Blah, blah, Ginger, blah blah, blah, blah, blah, blah, blah, blah, Ginger, blah, blah, blah blah. . . ."[2]

This cartoon is so true and so much a part of our popular culture that I've even heard problems in the listening aspect of interpersonal communication referred to as the "Ginger Factor."

Unfortunately, it's not just people and their dogs that have trouble listening to each other. It's the bane of many human-to-human interactions as well. We think we're listening but more often we are pretending to listen or listening selectively to certain parts of another's communication. In his bestselling book *The Seven Habits of Highly Effective People*, author Stephen Covey says that communication is the most important skill in life and that effective people are those who seek first to understand, then to be understood.[3]

Intimacy and closeness are about knowing and being known. The predominant way we achieve that level of interpersonal knowledge is by communicating clearly and, most important, by active, connected listening. So friendships and their growth rely a great deal on listening and being listened to.

Think about the last time you felt really listened to by an acquaintance or friend. First of all, he stopped what he was doing. He didn't ask you to compete with his washing the dishes, checking his cell phone messages, glancing at the newspaper or a report on his desk or, worst of all, looking over your shoulder to catch what's on the TV. Chances are that everything about his body language said, "You are important to me. I want to know what you have to say. I'm interested and I care about your feelings." He made good eye contact with you. Perhaps he leaned forward as you reached an important point of your story or nodded or smiled at appropriate places as you told your story. He never once interrupted or "one-upped" you ("Oh, I can beat that!"). He let you know that he's listening to you. His verbal behavior probably included encouragement ("I see," "That's interesting"), restatements ("In other words, you felt as if you had to . . ."), and reflections ("You must have been really hurt when . . ."). Occasionally, he may have added an empathy statement that shows you he understands how you feel ("Oh, I know. I felt just like that when I lost my job.") or an open-ended question that encouraged you to continue ("What happened next?"). But you never once felt that he was moving the conversation toward himself; mostly you did the talking. There may have even been moments of silence between you but you never once thought his attention had wandered from that moment, that exquisite moment of intimacy. But even in the absence of these interactive listening skills, I'll bet you felt that his whole being was devoted to you during that moment.

Good listening skills are a lot like mindfulness—the experience of one-pointed attention, of being fully present in that exact moment in time. Our concentration is focused; we're in the flow of the present moment with all our senses tuned in to just that. We are not just "waiting to talk" or thinking about unrelated matters ("I wonder if I should get my oil changed this week, hmmm"). The greatest gift we can give to each other is the honor of our attention. Twentieth-century Indian sage and philosopher Krishnamurti understood how really listening to each other moves us from the mundane to the level of soul: "So when you are listening to somebody, completely, attentively, then you are listening not only to the words, but also to the feeling of what is being conveyed, to the whole of it, not part of it." And theologian Paul Tillich once rightly noted, "The first duty of love is to listen."

When people in a recent survey conducted by counselor Mary Ellen Copeland were asked, "What would keep you from wanting to be friends with someone you have met?" the answer was surprising. These survey respondents did not mention a lack of common interests or not having chemistry between them. What they mentioned were listening skills. The most common impediment to a blossoming friendship was that this person did all the talking and did not listen, or that this person did not listen long or attentively enough.[4] Among the specific communication problems cited were: people talking too much about themselves; trying to get too close too fast; or discussing personal information too soon. All of these issues, you will note, would be avoided with a greater emphasis placed on listening to another's autobiography rather than telling our story.

A University of Maine communication researcher, Dr. Marisue Pickering, identified four important characteristics of active and empathetic listeners:

1. Desire to be *other-directed*, rather than to project one's own feelings and ideas onto the other.
2. Desire to be *nondefensive*, rather than to protect the self. When the self is being protected, it is difficult to focus on another person.
3. Desire to *imagine the roles, perspectives, or experiences of the other*, rather than assuming they are the same as one's own.

4. Desire to *listen as a receiver, not as a critic,* and desire to understand the other person rather than to achieve either agreement from or change in that person.[5]

Put on your best other-directed, nondefensive, interested-in-others ears and listen as a receiver, not a critic. Look at your own listening skills.

1. How much of the time do you spend talking versus listening? What do you hear when a friend is talking? Is your attention devoted to your friend when he/she is talking with you?

2. Ask a close friend to give you feedback on your listening skills. What does he/she think of your ability to be a good, empathetic listener?

3. Our species is very reliant on visual input to make sense of our world. Spend some time taking in the world with your other senses to sharpen those. Nature is an excellent teacher. Sit outside, close your eyes, and really listen. What do you hear when your attention is focused? Can you hear the sound of birds, the trees rustling in the breeze? Later, describe to a friend what you heard.

4. Now here's a wacky exercise that Karen Jones—my coteacher for writing workshops—and I came up with to help writers hone their non-visual senses. Good writing, like all good communication, relies on all our senses. So put on a blindfold and walk around your town. Of course, have your good friend accompany you and pick safe, traffic-free areas—like a park or nature trail. You can even go to Nordstrom's near the Lancôme counter; just don't put yourself in any danger of stepping off a curb or running into a wall. This experience will give you an opportunity to take in the world through your other four senses. This is a fun exercise for two or more friends that will reinvigorate your sensory abilities. It can help you learn to hear and listen more attentively. And it is something of an exercise in trust with your friend.

Your communication and listening skills are the foundation of the interpersonal skills that are required to bring others into your inner fold of attached-at-the-heart friends and keep them there. These skills are essential because, as we'll see in the next chapter, all meaningful friendships go through changes and good and bad times.

ELEVEN

Good Times/Bad Times

Be more prompt to go to a friend
in adversity than in prosperity.

—*Chilo*

What kinds of friends do you have? Or perhaps more important, what kind of friend are you? Aristotle once said that a true friend is like one soul in two bodies. If that's the case, then one measure of a true friend must be that he/she will stick by you through thick and thin. No fair-weather friends are they. You can count on these friends when you're riding high, but they're also there to help you up when you fall.

So did you hear the story about the two friends who were hiking when an angry bear suddenly met them on their path? One guy ran for a tree and hid in the branches. The other one wasn't so lucky. The bear came right up to him, so he hit the ground and pretended to be dead—he'd heard that bears don't bother with dead things. This poor guy held his breath as the bear felt him with her snout and sniffed him all over. He almost lost it when the bear sniffed and tickled his ears. But he held his breath and didn't move. Finally the bear sauntered off and his friend jumped down from the tree. "Hey, what did that bear whisper in your ear?" he asked with a laugh. "He gave me this advice," his companion said. "Never travel with a friend who deserts you at the moment of truth."

Vivian understood the meaning of attached-at-the-heart friends when her kidneys failed. She had been on dialysis for years but it was becoming less effective in keeping her healthy and she was getting sicker and sicker. A previous kidney transplant had failed and she was losing energy and losing hope. But because Vivian had friends who loved her, they marched down to a clinic to be tested to see if they could donate a kidney to her. Unfortunately, no one matched her blood type, but Vivian told me once that she felt loved and protected by this powerful container of people who loved her. "No matter what happens," she said, "I know I'm not alone." During the years, Vivian and her friends had lots of good times and many difficult ones, but they went through them together. Two years ago, Vivian lost her struggle for health and died. Those same friends were there to grieve for the loss of such a loving soul, and they comforted one another.

Unless they are touched by grace, acquaintances may scatter when times get tough and friends for a season or reason are unlikely to offer a kidney no matter how much they may claim to like you. These less intimate friends may desert us during difficult times in our life ("Hey, I signed on to discuss our mutual love of Pez dispensers, not to help you through this divorce!"). One doesn't have to be confronted by a hungry bear to experience those challenging times. Life has a way of throwing enough loss and suffering everyone's way. We expect—and rightfully so—our attached-at-the-heart friends to stick by us through thick and thin. Lasting friends are those who have stood by our sides when our hearts were broken, supported us in hard times, cheered us on when we needed encouragement, and celebrated our successes and joys.

1. What will you do for your dearest friends?
2. What will your friends do for you?
3. What other powerful stories of friendship move and inspire you?

Ch-Ch-Ch-Changes

Carl Jung once said, "All true things must change and only that which changes remains true." During the course of lifelong friendships—of a true safe harbor—we will all change. One measure of the strength of our relationships is the ability to withstand the ways each of us changes over time. And change we will. We will move to new neighborhoods, take new jobs, age, and change interests over time. We go from one stage of life to another, our roles evolve, and our sense of who we are is, one hopes, transforming as we go. Some friendships will go the distance, will absorb these changes, take them in stride, and continue to grow with us. Others will break apart at the seams. When they are good, our attached-at-the-heart friendships carry us beyond ourselves. We grow in consciousness and spirit. The presence of our friend—whether down the street or a continent away—gives us an honest and gentle mirror for our own changes and a safe place to explore our developing Self.

All living things go through cycles of growth and change, and human beings are no exception, but perhaps the most startling example of this is the metamorphosis of the pudgy, creeping caterpillar into the magnificent, airborne butterfly. As a caterpillar grows, it sheds its skin. The final molt produces the chrysalis, the silken cocoon in which the caterpillar—through a brutal metamorphosis—emerges as a butterfly. Our deepest friendships are something like a chrysalis for our own psychological and spiritual change. These safe harbors protect and sustain us. Without them, it's unlikely that we would have the safety or security to grow or change at all. With our friends' loving containment we try on new aspects of self with the same trust that we try on a new dress—with the full knowledge that we can trust our friends to tell us the truth about how it fits. Still, as we change or as our friends change, the relationships themselves must transform to accommodate our new selves.

Sociologist Jan Yager has coined the term *friendshifts* to refer to the way friendships change as we go from one stage of life to another.[1] And author Lillian Rubin wrote about the ways intimate friends provide a reference, a stable port in a sometimes unstable world. Regardless of where we are in our life cycle, she says, it is our dearest friends—our safe harbor—that will contain us as we go. "Whether child or adult, it is friends who provide a reference outside the family against which to measure and judge ourselves; who help us during passages that require our separation and individuation; who support us as we adapt to new roles and new rules; who heal the hurts and make good the deficits of other relationships in our lives, who offer the place and encouragement for the development of parts of self that, for whatever reasons, are inaccessible in the family context. It's with friends that we test our sense of self-in-the-world, that our often inchoate, intuitive, unarticulated vision of the possibilities of a self-yet-to-become finds expression."[2]

Rebecca and Mary have been friends for more than sixty years. They met in grammar school and have declared themselves to be "best friends" every since. As you can imagine, a lot of changes have taken place over the more than half a century that they've been connected. And their friendship might not be so remarkable if they had both stayed put—living down the street from each other as their mothers did for all their lives. But that's not the case with this friendship. Both married, had children, and between them lived in fifteen states and two countries overseas. In spite of that, they have stayed in touch regularly—sometimes daily if the circumstances permitted. Regardless of where they find themselves, they are attached at the heart. When they described their friendship to me, they spoke about feeling "like sisters" and how their friendship seemed like a natural and healthy extension of family and of themselves. They have changed and grown together, they said, and been there for each other in many good times and other heartbreaking ones.

As I spoke with these two women—now in their seventies—I was reminded of a lyrical quotation by actor Douglas Fairbanks: "I remember you and recall you without effort, without exercise of will; that is by natural impulse, indicated by a sense of duty, or of obligation. And that, I take it, is the only sort of remembering worth the having. When we think of friends and call their faces out of the shadows, and their voices out of the echoes that faint along the corridors of memory, and do it without knowing why save that we love to do it, we content ourselves that friendship is a Reality and not a Fancy—that it is built upon a rock, and not upon the sands that dissolve away with the ebbing tides and carry their monuments with them."

I love what this silent-film star said with words. This is the language of soul that speaks of building our friendships upon a rock and memories that come by natural impulse. This is the nature of deep and enduring friendships that weather all of the events of our lives. These relationships are a sacred responsibility and a sacred trust.

1. Think about your closest friends. How have you both changed over time? Have you grown together or apart as you have moved through life?

2. Again, look through a box of old photographs with a close friend. Talk about the changes that each of you has been through. What do you learn about the friendship by looking at your shared history?

Reflect on the value of the connections in your life and make a decision as to whether you will expend the effort to build one that will go the distance and sustain you through life's ups and downs. If your answer is yes, then continue to the next chapter, which addresses a major obstacle to creating attached-at-the-heart friendships: that time thing.

TWELVE

That Time Thing

If you want to make good use of your time,
you've got to know what's most important
and then give it all you've got.

—*Lee Iacocca*

I once heard a story about a time management expert demonstrating an important point to a group of students. He pulled out a one-gallon wide-mouthed Mason jar and a dozen fist-sized rocks. Very carefully, he placed each of the rocks in the jar. "Is this jar full?" he asked. "Yes," the students answered. Then he pulled out a bucket of gravel. He dumped it in the jar and shook it, causing pieces of gravel to work themselves into the spaces between the big rocks. "Is it full now?" he asked the students. They had gotten smart by now, and answered, "Well, probably not." Then the expert poured sand into the jar and that filled the spaces around the gravel. Finally, he poured water into the jar until it was filled to the brim. "What have you learned here?" he asked. One eager student jumped at the chance and said, "No matter how much you have to do, if you try hard, you can always fit more in!" "Wrong," the expert said. "The lesson is that if you don't put the big rocks in first, you'll never get them in at all."

What are the big rocks in your life—your family, friends, spiritual life, community, a cause? Are they getting into your Mason jar in the amounts and ways you would like or is there no room for them at all after you take care of earning a living and taking care of your family?

Since you are reading this book, I can guess—and probably be right—that you value your relationships and want to nurture them. If

you are like most of us, one of the biggest problems in doing this is finding the time to spend with friends, slip a card in the mail for their birthdays, or enjoy a quiet evening playing cards or just talking.

Our lives are rushed and sometimes feel insane. We race to work and
spend eight to ten hours (or more) there, we speed home, many of us
picking up children on the way, rush to prepare dinner, clean up, throw
a load of laundry in the washer, put children to bed, look over our calendar for tomorrow, and fall into bed exhausted at 11:30. The next day
we go through the whole routine again. Weekends are crammed with
chores, responsibility, and errands. Those of us with kids run from soccer game to T-ball to gathering snacks for the Saturday night sleepover
with hardly a break in between.

When I think about the pace of our modern lives—including my
own—I recall images from the film *Koyaanisqatsi*, which vividly portrays
how this pace and attitude toward our everyday experience can be both
exhausting and inauthentic. *Koyaanisqatsi* is a Hopi word that means
"life out of balance," "crazy life," or "a way of life that calls for another
way of living." As the film opens, images portray, in real time, the beauty
of the Badlands—brown craggy mountains and fine sand blowing over
smooth dunes. The clouds move slowly overhead, casting their shadows
across the desert and a clear, mirror-smooth blue lake. Then slowly,
almost imperceptibly, everything begins to speed up. Images of the
desert give way to modern skyscrapers, factories, explosions of the land
as mining operations carve into the earth. The shadows of clouds begin
to move by so quickly that their shapes are no longer recognizable.
Images of faces in large, crowded cities are empty, lifeless, diminished,
grim. By the end of the film cars are speeding by on a huge cloverleaf in
an American city. It is nighttime and things are moving so quickly now
that the images of the cars are simply whirling ribbons of white and red
as they approach and retreat from the viewer's vantage point. The music
becomes frenetic and wild. By the time the credits roll, our hearts are
pounding and one experiences a profound sense of exhaustion.[1] This is
the way most of us live: "life out of balance." We are where, and for what
purpose?

Time is a fixed commodity. We all have the same number of hours in
the day, and yet some people seem to manage their time in ways that
allow them to nurture deep and strong friendships. How are you spending your time? Are there places in your hectic schedule that could be

used to create and maintain your connections? Do you realize that until you can manage your time, you can manage nothing else about your life?

Every morning each one of us is gifted with twenty-four blessed hours. On the Internet I've seen a story that asks you to imagine your time as being like a sum of money. They say that "time is money," so just imagine that there is a bank that credits your account each morning with $86,400 dollars. This bank carries over no balance from day to day. Every evening it deletes whatever part of the balance you failed to use during the day. What would you do with such an account? Draw out every single solitary cent, I'd say.

What are you going to do with your 86,400 seconds today? Will you prioritize the things in your life to achieve goals, to spend time with friends and family, to enjoy pleasure in your life?

Every second of your life is a valuable gift and if you don't realize the value of one minute, ask a person who just missed the train. If you don't realize the value of one second, ask the person who just avoided an accident. If you don't realize the value of one millisecond, ask the guy who won the silver medal in the Olympics.

Our difficulties in maintaining strong connections and creating new ones in our lives is not really about a lack of time; it's a failure to honor our priorities and values. The secret to using our time wisely lies in applying this limited resource to our highest priorities *first*. If we don't, we'll end up like that management consultant guy trying to jam fist-sized rocks into a Mason jar already filled with gravel, sand, and water. And that's what happens to most of us. We say we have certain values and priorities in our lives but their importance is not reflected in our decisions about where we will apply our resource of time.

I'm suggesting a five-step plan to incorporate the nurturing of your relationships into your already overflowing life: (1) **identify** how you are presently using your time; (2) **analyze** your behavior with regard to honoring priorities and setting goals; (3) **develop** action plans to realize your goals; (4) **implement** your plan; and (5) **reevaluate** your use of time.

Identify Your Use of Time

Start by honestly looking at how you spend your time. It can sometimes help to keep a little notebook—one that you can carry in your pocket or purse—that accurately shows you what you are doing at any given moment. Pick a few times each day—7:00 A.M., noon, 4:00 P.M., 7:00 P.M., for example—and write in the notebook exactly where you are, who you are with, and what you are doing at those times. Ergonomics consultants for businesses observe productivity on a minute-to-minute basis and can tell managers exactly how their employees spend every second of every day. You don't have to be quite this precise—after all, who has time for that! But begin to become more conscious of exactly how you are spending your time. If you don't like the little notebook idea, then keep a journal (a good idea for a self-examined life anyway) and make sure you add entries that focus on how you are spending your time.

The goal of this exercise is to become more cognizant of exactly what you do with the precious commodity of time.

Analyze Your Present Situation and Set Goals

Now take a look back at the friendship values exercise in the chapter "Your Friendship Values." What core friendship values did you identify? Write those values down and compare them to the activities you wrote down in your little notebook. Is there any correlation between these values and your actual activities with regard to the time you give to them? Where do those friendship values show up in your life? Are the most important values being addressed in your life through the application of time? In other words, are you spending a considerable amount of your time—even any of your time—on the things that you deem to be important? Which values do you sell out on first? Which are the most neglected? Which ones are being honored by your day-to-day priorities? Are you spending too much time on activities that don't reflect your core values?

Here's a short exercise that will help you make the connections between your core values and the time you devote to them. I'll start with an example using two of my own core friendship values: expression of feelings and reaching out. This will give you some sense of the kind of specificity necessary to really look at how your time is being applied to your values (or not).

Day and Date	Reaching Out	Expression of Feelings
Monday—add date here	Called my niece Katelyn (who is also my friend) to wish her a happy birthday and catch up with her life (time spent—15 minutes)	Sent 3 birthday cards to friends and wrote a personal and affectionate note on each (time spent—15 minutes)
Tuesday	Called my cousin Mike (also my friend) to see how his medical test went (time spent—10 minutes)	Called my friend Lisa to tell her how much help she is to me and that I love her (time spent—7 minutes)
Wednesday	Ran some cookies across the street to Rosalyn (time spent—5 minutes)	Brushed, petted, and told Dorothy (my dog and best friend) how much I love her (time spent—10 minutes)
Thursday	Nothing—too busy, not enough time	Sent a "thinking of you" card with a note to my friend who is going through a hard time (time spent—3 minutes)
Friday	Agreed to serve on the board of a community-based organization for improving literacy and encouraging writers in NC (time spent—10 minutes, and the meetings will be for 4 hours every quarter = estimate 16 hours plus another 10 hours preparation and follow-up)	Sent an e-mail to Ken, Ruth, and Karen to tell them how much I love working with them (time spent—1 minute)

Saturday	Cohosted the neighborhood pig pickin' and made it a point to talk to four new people and introduce our new neighbors to the others (time at event—4 hours)	Told my good friends— "tribe"—how much I love them and appreciate their patience with me while I was writing this book and unavailable to go fishing with them (time spent—1 minute; they were all in the same room at the time)
Sunday	Set up our next Dinner and a Movie night and made sure we knew whose turn it is to pick the film (time spent—6 minutes)	Went to the beach with my friends (time spent—4 hours)

The point here is not that I am some kind of superwoman. Anyone who knows me will quickly tell you that is simply not true. It's also true that I do not have young children to care for, which takes so much time and energy when it is done well. Nevertheless, I do have a few secret strategies that I'll reveal in a minute. But take a close look at the time it took to do these many things that let my friends know I love them and enabled me to reach out to them and other, potentially new friends. When you exclude my time spent socializing at the pig pickin' and on the beach with my friends (total—eight hours), then add up these activities that contributed a great deal to my personal social capital, they come to about an hour and twenty minutes. But I'm getting ahead of myself. I suggest that for the next week you fill in this chart with your own core friendship values and the behaviors that support those values. There is something important about writing these down. In fact, the mere act of writing them down may encourage you to do more of them. Weight loss, smoking cessation, and other behavior-change experts speak often of the power of this kind of self-observation to actually change behavior, not just assess it. There's something about having to write down that you ate a whole piece of cheesecake when you're on a diet that makes you not want to eat it. Pass the carrots, please!

Day and Date	(Your Core Value Here)	(Your Core Value Here)
Monday		
Tuesday		
Wednesday		
Thursday		
Friday		
Saturday		
Sunday		

Carefully look at the application of your precious time to your precious values. Can this be improved? How? The next step is to develop a specific short- and long-term action plan to put these values into action by setting goals. The goal is to walk the talk and not just talk the talk if we want to create and maintain true connections.

Develop a Plan

The notion of short- and long-term goals in the context of very busy (often overwhelming) time commitments is an important one. It is not possible to just run out and solicit best friends. Attached-at-the-heart friends require nurturance and time. But even best friends initially begin as strangers. Looking at the first two points, a variety of relationships in our lives is a short-term goal we can work on by reaching out, by becoming involved, by welcoming the stranger. Putting in the time to nurture potentially deep relationships takes time and effort. One is given the model in business, to try to work toward at least one short-term goal and one long-term goal a day (or a week or whatever). The same can be said for creating containers and bonds in our lives. It is an excellent first step to become conscious of both elements and to work toward both goals.

What do you need to do differently in order to honor your friendship values in your life and how will you proceed? Begin by establishing the goals and describing a plan. Let me give you an example and then space to work on your own goals.

Short-term goal: To boost up some of the relationships I already have by making them closer and more connected.

Action Plan for Short-Term Goal

1. E-mail or write to friends and relatives, asking them to give me a list of important dates (that you currently might have in various old calendars, address books, scraps of paper, your head, nowhere). Then put them all in one central calendar or in my Palm Pilot so that I always have a few days' notice to put a card in the mail.

2. Treat myself to a trip to the store I think has the best selection of cards and stock up on birthday, anniversary, get-well, blank note cards, etc. Put them in a box that I like, that is accessible, and that I can dive into often. Stick a book of stamps and a pen that I love in there, too. Take pride in the revelation that I can now, with little or no effort, become the type of person that I appreciate: one who remembers others in important ways and at meaningful times in their lives. (Note: This is one of my "secret" strategies at maintaining my connections. All effective time management begins with planning. I am not nearly so thoughtful as my friends might believe. But I'm prepared and ready. It takes me a few minutes to send a birthday card to a friend. I'm not sure I would be nearly so "thoughtful" if each one required a trip to the store for a card and the post office for a stamp.)

3. Schedule lunch with my good friends at the office even if it is weeks—or months—away and then put it on my schedule and give it high priority. Do it now.

4. Continue to have Saturday night for "Dinner and a Movie" with Nancy, Kay, Lu, and Judy. Buy DVD of *Amélie* for my pick and serve French food (French fries? French-cut green beans? French toast?).

5. Call David and Leigh and find out when they'll be on the East Coast next so we can get together. Then put it in my schedule.

6. Call Lisa and see when she and Jamie and the kids can come to visit for a long weekend, then schedule time for it.

7. Call Dad and Deanne (also my friends) so they have plenty of

advance notice about our trip to D.C. for business. Take them out to dinner.

Long-term goal: To develop even greater levels of closeness with my friends and to welcome new friends into our tribe. To always feel the deep sense of connection and love that only good friends can offer.

Action Plan for Long-Term Goal

1. Continue taking small but consistent steps because this is the way I will realize my goal for stronger connections to my friends. "The journey of a thousand miles begins with a single step."

2. Live my friendship values every day through specific actions. My connections are a priority in my life and must be honored.

3. Combine activities so that some tasks that must be done also become a time to talk and laugh together (continue to mow lawn with Nancy and Judy; ask Lu if she wants to start biking together for exercise).

4. Plan a trip to Ireland for our "five-pack" of friends. This will be a "memory-maker." Go on-line or call Katrina at Seabreeze Travel to get info.

5. Check my Palm Pilot for next year—make sure all birthdays, anniversaries, and special dates are noted.

6. Send Christmas cards this year. Make sure address list is up-to-date.

7. Respond to all e-mails from friends, even if it is just a short note about why I don't have time to write.

8. Plan a holiday party for friends and neighbors.

It will be helpful to you to specifically think about your own short- and long-term goals and the action plans that will get you there. Take a few moments to reflect on these and write them down.

Short-term goal:

Action Plan for This Week:

1.

2.

3.
4.
5.

Long-term goal:

Action Plan for Long-Term Goal:

1.
2.
3.
4.
5.

Implement Your Plan

It seems as if it should go without saying that we need to actually put our action plans into action in order to realize them. But if you've ever told yourself that you will lose weight, stop smoking, find a new job, or rearrange your living-room furniture only to find that weeks later you haven't changed a thing, then "Implement your plan" bears repeating. Spending time reflecting on our priorities, setting goals, and developing plans to reach them are important first steps, but until we do change our behavior not much else will happen. So make a commitment to actually start—right now—on your action plans. As you implement your plan, you return to the top of the model, which means to reevaluate how effective you have been in putting your values and priorities into action and realizing your dreams of connection.

There are some interesting things about time. I think we have more of it than we realize but often we squander it on things that, in the long run, are not of consequence to us, things that don't add to joy or growth in our lives. We waste time. Look at your own time analysis from this exercise. Where do you spend your time? Here are a few thoughts about how you can better live your values and priorities:

1. For the most part, turn off your TV. It's a time killer and time is too precious to kill. As Benjamin Franklin once said, "If time be of all things the most precious, wasting time must be the greatest prodigality."

You know from an earlier chapter that I love television and have several in my house, but I've stopped the mindless use of this amazing technology and discovered that I have time left for my friends, community, hobbies, and self-growth. If the average TV viewer spent half the amount of time shoring up connections and making new friends that she/he does in front of the tube, her/his social capital would skyrocket. Use television consciously—not as a time waster but because there's something on that you really love to watch. Even television can be an opportunity to interact with friends. If you all love to watch tennis, plan a potluck and watch the U.S. Open together.

2. Avoid perfectionism—life is not perfect and neither are you. If you have a full-time job and young children, you may have to let your standards of housekeeping slide for, oh, say, eighteen years or so and until the kids are out of the house. I have a friend who teaches college and is a single mom. Her compulsive housekeeping (e.g., she stresses if there are crumbs on the toaster) keeps her busy every waking hour. Relax a little. I'm not saying to live in a dump and in danger of the Health Department knocking on your door, but put first things first where your values and priorities are concerned.

3. Don't use lack of time as an excuse for disconnection—recognize that you are a lovable person and deserve to have loving friendships in your life. If you carry old wounds that prevent this self-knowledge, get some professional help to heal. Don't allow the excuse of "not enough time" to keep you from your rightful human destiny as a connected being.

Argentine poet and essayist Jorge Luis Borges wrote about time in a way that moves the soul and emphasizes our power to use it to serve our own will. "Time," he wrote, "is the substance from which I am made. Time is a river which carries me along, but I am the river; it is a tiger that devours me, but I am the tiger; it is a fire that consumes me, but I am the fire."

We are the river and the tiger. We are the fire. This is our one, exquisite life, and we have the power to shape it to serve our most deeply held values.

THIRTEEN

Finding Your Pack

> Wolves love to howl. When it is started, they
> instantly seek contact with one another, troop together,
> fur to fur. Some wolves will run from any distance,
> panting and bright-eyed, to join in,
> uttering, as they near, fervent little wows,
> jaws wide, hardly able to wait to sing.
>
> —*Lois Crisler*, Arctic Wild

We can learn a lot from wolves. They understand the importance of bonding with members of their pack and they know how to do it. In an ancient, haunting song fueled by both instinct and need, they howl to find one another, to reunite, to connect. The wolf call to reassemble is deep, guttural, and loud—sometimes heard for more than fifty square miles on a quiet night. Once together, they raise their voices in concert—accompanied by a great deal of tail-wagging, pawing, and pressing against each other. They howl for the joy of being together.

If we don't howl, we won't find our pack. It's true that our howls may not pierce the night as wolves' do, but we can only find our pack when we reach out for it, when we communicate our deepest need to belong, knowing that our lives depend on it.

During the course of this book, I've tried to offer some ideas about how to howl—how to extend our lives toward others. I've no illusions that the suggestions included here are the only ones. Once you've accepted the importance of deep and meaningful relationships to your happiness and longevity and are committed to making these essential relationships a priority, I've no doubt that you will discover many creative ways of living a richly connected life. This will not be a quick fix. Almost everything of value takes time, nourishment, and attention to

become strong. And so it is with establishing a network of connections—a constellation of others who are attached to your very heart.

As I come to the conclusion of this book, I again realize that statistics
and data about the importance of connections can only go so far in con-
vincing us to make our relationships strong and vibrant. There is a more
urgent wisdom that comes from our hearts: a realization that something
has gone missing; a longing for the attachments that make life rich and
full. You begin to know that life is transient, and even at its longest, far
too short. You may realize that, in response to obligations and pressures
on your time, you've retreated, cutting out the very heart of what makes
life precious. So, knowing this, you begin to make changes. You begin to
build your safe harbor, find your pack. You not only reach out, you allow
yourself to be found by others. You open your heart, your home, your
life to those who mean something to you. You begin to turn your life
around. You howl. Your house becomes a home where friends are welcomed, and laughter and loving permeate your very soul. You may suddenly realize that your life is in your own hands, and that it is you—and
you alone—who will determine your priorities. You are the one who can
cast the net to widen the support for you and your family. You are the
one who can manifest the richness of connections, this loving and
laughter in the minute particulars of your everyday life.

So go to your heart. Listen. There is the wisdom. There are the
answers. Take a moment now to sit quietly and reflect on this poem by
David Whyte.[1] To me, it elegantly captures the power of connection to
sustain and nourish us. It describes the inner dwelling place that is open
to love and connection. It's called "The House of Belonging."

> I awoke
> this morning
> in the gold light
> turning this way
> and that
>
> thinking for
> a moment
> it was one
> day
> like any other.

But
the veil had gone
from my
darkened heart
and
I thought

it must have been the quiet
candlelight
that filled my room,

it must have been
the first
easy rhythm
with which I breathed
myself to sleep,

it must have been
the prayer I said
speaking to the otherness
of the night

And
I thought
This is the good day
you could
meet your love,

this is the black day
someone close
to you could die.

This is the day
you realize
how easily the thread
is broken
between this world
and the next

and I found myself
sitting up
in the quiet pathway
of light,

the tawny
close grained cedar
burning round
me like fire
and all the angels of this housely
heaven ascending
through the first
roof of light
the sun has made

This is the bright home
in which I live,
this is where
I ask
my friends
to come,
this is where I want
to love all the things
it has taken me so long
to learn to love.

This is the temple
of my adult aloneness
and I belong
to that aloneness
as I belong to my life.

There is no house
like the house of belonging.

Godspeed on this journey that is your life.

Ask/Tell

Backgound for the Ask/Tell Game*

In 1955 a psychologist and psychiatrist working at the University of California's Western Training Lab, Joseph Luft, Ph.D., and Harry Ingham, M.D., came up with a conceptual model that describes ways in which we know ourselves and others know us. They used the first part of each of their first names ("Joe" and "Harry") and called it the Johari Window. It's a model that is used quite often by businesses for organizational development and team building. But it's also a good construct for understanding ourselves. The Johari Window offers a way of understanding how we project our personality to the world and how we give and receive information—how we disclose to others—for facilitating our self-awareness and self-knowledge. The Johari Window addresses awareness in interpersonal relationships and is composed of four panes, each pane containing aspects of your personality and other information known and unknown to others and to you. It's about what we choose to share with others and what we don't and what we know about ourselves and what we don't. It relies on the social skills of self-disclosure and the ability to receive and integrate feedback from others.

---

* Adapted from the **Ask/Tell Game**—copyright by Full Potential Organizations (FPO). Used with permission.

	Known to Yourself	Unknown to Yourself
Known to Others	**Open self**—known to yourself and others	**Blind self**—unknown to yourself but known to others
Unknown to Others	**Private self**—known to yourself and unknown to others	**Unknown self**—unknown to yourself and unknown to others

Open Self Pane

This is information that you and everyone else knows about you. It is our conscious self—our attitudes, behaviors, overt values, and motivations that we express openly and intentionally. It includes our physical appearance and other public details about our life. For example, acquaintances—even strangers who gaze upon you—know that you are tall or short, male or female, blue-eyed or brown, old or young (though, admittedly, that is a relative measure). If you are a doctor whose license plate says DR. and you arrive home in surgical scrubs carrying a doctor bag, even your remotest neighbors have some information about you. The Open Self Pane includes all of our façade, our "New Year's Resolution" self that we are happy to share with just about anyone. These may be strengths or weaknesses about ourselves, but everyone knows what they are.

Blind Self Pane

This includes information about you that others can see but you cannot. You're in the dark here. You're clueless. It's hard to imagine that this could be possible. How can other people know more about me than I do myself? But it's true. We communicate all kinds of information to others that we are unaware of through our mannerisms, nonverbal behavior, habits, and the ways we relate to them and others. Remember that we can often see another's shadow more easily than we can see our own. You have seen another person's "Blind Self" when you've said: "Oh, I know he always comes off like a know-it-all, but underneath he's a nice but insecure person" or "She can be hard to get along with but, deep down, she's really a good person" or "He'll always help you out, but he's keeping score." I've heard human resource professionals refer to this pane as the "bad breath" quadrant—you know it about me, but I don't know it about myself. Our good, close friends can in gentle and loving ways give us feedback that helps us to understand personal characteristics in this quadrant of our Johari Window. That process of feedback and disclosure is one of the ways we grow, not only in the relationship with our friend, but also as a person. As we become less blind to various aspects of our own personality, this quadrant shrinks and our Open Self quadrant grows—now we know more about ourselves. And, of course, we cannot change—cannot even address—what we do not know. And remember again, there is gold in them thar' hills. You may be blind not only to bad breath, but to wonderful and important strengths that your friends are perfectly well aware of but you cannot see.

Private Self Pane

This includes information you wish to keep private and are unlikely to disclose to anyone but your closest friends. This pane contains your dreams and ambitions, your insecurities, and your most deeply held beliefs. It's the stuff you don't want others to know about you and they won't know it unless you disclose it to them. We often resist disclosing information in this quadrant for fear of rejection. If someone really knew that I'm not as good as I appear, will they still like/love me? What if she/he knew that sometimes I can be selfish or mean-spirited? And yet, if we can work through these fears, this is the pane—the aspect of self—that contains the greatest material for self-disclosure when a relationship has reached a level of intimacy and trust that encourages and can contain it. This is where you tell your best friends, "I don't know that I'm happy with my job." "I wish I was closer to my grown children." "My doctor found a lump in my breast and I'm worried waiting until next week for the biopsy results." These disclosures would be too early in the relationship and, thus, inappropriate revelations to a casual friend or acquaintance, but in the realm of those attached-at-the-hearts, these are the conversations that bring us closer together. We have reached beyond the banal conversations about the weather and the latest movies. This is where we come to really know each other.

Unknown Self Pane

This is the deepest layer of the unconscious. We don't know, nor do others, these aspects of our personality and life. Discovering aspects of our self and our own personality that lie in this nether region requires real dedication to the idea of "knowing thyself." Deep in the unconscious lies our most authentic Self. As W. H. Auden noted, "The center I cannot find, is known to my unconscious mind." Meditation, dream work, reflection, and self-observation are the necessary tools to plumb these depths. This is the richest, most complex aspect of our psyche and it holds a wealth of unrealized potential, but getting to it requires commitment and a willingness to go beneath the surface of our present level of consciousness. But don't think that just because this pane is unknown that it does not exert a strong influence on your life and relationships. Precisely because it is not known, it is often projected onto others and becomes a source of conflict between people.

Now on these little tables, I've drawn all the four quadrants the same size but that is not entirely accurate. If we are striving for intimacy, our goal is to reduce the size of the Hidden Self Pane (by disclosing information about ourselves to others) and the Blind Self Pane (by seeking and receiving feedback from others and learning more about ourselves). As we do that, our Open Self Pane grows larger and the Hidden Self Pane automatically shrinks because we're learning more and more about ourselves and our own motivations, feelings, and personality.

Take a minute and just reflect on these panes in your life and write down some things in each of the quadrants. You should be able to fill in tons of information in the Open Self Pane: What do people know about you? How do you think they perceive you? Remember, these are things that you and everyone you know realize about you. The Hidden Self Pane will not be quite as easy to fill in and may require more thought. But you know what's in here. What do you hold back from your close friends? Why do you not reveal to them? Do you fear the withdrawal of their love if they were to know you this intimately? Is there something in that pane that you would like to share with a trusted friend? In what ways will the relationship change if your friend were to know this hidden thing about you?

Can you enlist the help of a close friend to help you better understand your Blind Self? Remember, when you were reading about the shadow, I suggested asking a friend to talk about your greatest flaw. This time ask your friend to tell you anything he/she knows about you that he/she doesn't think you know about yourself. I think you will find this exercise revealing and powerful.

Filling in anything in the Unknown Self Pane is difficult, if not impossible, because it is precisely the things we don't know about ourselves. Still, we may have an inkling about what's in there and we can look at patterns in our lives and the symbols in dreams and images to help point the way. For right now, you can just put a big old question mark in that quadrant.

	Known to Yourself	Unknown to Yourself
Known to Others	Open self—known to yourself and others	Blind self—unknown to yourself but known to others
Unknown to Others	Private self—known to yourself and unknown to others	Unknown self—unknown to yourself and unknown to others

Directions: In order to be more open with others, it's critical to become more open and disclosive with yourself. This Ask/Tell game is based upon the Johari Window, a model of awareness based on disclosure and feedback and named after Joseph Luft and Harry Ingham.

This exercise is best conducted with two or more close friends (four to six is ideal). Get some small pieces of paper or index cards and on each one write a number from A1 to A25 (the Ask Questions) and T1 to T25 (the Tell Questions). In turn, have each person draw a piece of paper and respond to the question for the group. It's clear that some people will respond to these questions at a fairly superficial level while others will reveal deeper truths about themselves.

As you disclose information or learn about how your friends perceive you, just jot a word or two to remind you of that response in that section of the Johari Window on page 245.

When you have finished, just talk—have a conversation—about what each of you learned about yourselves and one another. Take a look at the Johari Window you completed in the earlier exercise and compare the results. Was there any new information there for you? How did you feel playing this game?

Serve chips and salsa and it will be a satisfying evening with your friends!

Ask Questions

1. Ask the person to your right and left what they think of you.
2. Ask someone what career they would choose for yourself besides the one you are in. Why?
3. Ask someone what hobby or interest they would choose for you besides the one you currently enjoy. Why?
4. Ask one person how his/her life would be different if you weren't in it.
5. Ask someone what he/she thinks you can teach him/her.
6. Ask one person what they think you feel about them as a person.
7. Ask each person in the group to tell you three things they like/admire about you and why.
8. Ask one person how he/she feels about giving you criticism or bad news.
9. Ask one person in the group to describe an occasion when they really counted on you and what the result was.
10. Ask one person in the group to comment on how they think you receive praise/compliments.
11. Ask everyone in the group to describe you with a single adjective.
12. Ask one person in the group to express his/her feelings toward you nonverbally—without words.
13. Ask the person to your left how he/she thinks you feel being part of this friendship group (or friends with you).

14. Ask the group members to guess what you really want to do with your life.
15. Ask one person in the group to share something about him-/herself that he/she thinks the others do not know.
16. Ask one person in the group to describe something memorable about you.
17. Ask one person in the group to describe what he/she thinks your core values are.
18. Ask the person to your right what he/she thinks you do well and why.
19. Ask one person to describe how you cope with change.
20. Ask one person to describe something about you that bothers them.
21. Ask the person to your left to guess about how you feel meeting new people.
22. Ask one person in the group to guess about what you miss most when you travel away from home.
23. Ask one person in the group to describe how he/she has benefited from the feedback you have given them during this game.
24. Ask one person in the group if he/she thinks you have been completely honest in your responses in this game.
25. Ask each of the group members to describe you as a kind of animal and discuss why they chose that one.

Tell Questions

1. Tell the group what you would do if you had less than six months to live.
2. Tell the group about something you've always wanted to do, whether you've done it, and if not, why.
3. Tell the group three things about yourself that you think they do not know.
4. Tell the group where you grew up (what kind of community, house, family).
5. Tell the group how you like to enjoy your spare time.
6. Tell the group how you're feeling right now.
7. Tell one person in the group how you feel about him/her without using words.

8. Tell the group about something you missed in your childhood and how this affected you.

9. Tell the group how you feel about receiving feedback from them (the Ask Questions) and why.

10. Tell the group about an experience or significant event in your life.

11. Describe one member of the group with a single adjective.

12. Tell the group what makes you most proud and describe a situation in which you felt proud of yourself.

13. Tell the group how you like to have fun.

14. Tell the group what makes you angry.

15. Tell the group what frightens you.

16. Tell the group what changes you would make in your life if you could.

17. Tell the group about the last time you cried, why you cried, and what feelings you had.

18. Tell the group about the last thing that made you really laugh.

19. Tell the group about one thing you excel in, one thing you think you're average in, and one thing that you don't do well.

20. Tell the group what makes you happy.

21. Tell the group about two things you did well lately.

22. Tell the group about a childhood experience you remember well.

23. Tell the group how you imagine your life will be ten years from now.

24. Tell the group how you feel about talking about yourself and why you feel that way.

25. Tell the group what you learned about yourself during this exercise. (Put this card back if you have just started the game.)

Notes

Epigraph

From Jalal al-Din Rumi, "The Pattern Improves." In *The Soul of Rumi*, Coleman Barks (trans.) (New York: HarperCollins, 2001), p. 33. Reprinted with permission.

Introduction

1. Recounted in Mark Nepo, *The Book of Awakening: Having the Life You Want by Being Present to the Life You Have* (Berkeley, Calif.: Conari Press, 2000).

Chapter One: The Psychology and Biology of Belonging

1. J. Madeleine Nash, "Fertile Minds." *Time*, February 3, 1997.
2. Cited in T. Lewis, F. Amini, and R. Lannon, *A General Theory of Love* (New York: Random House, 2001), p. 70.
3. John Bowlby, *Attachment*. Vol. 1. *Attachment and Loss* (New York: Basic Books, 1973).
4. James W. Prescott, "Alienation of Affection." *Psychology Today*, December 1979.
5. A. Montagu, *Touching: The Human Significance of the Skin* (New York: Columbia University Press, 1971), p. 35.
6. The brain can be thought of as consisting of three distinct sub-brains: the triune brain. The oldest part of the brain is called the reptilian brain and controls basic functions of life like breathing, swallowing, and heart rate. The limbic brain (or the mammalian brain) controls the body's autonomic nervous system, is the seat of emotions, and responds to rewards and punishment. The most recently evolved sub-brain, the neocortex, controls the higher forms of human cognition and the capacity for reason. You might call this our "thinking cap."

7. E. B. Keverne, C. M. Nevison, and F. L. Martel, "Early Learning and the Social Bond." In *The Integrated Neurobiology of Affiliation*, C. S. Carter, I. I. Lederhendler, and B. Kirkpatrick (eds.) (Cambridge, Mass.: MIT Press, 1999), pp. 263–74. Cited in S. E. Taylore, S. S. Dickerson, and Laura Cousino Klein, "Toward a Biology of Social Support." In *Handbook of Positive Psychology*, C. R. Snyder and S. J. Lopez (eds.) (Oxford: Oxford University Press, 2002).

8. www.heartmath.org.

9. Antoine de Saint-Exupery, *The Little Prince* (New York: Harcourt Paperbacks, 2000).

10. R. McCraty, M. Atkinson, and W. Tiller, "The Role of Physiological Coherence in the Detection and Measurement of Cardiac Energy Exchange between People." *Proceedings of the Tenth International Montreux Congress on Stress*. Montreux, Switzerland, 1999. For more see: D. R. Childre and H. Martin, *The HeartMath Solution* (New York: HarperCollins, 1999) and the Institute of HeartMath, www.heartmath.org.

11. A. Motluk, "Natural Born Fathers." *New Scientist*, Vol. 160, Issue 2164, December 18, 1998, p. 38.

12. M. Yogman, "Games Fathers and Mothers Play with Their Infants." *Infant Mental Health Journal* 2 (1981): 241–48.

13. P. Marton and K. Minde, "Paternal and Maternal Behavior with Premature Infants." Cited in Michael E. Lamb, "The Development of Father-Infant Relationships," *The Role of the Father in Child Development*, Michael E. Lamb (ed.) (New York: Wiley & Sons, 1997).

14. A. E. Storey, C. I. Walsh, R. L. Quinton, and K. E. Wynne-Edwards, "Hormonal Correlates of Paternal Responsiveness," *Evolution and Human Behavior*. Cited in A. Motluk, "Fatherly Love," *New Scientist*, Vol. 165, Issue 2220, January 8, 2000, p. 8.

15. R. A. Spitz and K. M. Wolf, "The Smiling Response." *Genetic Psychology Monographs*, Vol. 34 (1946). Cited in Joseph Campbell, *Primitive Mythology: The Masks of God* (New York: Penguin Books, 1959), p. 46.

16. T. Lewis, F. Amini, and R. Lannon, *A General Theory of Love* (New York: Random House, 2001), pp. 39–40.

17. www.schematherapy.com. Also see T. Bennett-Goleman, *Emotional Alchemy* (New York: Harmony Books/Random House, 2001).

18. N. L. Collins and S. J. Read, "Adult Attachment: Working Models and Relationship Quality in Dating Couples." *Journal of Personality and Social Psychology* 58 (4) (1990): 644–63.

19. *USA Today*, May 3, 2001, p. 3A.

20. Hierarchy of Needs Pyramid reprinted with permission from C. George Boeree, "Abraham Maslow," www.ship.edu/~cgboeree/maslow.html.

21. A. Maslow, *Toward a Psychology of Being* (New York: Van Nostrand Reinhold, 1968), p. 41.

22. Antoine de Saint-Exupery, *The Little Prince*.

23. A. Maslow, *Motivation and Personality*, 3rd ed. (New York: Addison Wesley Longman, 1954), p. 22.

24. A. Maslow, *The Farther Reaches of Human Nature* (New York: Penguin Books, 1971).

25. A. Maslow, *Toward a Psychology of Being*, p. 26.

26. V. Frankl, *Man's Search for Meaning* (New York: Simon and Schuster, 1959; first published in Austria, 1946).

27. Ibid., p. 23.

28. Ibid., p. 57.

29. F. De Waal, *Good Natured: The Origins of Right and Wrong in Humans and Other Animals* (Cambridge, Mass.: Harvard University Press, 1996), p. 12.

30. E. Durkheim, *Suicide* (New York: Free Press, 1951).

31. Cited in Clarke Johnson, Ph.D., "The Roseto Effect," University of Illinois at Chicago, 1999. http://www.uic.edu/classes/osci/osci590/14_2%20The%20Roseto%20Effect.htm.

32. S. Wolf, "Predictors of Myocardial Infarction over a Span of 30 Years in Roseto, Pennsylvania." *Integrative Physiological & Behavioral Science* 27 (3) (1992): 246–57.

33. D. Spiegel, J. R. Bloom, H. D. Kraemer, and E. Gottheil, "Effect of Psychosocial Treatment on Survival of Patients with Metastatic Breast Cancer." *The Lancet* 2 (1989): 888–91. Also see David Spiegel, *Living beyond Limits: New Hope and Help for Facing Life-Threatening Illness* (New York: Ballantine, 1994).

34. A. Deaton and C. H. Paxson, "Aging and Inequality in Income and Health." *American Economic Review* 88 (1998): 252.

35. E. M. Hallowell, *Connect* (New York: Pantheon Books, Random House, 1999), pp. 6–7.

36. S. Taylor, S. S. Dickerson, and L. C. Klein, "Toward a Biology of Social Support." In *Handbook of Positive Psychology*, C. R. Snyder and S. J. Lopez (eds.) (New York: Oxford University Press, 2002).

37. U.S. Department of Health and Human Services, "Toward a Blueprint for Youth: Making Positive Youth Development a National Priority," http://www.acf.dhhs.gov/programs/fysb/youthinfo/blueprint2.htm.

38. Cited in M. E. Copeland, *The Loneliness Workbook* (Oakland, Calif.: New Harbinger Publications, 2000), p. 7.

Chapter Two: Are We Bowling Alone?

1. Robert D. Putnam, *Bowling Alone* (New York: Simon and Schuster, 2000). This is a fantastic book with more information than you can possibly absorb in a single reading. I highly recommend this book to all those who want to know more about our eroding social capital in America.

2. Carlos Castaneda, *The Wheel of Time* (New York: Washington Square Press, Simon and Schuster, 1998), p. 32. Originally cited in Carlos Castaneda, *A Separate Reality* (New York: Pocket Books, Simon and Schuster, 1971).

3. Putnam, *Bowling Alone*, p. 19.

4. The Social Capital Community Benchmark Survey. Saguaro Seminar, John F. Kennedy School of Government, Harvard University, 2000. http://www.cfsv.org/communitysurvey/index.html.

5. The New Hampshire Charitable Foundation, 37 Pleasant Street, Concord, NH 03301-4005, 603-225-6641. http://www.nhcf.org/ and http://www.bettertogethernh.org/.

6. Social Capital Community Benchmark Survey. The Saguaro Seminar of the John F. Kennedy School of Government at Harvard University. www.ksg.harvard.edu/saguard/communitysurvey/

7. R. Putnam, "The Strange Disappearance of Civic America." *The American Prospect*, Vol. 7, Issue 24, December 1, 1996.

8. http://www.sleepfoundation.org/publications/2001poll.html#3. Poll conducted between October 25, 2000, and January 3, 2001.

9. http://www.sciencedaily.com/releases/2000/09/000919080457.htm. Original source is Center for the Advancement of Health, www.cfah.org.

10. R. Kubey and M. Csikszentmihalyi, "Television Addiction Is No Mere Metaphor." *Scientific American*, February 2002.

11. "Feeling Sociable," *The Industry Standard*, May 15, 2000.

12. The Benton Foundation, 2001. www.benton.org.

13. National Telecommunications and Information Administration (NTIA), U.S. Department of Commerce, 2001. www.ntia.doc/gov.

14. R. Kraut, "Internet Parody: A Social Technology That Reduces Social Involvement and Psychological Well-being." *The American Psychologist*, Vol. 53(9), September 1988, pp. 1017–1031.

15. Stanford Institute for the Quantitative Study of Society (SIQSS): http://www.stanford.edu/group/siqss/.

16. "Feeling Sociable."

17. J. B. Horrigan and L. Rainie, "Getting Serious Online." Pew Internet and American Life Project, March 3, 2002. www.pewinternet.org.

18. Putnam, *Bowling Alone*.

19. U.S. Department of Labor, Women's Bureau.

20. AFL-CIO. www.aflcio.org/women/wwfacts.htm.

21. J. Carter, "The Crisis of Confidence." Presidential Speech, July 15, 1979. National Archives and Records Administration, www.nara.gov and www.jimmycarter-library.org.

22. R. Polenberg, *War and Society: The United States 1941–1945* (New York: J. B. Lippincott, 1972), p. 132, citing W. Lloyd Warner, "The American Town," in *American Society in Wartime*, William Fielding Ogburn (ed.) (Chicago: University of Chicago Press, 1943), pp. 45–46. R. Putnam, *Bowling Alone*, p. 271.

23. Putnam, *Bowling Alone*, p. 402.

Chapter Three: A Changed and Changing World?

1. *Talk Magazine*, November 2001.

2. Gallup poll results cited in David Van Biema, "Faith after the Fall." *Time*, October 8, 2001.

3. Gallup poll, the Gallup Organization, December 21, 2001. www.gallup.com.

4. Gallup poll, the Gallup Organization, January 2, 2002. www.gallup.com.

5. Gallup poll, the Gallup Organization, March 11, 2002. www.gallup.com.

6. Carole Kammen and Jodi Gold, *Call to Connection: Bringing Sacred Tribal Values into Modern Life* (Salt Lake City, Utah: Commune-A-Key Publishing, 1998), p. 6.

7. William Crocker and Jean Crocker, *The Canela: Bonding through Kinship, Ritual, and Sex* (New York: Harcourt College Publishers, 1994), p. 61. Also see the documentary film *Intimate Truths of the Canela Indians of Brazil*, produced by the Human Studies Film Archives and Schecter Films. Aired on the Discovery Channel October 17, 1999, and distributed under the title *Mending Ways: The Canela Indians of Brazil*, by Films for the Humanities and Social Sciences, www.films.com/Films_Home/item.cfm?s=1&bin=9335.

8. Crocker and Crocker, ibid., p. 143.

9. C. G. Jung, *Psychological Reflections: A New Anthology of His Writings 1905–1961*, Joland Jaffe and R. F. C. Hull (eds.) (Princeton, N.J.: Princeton University Press, 1970).

10. Riane Eisler, *The Chalice and the Blade* (New York: Harper and Row, 1987), p. xiii. Also see http://www.partnershipway.org/.

11. Eisler, p. xx.

12. *I Ching*. Hsi-tz'u Chuan.

Chapter Four: A Thousand Words for Snow:
A Model for Understanding Our Relationships

1. Ralph Waldo Emerson, "Friendship," *The Writings of Ralph Waldo Emerson, Vol. 1 (Essays, First and Second Series)* (New York: Brentano's, 1910), p. 131. For a more contemporary and readily available citation, see William J. Bennett, *The Book of Virtues* (New York: Simon and Schuster, 1993), pp. 336–37.

2. His Holiness the Dalai Lama, *Ethics for the New Millennium* (New York: Riverhead Books, 1999), p. 41.

3. G. K. Chesterton, "Defendant," in *The Collected Works of G. K. Chesterton*, Vol. 34, George Marlin, Lawrence Clipper, Richard P. Rabatin, and John L. Swan (eds.) (Fort Collins, Colo.: Ignatius Press, 1991).

4. Barry Edmonston, "The New Americans: Economic, Demographic and Fiscal Effects of Immigration." Study by the National Research Council of the American Academy of Sciences. See: http://www4.nationalacademies.org/onpi/news.nsf/0a254 cd9b53e0bc585256777004e74d3/f3d7f5f7b08b997585256774006354e0?OpenDocument.

5. Data from the Civil Rights Project at Harvard University and U.S. Census data cited in Ron Stodghill and Amanda Bower, "Where Everyone's a Minority." *Time*, September 2, 2002, pp. 26–30.

6. Alvin Toffler, *Future Shock* (New York: William Morrow, 1980), p. 25.

7. "Noetic" comes from the Greek word "nous" meaning "intuitive knowing." See: www.ions.org.

8. Edgar Mitchell, *The Way of the Explorer* (New York: Putnam, 1996).

9. Ibid., p. 4.

10. C. G. Jung, *Memories, Dreams, Reflections* (New York: Vintage Books, 1965), p. 304.

11. Pierre Teilhard de Chardin, *The Phenomenon of Man* (New York: Harper and Row, 1955), p. 245.

12. Pierre Teilhard de Chardin, *The Evolution of Chastity*, Rene Hague (trans.) (London: William Collins, 1972). Reprinted in Pierre Teilhard de Chardin, *On Love and Happiness* (San Francisco: HarperCollins, 1984), p. 16.

13. A. S. Berman, "Did September 11 Events Refocus Global Consciousness?" *USA Today*, December 6, 2001, p. 3D.

14. Roger Nelson, "Terrorist Disaster, September 11, 2001," http://noosphere. princeton.edu. Also see www.ions.org.

15. Aldous Huxley, *The Perennial Philosophy* (New York: Harper and Row, 1944), p. 36.

16. Chief Seattle, letter to President Franklin Pierce, 1855. Cited in Joseph Campbell with Bill Moyers, *The Power of Myth* (New York: Doubleday, 1988), pp. 34–35.

17. Bede Griffiths, *Return to the Center* (Springfield, Ill.: Templegate, 1976), pp. 60–61.

18. John Gribbon, *In Search of Schroedinger's Cat: Quantum Physics and Reality* (New York: Bantam Books, 1984), p. 5, frontispiece.

19. Robert Brain, "Friends and Twins in Bangwa." In *Man in Africa*, Mary Douglas (ed.) (London: Tavistock, 1970). Also cited in footnotes: Lillian Rubin, *Just Friends* (New York: Harper and Row, 1985), p. 199.

20. Jan Yager, *Friendshifts* (Stamford, Conn.: Hannacroix Creek Books, 1999), p. 15.

21. Ibid., p. 5.

22. Quoted in Muriel James and Louise M. Savary, *The Heart of Friendship* (New York: Harper and Row, 1976).

23. You might be curious to know Americans eat more than 3 billion Pez candies every year and that these tasty morsels and their unique dispensers are available in more than sixty countries around the world. First marketed in Vienna, Austria, more than seventy years ago, the name *Pez* comes from the German word for peppermint, PfeffErminZ. "The official website of Pez Candy," www.pez.com (what else?).

24. Yager, *Friendshifts*, p. 36.

25. Beth Kephart, *Into the Tangle of Friendship: A Memoir of the Things That Matter* (New York: Houghton Mifflin, 2000), p. 87.

26. Ken DeBarth, unpublished e-mail correspondence, February 15, 2001.

27. Amanda Ripley, "Aftershocks: Proof of Life in Oklahoma." *Time*, September 11, 2002, p. 19.

28. *American Heritage Dictionary of the English Language*, 4th ed. (New York: Houghton Mifflin, 2000).

29. John O'Donohue, *Anam Cara: A Book of Celtic Wisdom* (New York: Harper-Collins, 1997), p. 14.

30. Bernat Rosner and Frederic C. Tubach, *An Uncommon Friendship* (Los Angeles: University of California Press, 2001).

31. Hannah Arendt, *Eichmann in Jerusalem: A Report on the Banality of Evil* (New York: Penguin Books, 1963).

32. Carole Kammen and Jodi Gold, *Call to Connection: Bringing Sacred Tribal Values into Modern Life* (Salt Lake City, Utah: Commune-A-Key Publishing, 1998), p. 27.

Chapter Five: Your Friendship Values

1. Laura Whitworth, Henry Kimsey-House, and Phil Sandahl, *Co-active Coaching* (Palo Alto, Calif.: Davies-Black Publishing, 1998), p. 121.

Chapter Six: Know Thyself

1. Thomas à Kempis, *The Imitation of Christ*, Joseph N. Tylenda (trans.) (reprint edition, New York, Vintage Books, 1998.)

2. Daniel Goleman, *Emotional Intelligence: Why It Can Matter More than IQ* (New York: Bantam Books, 1995), p. 41.

Chapter Seven: Social Skills

1. "Grace: The Social Robot." Swarthmore University. http://www.palantir. swarthmore.edu/GRACE/.

2. Judy Lin (Associated Press), "New Robot to Exhibit Basic Social Skills during Symposium." Cited at www.nandotimes.com/healthscience/story/477942phttp: //-3818002c.html.

3. Edward T. Hall, *The Hidden Dimension* (New York: Anchor Press, 1966; reissued 1990).

4. David B. Givens, Center for Nonverbal Studies. http://members.aol.com/ nonverbal2/.

Chapter Eight: Acceptance: Are You a Friend?

1. Beth Kephart, *Into the Tangle of Friendship* (New York: Houghton Mifflin, 2000), p. 33.
2. Paramahansa Yogananda: The Self-Realization Fellowship. http://www.yogananda-srf.org/index.html.
3. Mickey Baker, unpublished e-mail correspondence, September 23, 2002.

Chapter Ten: Communication Revolution

1. Communication specialist Donnell King. http://www2.pstcc.cc.tn.us/~dking/interpr.htm.
2. Gary Larson, *In Search of the Far Side (Collection #3)* (Kansas City, Mo.: Andrews and McMeel, 1984).
3. Stephen R. Covey, *The Seven Habits of Highly Effective People* (New York: Fireside, Simon and Schuster, 1989).
4. Mary Ellen Copeland, *The Loneliness Workbook* (Oakland, Calif.: New Harbinger Publications, 2000), p. 93.
5. Marisue Pickering, "Communication." *Explorations: A Journal of Research of the University of Maine* 1 (3) (Fall 1986): pp. 16–19. Cited at http://crs.uvm.edu/gopher/nerl/personal/comm/e.html.

Chapter Eleven: Good Times/Bad Times

1. Jan Yager, *Friendshifts* (Stamford, Conn.: Hannacroix Creek Books, 1997), p. 4.
2. Lillian B. Rubin, *Just Friends* (New York: Harper and Row, 1985), p. 13.

Chapter Twelve: That Time Thing

1. *Koyaanisqatsi*, directed by Godfrey Reggio, music by Philip Glass. This short film is distributed by MGM/UA and is available on DVD from a number of retailers including www.amazon.com.

Chapter Thirteen: Finding Your Pack

1. "House of Belonging," from *The House of Belonging* by David Whyte. Copyright © 1997 by David Whyte. Used by permission of the author and Many Rivers Press.

Acknowledgments

My life is enveloped by so many rich and nourishing relationships that to name each one in that web of belonging would take many pages. Suffice it to say that my family and attached-at-the-heart friends fill my life with such joy that language is inadequate to express my feelings, for as Thoreau aptly pointed out, "The language of friendship is not words, but meanings." And so, I thank you for the meaning and texture and celebration you give me in all my days of both happiness and sorrow. I could not be who I am and who I am trying to become without your love. I hold each of you in the cradle of my heart.

To my literary agent and dear friend, Lisa Ross, I offer my sincere thanks for your long-held belief in my work and your unfailing support and caring. We have gone down quite a road over the past years and I am eager to continue to follow this path together.

To my editor, Deborah Brody, thank you for your collaboration, intelligence, humor, and belief in this project. Your contribution has made this a far better book than I could have ever written without you. I offer my sincere thanks also to John Sterling, Maggie Richards, Elizabeth Shreve, Tracy Locke, Daniel Reid, and my other friends at Henry Holt and Company. Your enthusiastic support of my work and your commitment to publishing books that enlighten, enrich, and bring positive energy to the world does not go unnoticed or unappreciated.

Mitakye Oyasin.

Index